The Gallup Poll

Public Opinion 1990

Other Gallup Poll Publications Available from Scholarly Resources

The Gallup Poll: Public Opinion Annual Series

1989 (ISBN 0-8420-2344-5)   *1982* (ISBN 0-8420-2214-7)
1988 (ISBN 0-8420-2330-5)   *1981* (ISBN 0-8420-2200-7)
1987 (ISBN 0-8420-2292-9)   *1980* (ISBN 0-8420-2181-7)
1986 (ISBN 0-8420-2274-0)   *1979* (ISBN 0-8420-2170-1)
1985 (ISBN 0-8420-2249-X)   *1978* (ISBN 0-8420-2159-0)
1984 (ISBN 0-8420-2234-1)   *1972–77* (ISBN 0-8420-2129-9, 2 vols.)
1983 (ISBN 0-8420-2220-1)   *1935–71* (ISBN 0-394-47270-5, 3 vols.)

International Polls

The International Gallup Polls: Public Opinion, 1979
ISBN 0-8420-2180-9 (1981)

The International Gallup Polls: Public Opinion, 1978
ISBN 0-8420-2162-0 (1980)

The Gallup International Public Opinion Polls:
France, 1939, 1944–1975
2 volumes ISBN 0-394-40998-1 (1976)

The Gallup International Public Opinion Polls:
Great Britain, 1937–1975
2 volumes ISBN 0-394-40992-2 (1976)

—— The —— Gallup —— Poll ——

Public Opinion 1990

George Gallup, Jr.

SR Scholarly Resources Inc.
Wilmington, Delaware

The paper used in this publication meets the minimum requirements of the American National Standard for permanence of paper for printed library materials, Z39.48, 1984.

Scholarly Resources Inc.
104 Greenhill Avenue
Wilmington, DE 19805-1897

Library of Congress Catalog Card Number: 79-56557
International Standard Serial Number: 0195-962X
International Standard Book Number: 0-8420-2368-2

CONTENTS

DESIGN OF THE SAMPLE

The Gallup Poll gathers information both in personal interviews and in interviews conducted by telephone. Although the method for selecting households in which to conduct interviews is different, the goal is the same: to provide representative samples of adults living in the United States. In either case the standard size for Gallup Polls is 1000 interviews. More interviews are conducted in specific instances where greater survey accuracy is desired.

Design of the Sample for Personal Surveys

The design of the sample for personal (face-to-face) surveys is that of a replicated area probability sample down to the block level in the case of urban areas and to segments of townships in the case of rural areas.

After stratifying the nation geographically and by size of community according to information derived from the most recent census, over 350 different sampling locations are selected on a mathematically random basis from within cities, towns, and counties that, in turn, have been selected on a mathematically random basis.

The interviewers are given no leeway in selecting the areas in which they are to conduct their interviews. Each interviewer is given a map on which a specific starting point is marked and is instructed to contact households according to a predetermined travel pattern. At each occupied .dwelling unit, the interviewer selects respondents by following a systematic procedure that is repeated until the assigned number of interviews has been completed.

Design of the Sample for Telephone Surveys

The samples of telephone numbers used in telephone interview surveys are based on a random digit stratified probability design. The sampling procedure involves selecting listed "seed" numbers, deleting the last two digits, and randomly generating two digits to replace them. This procedure provides telephone samples that are geographically representative. The random digit aspect, since it allows for the inclusion of unlisted and unpublished numbers, protects the samples from "listing bias"—the unrepresentativeness of telephone samples that can occur if the distinctive households whose telephone numbers are unlisted or unpublished are excluded from the sample.

Weighting Procedures

After the survey data have been collected and processed, each respondent is assigned a weight so that the demographic characteristics of the total weighted sample of respondents match the latest estimates of the demographic characteristics of the adult population available from the U.S. Census Bureau. Telephone surveys are weighted to match the characteristics of the adult population living in households with access to a telephone. The weighting of personal interview data includes a factor to improve the representation of the kind of people who are less likely to be found at home.

The procedures described above are designed to produce samples approximating the adult civilian population (18 and older) living in private households (that is, excluding those in prisons, hospitals, hotels, religious and educational institutions, and those living on reservations or military bases)—and in the case of telephone surveys, households with access to a telephone. Survey percentages may be applied to census estimates of the size of these populations to project percentages into numbers of people. The manner in which the sample is drawn also produces a sample that approximates the distribution of private households in the United States. Therefore, survey results also can be projected to numbers of households.

Sampling Tolerances

In interpreting survey results, it should be borne in mind that all sample surveys are subject to sampling error—that is, the extent to which the results may differ from what would be obtained if the whole population surveyed had been interviewed. The size of such sampling errors depends largely on the number of interviews.

The following tables may be used in estimating the sampling error of any percentage. The computed allowances have taken into account the effect of the sample design upon sampling error. They may be interpreted as indicating the range (plus or minus the figure shown) within which the results of repeated samplings in the same time period could be expected to vary, 95 percent of the time, assuming the same sampling procedure, the same interviewers, and the same questionnaire.

Table A shows how much allowance should be made for the sampling error of a percentage. Let us say a reported percentage is 33 for a group that includes 1000 respondents. First, we go to the row headed "percentages near 30" and then go across to the column headed "1000." The number here is 4, which means that the 33 percent obtained in the sample is subject to a sampling error of plus or minus 4 points. Another way of saying it is that very probably (95 chances out of 100) the average of repeated samplings would be somewhere between 29 and 37, with the most likely figure being the 33 obtained.

In comparing survey results in two samples, such as for men and women, the question arises as to how large must a difference between them be before one can be reasonably sure that it reflects a real difference. In Tables B and C, the number of points that must be allowed for in such comparisons is indicated. Table B is for percentages near 20 or 80, and Table C is for percentages near 50. For percentages in between, the error to be allowed for is between those shown in the two tables.

TABLE A

Recommended Allowance for Sampling Error of a Percentage

In Percentage Points
(at 95 in 100 confidence level)*
Sample Size

	1000	750	600	400	200	100
Percentages near 10	2	3	3	4	5	7
Percentages near 20	3	4	4	5	7	9
Percentages near 30	4	4	4	6	8	10
Percentages near 40	4	4	5	6	8	11
Percentages near 50	4	4	5	6	8	11
Percentages near 60	4	4	5	6	8	11
Percentages near 70	4	4	4	6	8	10
Percentages near 80	3	4	4	5	7	9
Percentages near 90	2	3	3	4	5	7

*The chances are 95 in 100 that the sampling error is not larger than the figures shown.

TABLE B

Recommended Allowance for Sampling Error of the Difference

In Percentage Points
(at 95 in 100 confidence level)*
Percentages near 20 or percentages near 80

	750	600	400	200
Size of sample				
750	5			
600	5	6		
400	6	6	7	
200	8	8	8	10

TABLE C

	Percentages near 50			
	750	600	400	200
Size of sample				
750	6			
600	7	7		
400	7	8	8	
200	10	10	10	12

*The chances are 95 in 100 that the sampling error is not larger than the figures shown.

Here is an example of how the tables would be used: Let us say that 50 percent of men respond a certain way and 40 percent of women also respond that way, for a difference of 10 percentage points between them. Can we say with any assurance that the 10-point difference reflects a real difference between men and women on the question? The sample contains approximately 600 men and 600 women.

Since the percentages are near 50, we consult Table C, and since the two samples are about 600 persons each, we look for the number in the column headed "600" that is also in the row designated "600." We find the number 7 here. This means that the allowance for error should be 7 points, and that in concluding that the percentage among men is somewhere between 3 and 17 points higher than the percentage among women, we should be wrong only about 5 percent of the time. In other words, we can conclude with considerable confidence that a difference exists in the direction observed and that it amounts to at least 3 percentage points.

If, in another case, men's responses amount to 22 percent and women's 24 percent, we consult Table B because these percentages are near 20. We look in the column headed "600" that is also in the row headed "600" and see that the number is 6. Obviously, then, the 2-point difference is inconclusive.

RECORD OF
GALLUP POLL ACCURACY

Year	Gallup Final Survey*		Election Result*	
1988	56.0%	Bush	53.9%	Bush
1984	59.0	Reagan	59.2	Reagan
1982	55.0	Democratic	55.8	Democratic
1980	47.0	Reagan	50.8	Reagan
1978	55.0	Democratic	54.0	Democratic
1976	48.0	Carter	50.0	Carter
1974	60.0	Democratic	58.9	Democratic
1972	62.0	Nixon	61.8	Nixon
1970	53.0	Democratic	54.3	Democratic
1968	43.0	Nixon	43.5	Nixon
1966	52.5	Democratic	51.9	Democratic
1964	64.0	Johnson	61.3	Johnson
1962	55.5	Democratic	52.7	Democratic
1960	51.0	Kennedy	50.1	Kennedy
1958	57.0	Democratic	56.5	Democratic
1956	59.5	Eisenhower	57.8	Eisenhower
1954	51.5	Democratic	52.7	Democratic
1952	51.0	Eisenhower	55.4	Eisenhower
1950	51.0	Democratic	50.3	Democratic

* The figure shown is the winner's percentage of the Democratic-Republican vote except in the elections of 1948, 1968, and 1976. Because the Thurmond and Wallace voters in 1948 were largely split-offs from the normally Democratic vote, they were made a part of the final Gallup Poll preelection estimate of the division of the vote. In 1968, Wallace's candidacy was supported by such a large minority that he was clearly a major candidate, and the 1968 percentages are based on the total Nixon-Humphrey-Wallace vote. In 1976, because of interest in McCarthy's candidacy and its potential effect on the Carter vote, the final Gallup Poll estimate included Carter, Ford, McCarthy, and all other candidates as a group.

1948	44.5	Truman	49.9	Truman
1946	58.0	Republican	54.3	Republican
1944	51.5	Roosevelt	53.5*	Roosevelt
1942	52.0	Democratic	48.0	Democratic
1940	52.0	Roosevelt	55.0	Roosevelt
1938	54.0	Democratic	50.8	Democratic
1936	55.7	Roosevelt	62.5	Roosevelt

*Civilian vote 53.3, Roosevelt soldier vote 0.5 = 53.8% Roosevelt. Gallup final survey based on civilian vote.

Average Deviation for 26
  National Elections ....2.2 percentage points

Average Deviation for 19
  National Elections
  Since 1950, inclusive ....1.5 percentage points

Trend in Deviation

Elections	Average Error
1936–1950	3.6
1952–1960	1.7
1962–1970	1.6
1972–1988	1.4

CHRONOLOGY

This chronology is provided to enable the reader to relate poll results to specific events, or series of events, that may have influenced public opinion.

1989

November 26   Hungary holds free elections, its first in forty years.

December 2–3   Presidents George Bush and Mikhail Gorbachev meet at sea off the coast of Malta.

December 8   The Labor Department reports a slight increase to 5.3% in the November unemployment rate.

December 20   President Bush dispatches U.S. troops to Panama to overthrow the government of General Manuel Noriega.

December 24   General Noriega takes refuge in the Vatican's diplomatic mission in Panama City.

December 25   In Romania, President Nicolae Ceausescu and Communist party leaders are overthrown.

1990

January 3   Ousted Panamanian dictator General Noriega surrenders to U.S. officials.

January 5   The U.S. unemployment rate for December 1989 was 5.3%, unchanged from November.

January 9   The federally funded National Assessment of Educational Progress declares that the reading and writing ability of U.S. students had improved very little during the 1980s, despite some advance by minority groups.

January 12	The increase in 1989 wholesale prices was up from 4% in 1988 to 4.8% in 1989.
January 15	The Soviet-government dispatches troops to the southern Republic of Azerbaijan to quell an ethnic war between Moslem and Christian Armenians.
January 17	The November 1989 U.S. trade deficit was the largest of 1989, according to the Commerce Department.
January 18	The Labor Department reports that the government's consumer price index was 4.6% in 1989, the highest since 1981.
January 22	President Bush reiterates his opposition to abortion.
January 25	A $1-billion aid program to help the Panamanian economy is announced by President Bush.
January 29	President Bush sends Congress a $1.23-trillion budget for fiscal 1991 that does not raise taxes.
January 31	The Savings and Loan scandal grows as the government revises upward the number of thrift institutions that will have to be taken over.
February 11	South African black nationalist leader Nelson Mandela is freed after twenty-seven years in prison.
February 13	Ford, Chrysler, and General Motors report sharply reduced profits in the fourth quarter of 1989.
February 15	President Bush and the presidents of Peru, Bolivia, and Colombia sign an accord to cooperate against illegal narcotics trafficking.
February 16	The Commerce Department reports that the U.S. 1989 trade deficit was the smallest since 1984.
February 18–22	Czechoslovak President Vaclav Havel visits the United States and addresses a joint session of Congress on February 21.
February 24	Lithuanian nationalists win a majority of the seats in parliamentary elections.
February 25	In Nicaragua, the Sandinista government is defeated in a major election.

March 4	The U.S. space shuttle *Atlantis* completes a secret military mission that includes the deployment of a $500-million spy satellite. The satellite fails to achieve orbit.
March 5	For the second time in two weeks, a federal district judge declares unconstitutional a law that would make it a crime to burn the American flag.
March 11	Lithuania declares its independence from the Soviet Union. Soviet President Gorbachev calls the move "alarming" and deplores the action.
March 16	The Commerce Department reports that new housing starts fell 7% in February.
March 26	The Office of Thrift Supervision announces that the cost of the U.S. Savings and Loan crisis had surged to a record $19.17 billion in 1989.
April 1	The International Monetary Fund reports that in 1989 the United States had regained the lead from Germany as the world's largest exporter.
April 3	The Commerce Department reports that its index of leading economic indicators fell 1% in February, the sharpest decline in nine months.
April 6	The Labor Department announces that unemployment figures in March edged down to 5.2%.
April 7	A federal jury convicts former National Security Adviser John Poindexter of criminal charges in connection with the Iran-contra arms scandal.
April 13	The Soviet Union threatens economic sanctions against Lithuania.
April 27	The Commerce Department reports that inflation in the first three months of 1990 soared to its highest quarterly rate since 1981.
May 10	A Senate Judiciary Committee report estimates that 2.2 million Americans use cocaine at least once per week. The figure is more than double previous government estimates.
May 22	The Federal Deposit Insurance Corporation announces that its insurance fund to protect bank depositors has fallen to 70¢ in assets for every $100 in insured deposits.

May 27– June 7	Ethnic violence tears apart the Soviet republics of Armenia and Kirghizia.
May 30	Soviet President Gorbachev arrives in Washington for a four-day summit with President Bush.
	The Commerce Department reports that the sale of new houses declined 1.6% in April, the lowest rate of sales of new homes since December 1982.
June 1	The Labor Department announces that the unemployment rate fell to 5.3% in May, but that the economy had added few new jobs.
June 7	The Federal Reserve Board reports that consumer credit rose $584 million in April.
June 11	The Supreme Court strikes down as unconstitutional a 1989 federal law that forbid the desecration of the American flag.
June 13	Thirty-year U.S. Treasury bonds fall to 8.37%, the lowest yields since mid-February.
June 15	Donald Trump's real estate empire seems to be on the verge of bankruptcy, sending shock waves through the nation's real estate and bond industries.
	The Labor Department reports that the consumer price index rose 0.2% in May.
June 16	The Federal Reserve Board announces that its industrial production index, gauging output at the nation's factories, mines, and utilities, rose 0.6% in May.
June 19	The Commerce Department reports that housing starts fell 1.4% in May. The decline left housing starts at their lowest monthly level since October 1982.
June 20	President Bush suspends the U.S. diplomatic dialogue with the Palestine Liberation Organization.
	South African black nationalist leader Mandela arrives in the United States for an eleven-day, eight-city tour. On June 26 he addresses a joint session of Congress.
June 20–24	The Sixth International AIDS Conference is held in San Francisco. More than ten thousand researchers and public health officials attend.

June 26	President Bush moves away from his campaign vow against new taxes by issuing a statement that reducing the budget deficit now requires "tax revenue increases."
	President Bush announces a moratorium on offshore oil exploration for large areas of the coastal United States.
July 1	A unified economic and monetary system for East and West Germany goes into effect.
	Most large American corporations, including Chrysler and Exxon, report losses during the first half of 1990.
July 5–6	NATO nations agree to a dramatic series of changes in military strategy and say that they will seek a nonaggression agreement with the Warsaw Pact nations.
July 9	The Labor Department announces that unemployment fell to 5.2% in June even though few new jobs were created. Service industries continued to show some strength, adding forty thousand workers in the health services industry.
	The Federal Reserve Board reports that outstanding consumer credit rose $3.91 billion in May.
July 9–10	Leaders of the major industrial democracies meet in Houston for their sixteenth annual summit on world economic issues.
July 16	Soviet President Gorbachev agrees to conditions that would allow a reunified Germany to become a member of NATO.
July 18	The Commerce Department reports that housing starts in June fell 2.3%.
	Iraqi President Saddam Hussein threatens to use force against Kuwait to stop Iraq's southern neighbor from lowering oil prices. He charges that certain Persian Gulf leaders have been "inspired by America" to plot to keep oil prices low through overproduction.
July 19	Pete Rose, major league baseball's all-time leader in hits, is sentenced to five months in jail on federal tax-evasion charges.
July 20	Justice William Brennan resigns from the Supreme Court after almost thirty-four years of service.

July 23	Iraq masses some thirty thousand troops on its frontier with Kuwait. (The force later will grow to nearly one hundred thousand.)
	President Bush nominates David Souter, a little-known judge from New Hampshire, as his choice to fill the Supreme Court vacancy.
July 26	President Bush signs into law a landmark civil rights bill that prohibits discrimination against people with disabilities.
July 30	Government banking officials report that they will need as much as $100 billion in 1991 to continue the Savings and Loan bailout.
August 2	Iraqi troops invade Kuwait and quickly seize control of the oil-rich desert sheikdom at the head of the Persian Gulf. President Bush blasts the invasion as "naked aggression" and announces that the United States will consider economic and diplomatic sanctions against Iraq.
August 6	President Bush orders U.S. military forces to Saudi Arabia to defend its oil fields from a feared Iraqi attack.
August 8–16	Arab nations led by Egypt agree to send troops to join in the defense of Saudi Arabia. President Bush orders a trade embargo against Iraq.
August 10	Hussein urges the "Moslem masses" to launch a "holy war" against "corrupt" Arab rulers.
August 12	Hussein links a possible Iraqi withdrawal from Kuwait to "an immediate and unconditional" Israeli pullout from the Arab-occupied territories in Palestine, Syria, and Lebanon.
August 17–23	The confrontation in the Persian Gulf continues to worsen as Hussein declares his intention to use foreigners trapped in Kuwait and Iraq as "human shields" against any attack.
August 24–29	On August 25 the United Nations Security Council authorizes a U.S.-led Western naval armada in and around the Persian Gulf to use force to prevent violations of UN economic sanctions against Iraq. U.S. warships shadow Iraqi tankers in the Persian Gulf as Soviet President Gorbachev warns Hussein that tougher UN measures will follow unless Iraq withdraws its troops.

Attempts at a diplomatic settlement seem to fail. Iraqi troops surround at least nine foreign embassies in Kuwait City and order them to shut down. Iraqi authorities continue to round up Western civilians in Iraq and occupied Kuwait and to place them in strategic locations to deter any U.S.-led military attack.

August 28   Iraq announces that Kuwait has become the nineteenth Iraqi province.

September 1–30   President Bush begins an impressive military buildup in the Persian Gulf area. While scores of refugees try to flee Iraq into Jordan, the president uses some of his toughest language so far in the crisis, vowing that Iraq's aggression will not be allowed to succeed.

September 7   The Labor Department reports that the nation's unemployment rate rose to 5.6% in August.

October 1–31   The Persian Gulf crisis overshadows all world news.

October 3   Germany becomes a united nation for the first time since 1945.

October 22   President Bush vetoes the Civil Rights Act of 1990 and, on October 24, the Senate fails to override the veto.

October 24   Secretary of Labor Elizabeth Dole resigns, the first cabinet member to leave the Bush administration. Dole will become president of the American Red Cross.

November 1–30   The Persian Gulf crisis continues to dominate world news. More than four hundred thousand American troops have been deployed to the area.

November 22   Margaret Thatcher, the longest-serving British prime minister of the twentieth century, announces that she will resign her post within one week.

November 28   John Major becomes the new prime minister of Great Britain.

December 1–31   In the Persian Gulf crisis, more than one million troops face off across the Saudi-Kuwaiti border. The United Nations establishes a January 15, 1991, deadline for an Iraqi withdrawal from Kuwait.

JANUARY 1
LOOKING AHEAD TO THE YEAR 2000

Interviewing Date: 11/16–19/89
Survey #GO 89140-2

Now, I'd like you to think ahead to the year 2000—that is, ten years from now—and I'm going to ask you some questions about how optimistic or pessimistic you are about the future. First, are you very optimistic, somewhat optimistic, somewhat pessimistic, or very pessimistic about:

Your future?

Very optimistic	44%
Somewhat optimistic	38
Somewhat pessimistic	7
Very pessimistic	3
No opinion	8

The future of the United States?

Very optimistic	29%
Somewhat optimistic	42
Somewhat pessimistic	17
Very pessimistic	6
No opinion	6

The future of the world?

Very optimistic	23%
Somewhat optimistic	43
Somewhat pessimistic	18
Very pessimistic	9
No opinion	7

Compared to the way things are now, please tell me whether you expect each of the following areas of your life to be better or worse in the year 2000:

	Better	Worse	Same	No opinion
Financial situation	74%	14%	9%	3%
Family life	77	4	15	4
Health	51	24	21	4
Job*	82	7	9	2
Overall quality of life	77	8	12	3
Environment, pollution	62	34	2	2
Homelessness	62	32	4	2
Poverty	67	25	6	2
Crime rate	71	23	4	2
Tensions between racial and ethnic groups	39	52	6	3
Peace between countries	68	26	4	2
International terrorism	50	40	5	5

*Based on those who are employed

Again, looking ahead to the year 2000, which of these things do you think will have happened by then?

	Will have happened by 2000
Soviet Union and West living peacefully together	68%
Cure for AIDS found	67
New, clean energy source developed	65
Another energy crisis will occur	64
Major change in the earth's climate	61
Cure for cancer found	56
Most assembly-line workers replaced by robots	52
U.S. forces drawn into military conflict in Central America	50
Life expectancy will have risen to 100 years	42
Worldwide economic depression	34

Nuclear war started by country other than
United States or Soviet Union 33
Soviet communism will have vanished ... 32
All countries will have ceased to
manufacture nuclear weapons 29
Peace between the Israelis and Arabs 28
World hunger eliminated through
agricultural advances 27
Civilization as we know it in ruins 13
Nuclear war between the Soviet Union
and United States 8

*Do you expect the 1990s to be a decade when
life gets easier or harder for you?*

Easier 53%
Harder 38
Both 6
No opinion 3

*Everything considered, do you expect life in
the year 2000 to be very different, somewhat
different, or not too different from what life
is like now?*

Very different 23%
Somewhat different 50
Not too different 26
No opinion 1

*For each item I read, please tell me how
different you expect it to be by the year 2000.
First, do you expect life to be very different
by the year 2000, somewhat different, or not
too different?*

	Very different
Way children are taught in school	40%
Type of medical care people receive	39
Types of cars people drive	38
Way the elderly are cared for	34
Kinds of programs people watch on television	32
Way people dress	30
Kinds of music people listen to	29
Way children are raised	29
Way people shop	26
Kinds of jobs people have	25

Types of homes people live in 22
Kinds of food people eat 21
Way people spend their free time 19
Way people worship 17

*By the year 2000 do you think people will
be spending more or less time on:*

Leisure and recreational activities?

More 68%
Less 24
Same 6
No opinion 2

Their families?

More 58%
Less 34
Same 6
No opinion 2

Household chores?

More 13%
Less 75
Same 9
No opinion 3

Their jobs?

More 38%
Less 49
Same 10
No opinion 3

*By the year 2000 do you think it will be
easier or harder:*

For young people to find jobs?

Easier 28%
Harder 64
Same 6
No opinion 2

For parents to raise children and have jobs at the same time?

Easier	28%
Harder	64
Same	7
No opinion	1

For parents to afford college for their children?

Easier	8%
Harder	89
Same	2
No opinion	1

To buy a house?

Easier	14%
Harder	81
Same	3
No opinion	2

To afford retirement?

Easier	15%
Harder	79
Same	3
No opinion	3

To afford medical care?

Easier	18%
Harder	79
Same	2
No opinion	1

For each of the following social conditions, please tell me whether you think it will increase or decrease by the year 2000:

Divorce rate?

Increase	58%
Decrease	32
Stay the same	8
No opinion	2

Number of young couples choosing not to have children?

Increase	69%
Decrease	22
Stay the same	5
No opinion	4

Number of working mothers?

Increase	87%
Decrease	10
Stay the same	2
No opinion	1

Problems with alcohol and drug abuse?

Increase	58%
Decrease	36
Stay the same	4
No opinion	2

Unemployment rate?

Increase	59%
Decrease	31
Stay the same	7
No opinion	3

Rate of inflation?

Increase	74%
Decrease	17
Stay the same	7
No opinion	2

Note: Most Americans see a better life for themselves in the 1990s. They expect to spend fewer hours at work and more with their families. They predict improvements in their finances, careers, and general quality of life. Cures are anticipated for AIDS and cancer. Overall, when asked to forecast their personal futures by the year 2000, optimists outnumber pessimists by eight to one.

However, those rosy expectations often do not extend to society as a whole, according to a new Gallup Mirror of America survey. Most people are pessimistic that substantial progress will be made during the 1990s in solving the country's major domestic problems, including drug abuse, poverty, and homelessness. Moreover, the divorce rate is expected to climb, and six in ten fear that there will be an environmental disaster in the next decade.

While a majority does not foresee an economic calamity such as a worldwide recession, many expect that inflation and unemployment will increase over the ten years. Furthermore, most think that it will become more difficult for people in general to afford a college education, good housing, medical care, and retirement.

These reservations notwithstanding, the Gallup Poll on expectations for the year 2000 reveals a spirit of hopefulness and enthusiasm about the future in the country today. On balance, Americans are eagerly anticipating the turn of the century as a time when their own lives will be different, better, and often easier than they are now.

JANUARY 10
MILITARY SPENDING

Interviewing Date: 1/4–7/90
Survey #GO 922001

In determining America's strength in the future, say twenty-five years from now, how important do you feel each of the following factors will be—very important, fairly important, not too important, or not at all important:

Developing the most efficient industrial production system in the world?

Very important 61%
Fairly important 32
Not too important 3
Not at all important 1
No opinion 3

Selected National Trend
May 1984

Very important 70%
Fairly important 23
Not too important 3
Not at all important 1
No opinion 3

Building the strongest military force in the world?

Very important 36%
Fairly important 38
Not too important 18
Not at all important 5
No opinion 3

Selected National Trend
May 1984

Very important 45%
Fairly important 36
Not too important 13
Not at all important 3
No opinion 3

Developing the best educational system in the world?

Very important 91%
Fairly important 7
Not too important 1
Not at all important .... *
No opinion 1

Selected National Trend
May 1984

Very important 82%
Fairly important 14
Not too important 2
Not at all important .... *
No opinion 2

*Less than 1%

Do you feel that our national defense is stronger now than it needs to be, not strong enough, or about right at the present time?

Stronger than it needs to be 16%
Not strong enough 17
About right 64
No opinion 3

Selected National Trend
1984*

Stronger than it needs to be 15%
Not strong enough 36
About right 46
No opinion 3

*This survey was conducted for *Newsweek* by the Gallup Organization.

There is much discussion as to the amount of money the government in Washington should spend for national defense and military purposes. How do you feel about this? Do you think we are spending too little, about the right amount, or too much?

Too little 9%
Right amount 36
Too much 50
No opinion 5

Selected National Trend

	Too little	Right amount	Too much	No opinion
1987	14%	36%	44%	6%
1986	13	36	47	4
1985	11	36	46	7
1983	21	36	37	6
1982	16	31	41	12
1981	51	22	15	12
1976	22	32	36	10
1973	13	30	46	11
1971	11	31	50	8
1969	8	31	52	9

How likely do you think it is that government spending on defense will be greatly reduced as a result of improving relations with the Soviet Union and the changes in Eastern Europe?

Very likely 24%
Somewhat likely 44
Not very likely 19
Not at all likely 8
No opinion 5

How do you think U.S. defense spending should be affected by the changes taking place in Eastern Europe? Do you think the United States should make sharp cuts in defense spending right away, or do you think the United States should wait and see how things develop before making any sharp cuts, or do you oppose making any sharp cuts in defense spending in the foreseeable future?

Make cuts right away 8%
Wait and see before making cuts 78
Oppose making cuts in the foreseeable
  future 12
No opinion 2

If government spending on defense is greatly reduced, how concerned are you that our national security might become threatened? Are you very concerned, somewhat concerned, not very concerned, or not at all concerned?

Very concerned 33%
Somewhat concerned 39
Not very concerned 18
Not at all concerned 8
No opinion 2

As one of the ways to reduce the amount the government spends on defense, would you approve or disapprove of reducing the number of U.S. troops based in Europe?

Approve 57%
Disapprove 34
No opinion 9

If government spending on defense is greatly reduced, do you think this will hurt the U.S.

economy, help the U.S. economy, or won't it make any difference to the U.S. economy?

Hurt the economy 35%
Help the economy 28
Won't make any difference 30
No opinion 7

If government spending on defense is greatly reduced, do you think this will hurt the economy in your local area, help the economy in your local area, or won't it make any difference to the economy in your local area?

Hurt local economy 27%
Help local economy 13
Won't make any difference 57
No opinion 3

If government spending on defense is greatly reduced, do you think this will hurt your household's financial situation, help your household's financial situation, or won't it make any difference to your household's financial situation?

Hurt household's financial situation 13%
Help household's financial situation 12
Won't make any difference 72
No opinion 3

If the defense budget is cut sharply, money would be available to be spent in other ways. Do you think this money should mainly be used to increase spending on social problems such as homelessness, poverty, drugs, and education; or should this money mainly be used to reduce the federal budget deficit?

Increase spending on social problems 62%
Reduce the federal budget deficit 27
Both equally 8
No opinion 3

Note: A new Gallup Poll finds that most Americans are cautious about cutting too much from the defense budget too soon in response to events in Eastern Europe. Although roughly two thirds (68%) believe that the situation eventually will lead to large cuts in defense spending, close to eight in ten (78%) say that it is prudent to wait and see how things develop before making deep reductions in the Pentagon's budget.

Sentiment for cutting military spending is as great as it has been at any time since the latter stages of the U.S. involvement in Vietnam. Today, 50% of Americans think that defense spending is too high, while only 9% reply that it is too low.

Since the mid-1980s a plurality has thought that we are overspending on defense. One must look back to 1971, however, to find the last time that such a plurality reached 50% in the Gallup Poll. The belief then that the defense budget should be cut was associated with a growing perception that the United States should get out of Vietnam.

Now, in the context of events in Eastern Europe, U.S. military power seems less critical than it did in the past. Since 1984 the percentage who believe that building the strongest military force in the world is very important to our nation's future has declined from 45% to 36%. Over the same period the percentage who say that it is very important to develop the best educational system in the world—often cited as a key to solving our competitiveness problems—has increased from 82% to 91%.

JANUARY 10
PRESIDENT BUSH

Interviewing Date: 1/4–7/90
Survey #GO 922001

Do you approve or disapprove of the way George Bush is handling his job as president?

Approve 80%
Disapprove 11
No opinion 9

Selected National Trend

	Approve	Dis- approve	No opinion
1989			
December	71%	20%	9%
November	70	17	13
October	68	20	12
September	70	17	13
August	69	19	12
July	66	19	15
June	70	14	16
May	56	22	22
April	58	16	26
March	56	16	28
February	63	13	24
January	51	6	43

Presidential Performance Ratings
(In January of Second Year in First Fully Elected Term)

		Approve	Dis- approve	No opinion
Bush	1990	80%	11%	9%
Reagan	1982	49	40	11
Carter	1978	55	27	18
Nixon	1970	61	22	17
Johnson	1966	59	24	17
Kennedy	1962	78	9	13
Eisenhower	1954	71	19	10
Truman	1950	45	40	15

Now, let me ask you about some specific problems facing this country. As I read off each one, would you tell me whether you approve or disapprove of the way President Bush is handling that problem:

Situation in Eastern Europe?

Approve 73%
Disapprove 13
No opinion 14

Selected National Trend

	Approve	Dis- approve	No opinion
November 1989	63%	16%	21%

Situation in Central America?

Approve 66%
Disapprove 21
No opinion 13

Selected National Trend

	Approve	Dis- approve	No opinion
1989			
November	40%	39%	21%
March	37	33	30

Note: President George Bush's current job approval rating of 80% is his all-time high and the second highest ever recorded in the Gallup Poll. The highest rating was President John F. Kennedy's (83%) at the time of the Bay of Pigs invasion of Cuba in April 1961. This is also the highest rating for a president at the beginning of his second year in office. President Kennedy achieved a comparable rating of 78% in January 1962.

President Bush's overall approval has experienced two significant increases since he took office in January of last year. His job rating held steady at just below 60% throughout the first five months of his presidency. Then, in June 1989, his rating jumped to 70%—a level that he more or less maintained for the remainder of 1989. The second significant increase occurred in January 1990, when Bush's approval rating increased 9 percentage points.

There is also a sharp increase in those who approve of the president's handling of the situation in Central America. Two thirds (66%) of respondents approve of Bush's actions in that region, up from 40% last November and only 37% in March 1989. For his handling of the situation in Eastern Europe the president's approval rating also rose, from 63% in November 1989 to 73% in the current survey.

JANUARY 17
DRUG PROBLEM

Interviewing Date: 1/4–7/90
Survey #GO 922001

Do you approve or disapprove of the way George Bush is handling the drug problem?

Approve 69%
Disapprove 24
No opinion 7

Selected National Trend

	Approve	Dis-approve	No opinion
1989			
November	53%	41%	6%
September	72	18	10

How much progress, if any, do you think the Bush administration has made in combating drugs? Would you say it has made a lot of progress, some progress, not too much, or none at all?

A lot 10%
Some 53
Not too much 26
None at all 9
No opinion 2

Selected National Trend
November 1989

A lot 7%
Some 48
Not too much 30
None at all 12
No opinion 3

There are many things that our government is doing to fight drug use. Which one of the following activities in the government's fight against drugs do you think deserves the most money and effort?

Teaching young people about the
  dangers of drugs 40%
Helping drug users overcome their
  addiction to drugs 5
Working with foreign governments
  to stop the export of drugs to this
  country 28
Arresting people in this country
  who sell drugs 19
Arresting the people who use drugs 4
No opinion 4

Selected National Trend
July 1986*

Teaching young people about the
  dangers of drugs 42%
Helping drug users overcome their
  addiction to drugs 4
Working with foreign governments
  to stop the export of drugs to this
  country 28
Arresting people in this country
  who sell drugs 19
Arresting the people who use drugs 4
No opinion 3

*This survey was conducted for *Newsweek* by the Gallup Organization.

Which one of these government activities is the next most important?

Teaching young people about the
  dangers of drugs 24%
Helping drug users overcome their
  addiction to drugs 15
Working with foreign governments
  to stop the export of drugs to this
  country 24
Arresting people in this country
  who sell drugs 26
Arresting the people who use drugs 8
No opinion 3

Teaching young people about the
 dangers of drugs 24%
Helping drug users overcome their
 addiction to drugs 12
Working with foreign governments
 to stop the export of drugs to this
 country 23
Arresting people in this country
 who sell drugs 31
Arresting the people who use drugs 5
No opinion 5

*This survey was conducted for *Newsweek* by the
Gallup Organization.

*Many institutions in society are involved in
the fight against drugs. For each of the following, please tell me how much confidence
you have that it has the resources and the
ability to be effective in the fight against
drugs. First, how much confidence do you
have in the resources and ability of:*

Courts?

Great deal 11%
Some 39
Not too much 32
None at all 15
No opinion 3

Police?

Great deal 19%
Some 54
Not too much 20
None at all 6
No opinion 1

Public schools?

Great deal 19%
Some 47
Not too much 23
None at all 7
No opinion 4

Drug treatment centers?

Great deal 19%
Some 49
Not too much 19
None at all 7
No opinion 6

Border patrol?

Great deal 15%
Some 44
Not too much 24
None at all 9
No opinion 8

Federal drug agents?

Great deal 22%
Some 52
Not too much 15
None at all 5
No opinion 6

*Some people feel that current drug laws
haven't worked and that drugs like marijuana, cocaine, and heroin should be legalized and subject to government taxation and
regulation like alcohol and tobacco. Do you
think drug legalization is a good idea or a
bad idea?*

Good idea 14%
Bad idea 80
Some drugs should be legalized
 and others should not (volunteered) ... 2
No opinion 4

*How strongly do you feel about this issue?
Do you feel very strongly, fairly strongly, or
not at all strongly about drug legalization?*

Very strongly 72%
Fairly strongly 21
Not at all strongly 6
No opinion 1

*How closely have you followed the news cov-
erage about the idea of drug legalization?*

Have you followed it very closely, fairly closely, not too closely, or not at all closely?

Very closely 19%
Fairly closely 53
Not too closely 21
Not at all closely 6
No opinion 1

Now, I'd like you to think about what might happen if drugs were legalized. First, do you think the following would increase, decrease, or stay about the same:

Drug use in public schools?

Increase 65%
Decrease 12
Stay the same 20
No opinion 3

Selected National Trend
June 1988

Increase 65%
Decrease 13
Stay the same 19
No opinion 3

Number of addicts?

Increase 67%
Decrease 7
Stay the same 23
No opinion 3

Selected National Trend
June 1988

Increase 61%
Decrease 8
Stay the same 28
No opinion 3

Drug overdoses?

Increase 63%
Decrease 10
Stay the same 23
No opinion 4

Selected National Trend
June 1988

Increase 60%
Decrease 12
Stay the same 24
No opinion 4

Amount of drug-related crime?

Increase 52%
Decrease 25
Stay the same 20
No opinion 3

Selected National Trend
June 1988

Increase 49%
Decrease 27
Stay the same 20
No opinion 4

Now, I'd like you to think about what might happen if drugs were legalized. Do you think it would be easier, harder, or about the same to get drug addicts to participate in treatment programs?

Easier 19%
Harder 47
About the same 29
No opinion 5

How do you think legalization might affect the government's efforts to educate people about the dangers of drugs? Would it mostly improve things by generating tax revenue from drug sales that could be directed to drug education programs, or would it mostly make things worse by sending a message that it is okay to use drugs?

Legalization would improve things 20%
Legalization would make things worse ... 74
No opinion 6

Selected National Trend
June 1985

Legalization would improve things 23%
Legalization would make things worse ... 68
No opinion 9

Note: Americans, by a margin of almost six to one, reject the idea that drugs such as marijuana, cocaine, and heroin should be legal. While a growing number of experts and public officials make the case for legalization, most respondents think that it would result in increased drug use and are not convinced that crime would be reduced and addiction would be easier to identify and treat.

The public fails to endorse legalization despite its belief that the institutions engaged in the war on drugs are ill equipped to win. The latest Gallup Poll shows that few people are confident that these institutions—the courts, police, public schools, drug treatment centers, border patrol, and federal drug agents—have the resources and ability to be effective in the fight against drugs. The courts, in particular, are a source of public concern. Only one in ten people has a great deal of confidence that the courts can be effective in the drug war.

Seven in ten, however, approve of the way President George Bush is handling the drug problem. Support for his approach in the fight against drugs is up significantly from a November survey, where only one half of the respondents approved. Public approval of Bush's handling of the drug problem is as high as it was in September 1989, shortly after his televised speech to the nation about the war on drugs.

Compared with their views in November, Americans now also see a little more progress in combating the drug war. More than six in ten adults now think that the Bush administration has made either a lot or some progress in fighting drug use. In November only five in ten thought that this amount of progress had been made.

JANUARY 24
CHURCH/SYNAGOGUE MEMBERSHIP

Interviewing Date: Several Interviews during 1989
Various Surveys

Did you, yourself, happen to attend church or synagogue in the last seven days?

	Yes
National	43%*

Selected National Trend

	Yes
1988	42%
1987	40
1985	42
1983	40
1982	41
1981	41
1979	40
1972	40
1969	42
1967	43
1962	46
1958	49
1957	47
1955**	49
1954	46
1950	39
1940	37
1939	41

*The replies to this and the following two questions were given in 1989, not 1990.
**The audits from 1955 through 1989 were based on an average of several surveys each year. The figures prior to 1955 were based on a single survey. This is also the case with the next two selected national trends.

Do you happen to be a member of a church or synagogue?

	Yes
National	68%

Selected National Trend

	Yes
1988	65%
1987	69

1985	....	71
1983	....	69
1982	....	67
1979	....	68
1976	....	71
1965	....	73
1952	....	73
1947	....	76
1944	....	75
1940	....	72
1937	....	73

How important would you say religion is in your life—very important, fairly important, or not very important?

Very important	....	55%
Fairly important	....	30
Not very important	....	14
No opinion	....	1

Selected National Trend

	Very important	Fairly important	Not very important	No opinion
1988	54%	31%	14%	1%
1987	53	32	14	1
1986	55	30	14	1
1985	55	31	13	1
1984	56	30	13	1
1983	56	30	13	1
1982	56	30	13	1
1981	56	29	14	1
1980	55	31	13	1
1978	52	32	14	2
1965	70	22	7	1
1952	75	20	5	*

*Less than 1%

Note: A majority of Americans (55%) consider religion to be a very important part of their lives, according to a series of Gallup Polls conducted throughout 1989. Membership in a church or synagogue is reported by two out of three (68%) respondents, and 43% of all adults attended a church or a synagogue in a typical week during 1989. The polls indicate that religious involvement has remained remarkably stable throughout the 1980s. In fact, there has been little change in these measures since the late 1960s.

FEBRUARY 5
GENDER GAP

Interviewing Date: 12/18–21/89
Survey #GO 89141-2

All things considered, who have a better life in this country—men or women?

Men	....	49%
Women	....	22
Same	....	21
No opinion	....	8

Selected National Trend
1975

Men	....	32%
Women	....	28
Same	....	31
No opinion	....	9

Do you think the changes brought about by the women's movement have made men's lives easier or harder than they were twenty years ago?

Easier	....	36%
Harder	....	43
No change	....	15
No opinion	....	6

By Sex
Male

Easier	....	36%
Harder	....	42
No change	....	15
No opinion	....	7

Female

Easier	....	36%
Harder	....	43
No change	....	15
No opinion	....	6

Do you think the changes brought about by the women's movement have made women's lives easier or harder than they were twenty years ago?

Easier	54%
Harder	36
No change	5
No opinion	5

By Sex
Male

Easier	55%
Harder	38
No change	3
No opinion	4

Female

Easier	53%
Harder	35
No change	6
No opinion	6

For each of the following aspects of life, please tell me whether you think the women's movement has made things easier or harder in this country:

For women to lead satisfying lives?

Easier	56%
Harder	35
No change (volunteered)	3
No opinion	6

For families to earn a comfortable living?

Easier	47%
Harder	50
No change (volunteered)	2
No opinion	1

For men to lead satisfying lives?

Easier	41%
Harder	43
No change (volunteered)	9
No opinion	7

For women to combine jobs and family responsibilities?

Easier	30%
Harder	66
No change (volunteered)	2
No opinion	2

For marriages to be successful?

Easier	15%
Harder	76
No change (volunteered)	4
No opinion	5

For parents to raise children?

Easier	14%
Harder	82
No change (volunteered)	2
No opinion	2

As I read a list of common household chores, please tell me how much of each job you usually do yourself. If I read a chore that does not apply to your household, just tell me. First, do you usually do all of this yourself, most of it, about half, less than half, or none:

	Percent saying they do all or most of each chore	
	Men	*Women*
Doing laundry?	27%	79%
Preparing meals?	26	78
Paying bills?	47	65
Making decisions about savings or investments?	41	38
Washing dishes?	31	68
Doing yard work?	63	21
Making minor home repairs?	74	16
Grocery shopping?	26	72
Cleaning house?	22	69
Keeping car in good condition?	81	22

Caring for children on daily basis?*	12	72
Taking care of children when sick?*	10	78
Disciplining children?*	28	42
Buying gifts for birthdays and holidays?	24	78
Making decisions about vacations and entertainment?	25	34
Making decisions about furniture and decoration?	18	60

*Based on those with children living at home

Does your household have domestic help or a cleaning person that you pay to help with household chores?

	Yes
National	14%

Now, I'd like to ask about your preference— what kind of marriage do you think is the more satisfying way of life?

One where the husband provides for the family and the wife takes care of the house and children	37%
One where the husband and wife both have jobs and both take care of the house and children	57
Other	3
No opinion	3

Do you feel that women in this country have equal job opportunities with men, or not?

Yes	42%
No	56
No opinion	2

Selected National Trend
1975

Yes	48%
No	48
No opinion	4

If you were taking a new job and had your choice of a boss, would you prefer to work for a man or for a woman?

Man	48%
Woman	14
No difference (volunteered)	34
No opinion	4

By Sex
Male

Man	43%
Woman	12
No difference (volunteered)	41
No opinion	4

Female

Man	54%
Woman	15
No difference (volunteered)	27
No opinion	4

Now, I'm going to read several statements. As I read each one, please tell me whether you agree or disagree:

It is much better for everyone involved if the man is the achiever outside the home and the woman takes care of the home and family?

Agree	52%
Men	53
Women	51

A working mother can establish just as warm and secure a relationship with her children as a mother who does not work?

Agree	59%
Men	52
Women	66

Women get a greater sense of satisfaction from caring for their family than from a job well done at work?

Agree	60%
Men	59
Women	60

Men get a greater sense of satisfaction from caring for their family than from a job well done at work?

Agree 50%
Men 59
Women 42

Women are more capable of managing a household than men?

Agree 66%
Men 64
Women 68

Men who stay home and care for children rather than work are just as capable as women of being good parents?

Agree 78%
Men 75
Women 80

Men are more capable of being successful in the business world than women?

Agree 43%
Men 46
Women 40

Most women work only because their families need the money?

Agree 55%
Men 55
Women 55

Women are capable of being just as successful as men in the workplace?

Agree 91%
Men 90
Women 92

Women who have successful careers end up sacrificing too much of their family and personal life?

Agree 69%
Men 69
Women 69

Men who have successful careers end up sacrificing too much of their family and personal life?

Agree 66%
Men 68
Women 64

Now, I'd like you to think about men's and women's personalities, interests, and abilities. Not including purely physical differences, do you think men and women are basically similar or basically different?

Similar 40%
Different 58
No opinion 2

Now, I want to ask about some more specific characteristics of men and women. For each one I read, please tell me whether you think it is generally more true of men or more true of women:

Fifteen Characteristics Most Often Said to Describe Men

	Total	Men	Women
Aggressive	64%	68%	61%
Strong	61	66	57
Proud	59	62	55
Disorganized	56	55	57
Courageous	54	55	53
Confident	54	58	49
Independent	50	58	43
Ambitious	48	51	44
Selfish	47	49	44
Logical	45	53	37
Easygoing	44	48	40
Demanding	43	39	46
Possessive	42	38	45
Funny	40	47	34
Level-headed	39	36	34

Fifteen Characteristics Most Often Said to Describe Women

	Total	Men	Women
Emotional	81%	79%	83%
Talkative	73	73	74
Sensitive	72	74	71
Affectionate	66	69	64
Patient	64	60	68
Romantic	60	59	61
Moody	58	63	52
Cautious	57	55	59
Creative	54	48	60
Thrifty	52	51	53
Manipulative	51	54	48
Honest	42	44	41
Critical	42	43	41
Happy	39	38	39
Possessive	37	43	32

Asked of those who are employed: About how many hours per week do you work (count all jobs for pay)?

	Men	Women
30 or less	8	25
31 to 35	3	6
36 to 40	36	45
41 to 50	30	17
51 plus	22	6
No opinion	1	1

Asked of those who replied that men and women are basically different: What do you think is the main reason men and women have different personalities, interests, and abilities? Is it mainly because of the way men and women are raised, or are the differences part of their biological makeup?

The way they are raised	40%
Their biological makeup	45
Both equally	13
Other	1
No opinion	1

Asked of those who are married or living with a partner and both are employed: Do you and your husband/wife/partner each earn about the same amount of money at your jobs, is there a little difference in your earnings, or is there a big difference in your earnings?

Man and woman earn same amount	11%
Man earns a little more	21
Man earns a lot more	52
Woman earns a little more	9
Woman earns a lot more	7

Asked of those who are married or living with a partner: When it comes to household chores, do you and your husband/wife/partner share the work equally, do you do more of the work, or does he/she do more of the work?

	Total	Men	Women
Share equally	40%	46%	35%
Man does more	7	8	6
Woman does more	52	45	59
Other; no opinion	1	1	*

*Less than 1%

Note: In a remarkable shift of opinion compared to the mid-1970s, the American public now thinks that men have a better life than women in this country. According to a new Gallup Mirror of America Poll, today nearly one half of all adults believes that men have the better life, whereas in a 1975 Gallup Poll only one third thought that men had it best.

Fifteen years ago, there was no dominant view of which sex had the better life; opinion was fairly evenly split between the views that men had it better, women had it better, and neither sex had an advantage. Now, among both men and women the view that men have it better clearly dominates. Only a minority (22%) now believes that women have a better life, and 21% believe that men and women have a similar quality of life.

The women's movement is credited with improving women's lives but faulted for making family life more difficult. When asked about changes brought about over the past twenty years, majorities say that women's lives have become easier (54%) and more satisfying (56%) than they were two decades ago. But much larger majorities think that it has become harder for parents to raise children (82%), harder for marriages to be successful (76%), and harder for women to combine both job and family responsibilities (66%) as a result of the women's movement.

People are nearly evenly divided in opinion about whether the women's movement has made it easier (47%) or harder (50%) for families to earn a comfortable living. However, this split in opinion reflects the divergent perspectives of men and women on this issue. From the male point of view, the women's movement has allowed the responsibility for supporting a family to be shared between husband and wife, making things easier. On the other hand, women see the necessity of two incomes as creating more difficulties.

FEBRUARY 14
PRESIDENT BUSH

Interviewing Date: 2/8–11/90
Survey #GO 922003

Do you approve or disapprove of the way George Bush is handling his job as president?

Approve 73%
Disapprove 16
No opinion 11

By Sex
Male

Approve 78%
Disapprove 14
No opinion 8

Female

Approve 68%
Disapprove 18
No opinion 14

By Ethnic Background
White

Approve 75%
Disapprove 15
No opinion 10

Black

Approve 58%
Disapprove 25
No opinion 17

By Education
College Graduate

Approve 78%
Disapprove 15
No opinion 7

College Incomplete

Approve 76%
Disapprove 16
No opinion 8

High-School Graduate

Approve 74%
Disapprove 16
No opinion 10

Less Than High-School Graduate

Approve 63%
Disapprove 18
No opinion 19

By Income
$50,000 and Over

Approve 84%
Disapprove 13
No opinion 3

$30,000–$49,999

Approve 77%
Disapprove 14
No opinion 9

$20,000–$29,999

Approve 74%
Disapprove 17
No opinion 8

Under $20,000

Approve 63%
Disapprove 20
No opinion 18

By Political Affiliation
Republicans

Approve 91%
Disapprove 5
No opinion 4

Democrats

Approve 61%
Disapprove 27
No opinion 12

Independents

Approve 66%
Disapprove 18
No opinion 16

Moderate-to-Liberal White Democrats

Approve 56%
Disapprove 33
No opinion 11

Conservative White Democrats

Approve 73%
Disapprove 19
No opinion 8

By Political Ideology
Liberal

Approve 65%
Disapprove 25
No opinion 10

Moderate

Approve 78%
Disapprove 13
No opinion 9

Conservative

Approve 82%
Disapprove 10
No opinion 8

What do you think is President Bush's greatest achievement to date?*

Panama invasion, Noriega capture 18%
Drug war, fighting drugs 9
Changes in USSR; getting along with
   Gorbachev 7
General foreign policy; foreign affairs;
   peace in world 7
Getting elected 3
Leadership qualities 2
Changes in Eastern Europe;
   Berlin Wall 2
Abortion stand 1
Economy; budget 1
Taxes 1
Other 9
Nothing 6
No opinion 36

*Total does not add to 100% due to rounding.

Here is a list of some problems and responsibilities facing the president and his administration. After one year in office, do you think George Bush is making progress or is not making progress on handling each of these different problems:

	Is making progress		
	1988 Nov.	1990 Feb.	Difference
Keep the nation out of war	70%	77%	+7
Keep America prosperous	65	59	−6
Increase respect for United States abroad	64	73	+9
Improve educational standards	61	48	−13
Improve the quality of the environment	50	46	−4
Improve the lot of minorities and the poor	39	35	−4
Reduce the crime rate in the United States	36	37	+1
Reduce the federal budget deficit	33	30	−3
Get drug crisis under control	27	57	+30
Avoid raising taxes	24	54	+30

*The November 1988 question asked about the expectations for the administration of George Bush, which was to take office in January 1989.

Note: President George Bush's job approval is down slightly from his record January 1990 high, but it still remains at one of the higher levels recorded for any president since the Gallup Poll began using this approval measure in 1938.

Bush's February approval rating is 73%, off 7 percentage points from his 80% rating in January, the second highest ever recorded for an American president. Bush's February level is the second highest recorded during his administration, slightly ahead of the approval ratings given through the summer and fall of 1989.

Bush's approval and disapproval levels are fairly consistent throughout most subgroups of the population, with two exceptions: women and lower socioeconomic status groups (those with less than a high-school education and those with less than $20,000 per year in family income) give the president lower approval ratings than the national average. But these groups do not have abnormally high disapproval levels of Bush; they are simply more likely to have no opinion.

On the other hand, the data show that two other groups—blacks and moderate-to-liberal white Democrats—have lower approval and higher disapproval ratings of Bush. The poll thus suggests that it is among these groups that Bush has his only real image problems at this time.

The February poll also included a series of questions designed to shed light on the reasons why the president is currently enjoying such extraordinary job approval. In reply, more than one third discuss some aspect of foreign policy. This group is by far the largest response category given, particularly in view of the fact that over four out of ten respondents could not or would not name any achievement at all.

First is Bush's ordering the invasion of Panama and the subsequent capture of General Manuel Noriega (18%). This is followed by 7% who discuss Bush's foreign policy achievements in general, and another 7% who specifically relate his greatest achievement to some aspect of the changes in the Soviet Union. Another 2% talk about events in Eastern Europe.

The most frequently cited achievement after foreign policy and the only domestic one that is mentioned by over 1% is the war on drugs. About 9% discuss their perceptions of Bush's success in fighting the drug problem as his greatest achievement. (This does not include those respondents who mentioned drugs in connection with the invasion of Panama.)

President Bush has dramatically exceeded the public's expectations of what they thought he would be able to do in getting the drug crisis under control and avoiding new taxes. These findings are the result of comparison questions asking Americans immediately after his election how well they thought he would do on selected issues, and responses given after one year in office to how much progress they think Bush has made on the same issues.

In November 1988 respondents were not at all optimistic about Bush's likelihood of getting the drug crisis under control or avoiding raising taxes.

Now, they are significantly positive about the progress the president has made, after one year in office, in both these areas. Bush has, in short, overperformed on drugs and taxes.

FEBRUARY 14
BASEBALL STRIKE

Interviewing Date: 2/8–11/90
Survey #GO 922003

Have you heard or read anything about a possible baseball strike this season?

	Those who have heard
National	45%

Asked of those who replied in the affirmative: Do you think there will be a baseball strike this season, or not?

	Yes
National	61%

Asked of those who had heard about a strike and thought there would be one this season: If there is a strike, whose side do you favor—the owners or the players?

Owners	57%
Players	22
Both sides	5
No opinion	16

Note: At the height of press coverage of a major league baseball lockout and possible strike delaying spring training, the latest Gallup Poll finds that more than one half (55%) of Americans have not heard or read about the possibility of a strike by players. Only 45% say that they have heard or read anything about a strike.

Among those who are knowledgeable about baseball, a strike is seen as highly likely. Sixty-one percent of the informed group—those who have heard about the possibility—believe that it will happen this season. In the event of a strike, respondents overwhelmingly would support the owners over the players. Fifty-seven percent favor

the owners, while only 22% say that they would favor the players' side.

FEBRUARY 21
SOUTH AFRICA

Interviewing Date: 2/15–18/90
Survey #GO 922004

Is your overall opinion of South Africa very favorable, mostly favorable, mostly unfavorable, or very unfavorable?

Very favorable	5%
Mostly favorable	25
Mostly unfavorable	32
Very unfavorable	22
No opinion	16

Selected National Trend
February 1989

Very favorable	5%
Mostly favorable	28
Mostly unfavorable	29
Very unfavorable	21
No opinion	17

How closely have you followed recent events in South Africa: very closely, fairly closely, not too closely, or not at all closely?

Very closely	22%
Fairly closely	46
Not too closely	22
Not at all closely	9
No opinion	1

Asked of those who are following the situation very or fairly closely: In the South African situation, are your sympathies more with the black population or more with the South African government?

With the black population	72%
With the government	14
Both equally (volunteered)	6
Neither (volunteered)	4
No opinion	6

With the black population 73%
With the government 12
Both equally (volunteered) 6
Neither (volunteered) 3
No opinion 6

The following questions were asked of the aware group: Have you happened to have heard or read anything recently about African National Congress leader Nelson Mandela?

Have heard 93%
Have not heard 7
No opinion .... *

*Less than 1%

To the best of your knowledge, is Nelson Mandela currently in jail or has he been released?

In jail 1%
Has been released 96
Don't know 3

Do you think the United States should put more pressure on the South African government to end its apartheid racial system, less pressure, or about the same amount of pressure as now?

More pressure 41%
Less pressure 17
Same amount 39
No opinion 3

Selected National Trend
September 1986

More pressure 55%
Less pressure 14
Same amount 24
No opinion 7

How important do you think economic sanctions were in the recent South African government's decision to release Nelson Mandela from jail? Were they very important, somewhat important, not very important, or not at all important?

Very important 37%
Somewhat important 40
Not very important 10
Not at all important 7
No opinion 7

Do you think the South African government has or has not made significant progress during the last year in trying to resolve its racial problems?

Significant progress 59%
No significant progress 36
No opinion 5

Selected National Trend
September 1986

Significant progress 22%
No significant progress 72
No opinion 6

Some people feel that economic sanctions against South Africa should be lifted as a result of the changes that are taking place there now. Others think the economic sanctions should be maintained to pressure the government to make further changes. Which view comes closer to your own?

Sanctions should be lifted 27%
Sanctions should be maintained 66
No opinion 7

Many companies and investors have ended all investment in South Africa in a process called divestment. Should companies continue this process to pressure the government to make further changes, or should companies start to invest money in South Africa as a result of the recent changes?

Continue to pressure the government 60%
Start to invest 29
No opinion 11

President Bush has extended an invitation to South African President De Klerk to visit the United States. Do you approve or disapprove of the president's action?

Approve 88%
Disapprove 9
No opinion 3

Do you think the South African government will eventually grant full political power to the black majority by peaceful means, or that the blacks will only be able to achieve power by violent means?

By peaceful means 48%
By violent means 39
No opinion 13

Selected National Trend
September 1986

By peaceful means 31%
By violent means 57
No opinion 12

Note: A current Gallup Poll on American attitudes toward South Africa finds the aware public much more hopeful now than in September 1986 that the end of apartheid can be reached through peaceful means. However, although a majority believes that the South African government has made significant progress toward resolving its racial problems, most do not think that the changes implemented so far warrant the lifting of economic sanctions.

Nearly six in ten (59%) respondents who have closely followed the situation believe that the Pretoria government has made significant progress in improving racial matters. This figure is up from 22% in response to the same question in the 1986 survey. Fewer than three in ten (27%) of aware Americans now think that the situation has changed enough to justify removing the sanctions.

Unchanged since Nelson Mandela won his freedom is the degree to which respondents say that they support the black population over the white-run South African government. In both the 1986 and the current Gallup Polls, an identical 72% of the aware public sided with the black majority.

Also unchanged since Mandela's release is overall favorability toward South Africa as a country. The 30% who say that they have a very or mostly favorable attitude is statistically the same as the 33% figure from the September 1989 Gallup Poll.

President George Bush's decision to invite South African President F. W. De Klerk to come to the United States appears to be uncontroversial. Nearly nine in ten (88%) of those following events in South Africa approve of the decision.

FEBRUARY 21
GERMAN REUNIFICATION

Interviewing Date: 2/15–18/90
Survey #GO 922004

Do you think the reunification of East and West Germany would be a good thing for the United States and its Western allies, or a bad thing?

Good 72%
Bad 12
Neither good nor bad (volunteered) 4
No opinion 12

Selected National Trend
December 1989

Good 63%
Bad 21
Neither good nor bad (volunteered) 5
No opinion 11

How concerned are you that if East and West Germany are reunited into one country that it might become an aggressor nation like it was in World War II?

Very concerned 15%
Fairly concerned 23
Not too concerned 33
Not at all concerned 26
No opinion 3

Selected National Trend
December 1989

Very concerned 13%
Fairly concerned 22
Not too concerned 34
Not at all concerned 26
No opinion 5

Note: Nearly three quarters of Americans (72%) think that the reunification of East and West Germany would be a good thing for the United States and its Western allies, according to a recent Gallup Poll. This figure is up 9 percentage points since a similar poll was conducted in December 1989.

The latest survey was begun the day after the United States, the USSR, Britain, France, and representatives of both Germanys concluded a meeting that launched the process that is expected to lead to reunification of the nation divided at the end of World War II. Most Americans do not seem to be worried about the security implications that a reunified Germany might pose for Europe and the rest of the world. About six in ten (59%) are not too or not at all concerned that a reunified Germany might become an aggressor nation as it did in the 1930s and 1940s. Sixty percent thought that way in December.

FEBRUARY 28
HONESTY AND ETHICAL STANDARDS

Interviewing Date: 2/8–11/90
Survey #GO 922003

How would you rate the honesty and ethical standards of the people in these different fields: very high, high, average, low, or very low?

	Very high, high	Average	Low, very low	No opinion
Druggists, pharmacists	62%	31%	5%	2%
Clergy	55	35	7	3
Medical doctors	52	38	9	1
Dentists	52	41	4	3
College teachers	51	36	5	8
Engineers	50	36	4	10
Policemen	49	41	9	1
Funeral directors	35	44	11	10
Bankers	32	52	13	3
Television reporters, commentators	32	46	20	2
Journalists	30	51	15	4
Business executives	25	55	14	6
Newspaper reporters	24	54	18	4
Senators	24	52	20	4
Lawyers	22	43	31	4
Local political officeholders	21	56	20	3
Building contractors	20	50	21	9
Congressmen	20	52	24	4
State political officeholders	17	55	24	4
Real estate agents	16	54	25	5
Labor union leaders	15	37	39	9
Stockbrokers	14	50	22	14
Insurance salesmen	13	47	36	4
Advertising practitioners	12	48	31	9
Car salesmen	6	36	53	5

Selected National Trend
Percent Saying Very High or High

	1981	1983	1985	1988
Druggists, pharmacists	59%	61%	65%	66%
Clergy	63	64	67	60
Medical doctors	50	52	58	53

Dentists	52	51	56	51
College teachers	45	47	53	54
Engineers	48	45	53	48
Policemen	44	41	47	47
Funeral directors	30	29	32	24
Bankers	39	38	38	26
Television reporters, commentators	36	33	33	22
Journalists	32	28	31	23
Business executives	19	18	23	16
Newspaper reporters	30	26	29	22
Senators	20	16	23	19
Lawyers	25	24	27	18
Local political officeholders	14	16	18	14
Building contractors	19	18	21	22
Congressmen	15	14	20	16
State political officeholders	12	13	15	11
Real estate agents	14	13	15	13
Labor union leaders	14	12	13	14
Stockbrokers	21	19	20	13
Insurance salesmen	11	13	10	10
Advertising practitioners	9	9	12	7
Car salesmen	6	6	5	6

Note: Americans' overall opinion of the honesty and ethical standards of twenty-five leading professions has not changed significantly since 1988, according to a new Gallup Poll. While certain professions have gained on others, those most admired in the past, such as druggists and the clergy, remain at the top of the list. At the other extreme, advertising practitioners and car salesmen once again are at the bottom.

While the clergy are still the second most admired group, recent televangelist scandals may have been at least partially responsible for a significant change in opinion since 1985. The public's perception of the honesty and ethical standards of the police has increased from 1977,

as well as that of television reporters and funeral directors. And considering the lingering Savings and Loan crisis, the increase in the ratings for bankers is surprising.

MARCH 1
SATISFACTION INDEX/PERSONAL FINANCES

Interviewing Date: 2/8–11/90
Survey #GO 922003

In general, are you satisfied or dissatisfied with the way things are going in the United States at this time?

	Satisfied
National	55%

Selected National Trend

	Satisfied
September–October 1988	56%
August–September 1987	45
March 1986	66
November 1985	51
February 1984	50
August 1983	35
April 1982	25
January 1981	17

In general, are you satisfied or dissatisfied with the way things are going in your personal life?

	Satisfied
National	83%

Selected National Trend

	Satisfied
September–October 1988	87%
August–September 1987	83
March 1986	84
November 1985	82
February 1984	79

August 1983 77
April 1982 76
January 1981 81

We are interested in how people's financial situation may have changed. Would you say that you are financially better off now than you were a year ago, or are you financially worse off now?

Better 49%
Worse 24
Same (volunteered) 26
No opinion 1

Selected National Trend

	Better	Worse	Same	No opinion
June 1989	42%	25%	31%	2%
May 1988	47	24	28	1
June 1987	43	32	24	1
June 1986	46	28	25	1
June 1985	43	29	26	2
July 1984	40	25	34	1
June 1983	28	39	32	1
Aug. 1982	25	46	26	3
June 1981	33	35	30	2
Mar. 1980	30	45	24	1
June 1979	30	41	27	2
June 1978	35	32	31	2
June 1977	39	31	28	2
Sept. 1976	33	30	36	1

Now, looking ahead, do you expect that at this time next year you will be financially better off than now, or worse off than now?

Better 65%
Worse 13
Same (volunteered) 16
No opinion 6

Selected National Trend

	Better	Worse	Same	No opinion
June 1989	58%	13%	20%	9%
May 1988	63	9	17	11
June 1987	57	17	18	8

June 1986	57	20	17	6
June 1985	52	19	19	10
July 1984	52	12	28	8
June 1983	43	19	28	10
Aug. 1982	37	29	24	10
June 1981	41	26	25	8
Mar. 1980	36	31	24	9
June 1979	33	30	27	10
June 1978	38	20	30	12
June 1977	47	17	27	9
Sept. 1976	44	12	31	13

Note: A recent Gallup Poll records continuing high levels of satisfaction with the way things are going in the United States. Fifty-five percent of Americans are satisfied with the direction of the country, almost identical to the level measured in the fall of 1988 immediately before George Bush was elected president.

The general levels of satisfaction in this country have been high for the last six years, ranging from a high of 66% in March 1986 to a low of 45% in August and September 1987. The big change came in 1984 (50%); measures in 1981 (17% satisfied), 1982 (25% satisfied), and 1983 (35% satisfied) were all significantly lower.

On the other hand, while President Ronald Reagan's approval levels were relatively low in 1985 and 1986—fully 10 percentage points below President Bush's current ratings—the satisfaction measures in 1985 and 1986 still were roughly where they are today. Moreover, while satisfaction was almost exactly the same in September and October 1988 as it is today, Reagan's approval rating then was just 54%, compared to Bush's 73%. In short, it appears that President Bush's approval ratings are built on more than an overall sense of general satisfaction with how things are going in the country.

Americans are remarkably sanguine about their personal situation, regardless of how they may feel about the country as a whole. Gallup measures since the beginning of the 1980s have shown consistently that about 80% are satisfied with the way things are going in their lives.

During the same time, satisfaction with the way things are going in the country has undergone significant swings. Americans apparently have a unique ability to think positively about their own personal life situations, even while seeing things around them in a much more negative light. Thus, while 83% now claim to be satisfied with their lives today, almost as many (76%) said that they were satisfied in April 1982. At that time only 25% said that they were satisfied with the way things were going in the United States.

At a time of increased satisfaction with the way things are going and high presidential approval, respondents are also more positive and optimistic about their financial situation. Almost one half (49%) think that their financial situation has improved over the last year, and nearly two thirds (65%) think that they will be better off financially in one year.

Both of these measures are up to the highest level recorded by Gallup over the last fourteen years. And both reflect the continuing financial optimism found since 1984, in sharp contrast to the economic pessimism of the early 1980s and late 1970s.

MARCH 5
FRIENDSHIP

Interviewing Date: 1/18–21/90
Survey #GO 922002

How often do you ever feel lonely?

Frequently	10%
Sometimes	26
Seldom	40
Never	23
No opinion	1

Not counting your relatives, about how many close friends would you say you have?

One	4%
Two	9
Three	11
Four or five	24
Six to nine	14

Ten or more	33
None	3
No opinion	2

How easy is it for you to make new friends?

Very easy	41%
Fairly easy	40
Not very easy	14
Not at all easy	4
No opinion	1

How hard do you try to make new friends these days?

Very hard	6%
Fairly hard	21
Not very hard	42
Not at all hard	24
Don't try at all (volunteered)	5
No opinion	2

The following questions were asked of those who have at least one friend:

Are you satisfied with the number of friends you have, or would you like to have more?

Satisfied	75%
Like to have more	24
Like to have fewer (volunteered)	1
No opinion	*

*Less than 1%

Are you satisfied with the closeness of your relationship with your friends, or would you like to have closer relationships?

Satisfied with closeness	84%
Would like closer relationships	14
Would like less closeness (volunteered)	1
No opinion	1

Do you have one person you consider to be your best friend?

Yes 77%
No 22
No opinion 1

How often do you and your friends do each of the following:

Call each other when you need a favor?

Very often 37%
Somewhat often 37
Not very often 22
Never 4
No opinion .... *

Visit at each others' homes?

Very often 36%
Somewhat often 38
Not very often 22
Never 3
No opinion 1

Celebrate birthdays together?

Very often 31%
Somewhat often 27
Not very often 24
Never 18
No opinion .... *

Turn to each other with personal problems?

Very often 28%
Somewhat often 32
Not very often 30
Never 10
No opinion .... *

Go out to dinner together?

Very often 21%
Somewhat often 41
Not very often 29
Never 9
No opinion .... *

Spend time together watching television or listening to music?

Very often 18%
Somewhat often 28
Not very often 33
Never 21
No opinion .... *

Attend parties together?

Very often 18%
Somewhat often 34
Not very often 30
Never 17
No opinion 1

Participate in sports together, such as tennis, jogging, basketball, etc.?

Very often 14%
Somewhat often 22
Not very often 22
Never 42
No opinion .... *

Pray together?

Very often 14%
Somewhat often 20
Not very often 25
Never 41
No opinion .... *

Attend movies or sporting events together?

Very often 13%
Somewhat often 30
Not very often 30
Never 27
No opinion .... *

Take vacations together?

Very often 5%
Somewhat often 15
Not very often 31
Never 49
No opinion .... *

Borrow money from each other?

Very often 4%
Somewhat often 9
Not very often 24
Never 63
No opinion .... *

*Less than 1%

Do you ever get into serious arguments with your friends?

Yes 13%
No 80
Sometimes (volunteered) 7
No opinion .... *

*Less than 1%

Thinking about the amount of time you usually spend with your friends, do you think you spend too much time with them, about the right amount, or not enough time?

Too much 2%
About right 65
Not enough 32
No opinion 1

Think for a moment of your half dozen or so closest friends. How many of them live in your local community—all of them, most of them, some of them, or none?

All of them 19%
Most of them 33
Some of them 35
None 13
No opinion .... *

*Less than 1%

How long ago did you most recently make a new friend?

Within the past year 65%
One year ago 10
Two years ago 7
Three years ago 3

Four years ago 1
Five years ago 2
Six years ago .... *
Seven years ago 1
Eight or more years ago 4
No opinion 7

*Less than 1%

Asked of those who have a best friend: Is your best friend a man or a woman?

	Men	Women
Man	69%	18%
Woman	31	81
No opinion	*	1

*Less than 1%

Note: Loneliness strikes as many as one in three Americans today, and, although most people claim to be happy with the friends they have, there is a strong undercurrent of discontent among nearly one half of the public who complain that they either do not have enough time for friends, they want more friends, or they would like to have closer relationships with their friends.

A new Gallup Mirror of America survey recently polled adults across the nation to question them about their friendships. One in four (24%) would like to have more friends. People who want more friends already have as many as anyone else; what they often lack is time to spend with them.

The most popular activities among friends are those that provide lots of opportunity for conversation and mutual support. Majorities say that they often visit friends at home (74%), call on them for favors (74%), go out to dinner with them (62%), rely on their friends when they have personal problems (60%), and help friends celebrate their birthdays (58%).

Three out of four adults (75%) are satisfied with the number of friends they have, and an even larger proportion (84%) are satisfied with the closeness of their current relationships. However, although most adults claim that it is easy to make friends, many admit that they generally do not work at it very much. Only about one in four (27%) is trying very or fairly hard to make new friends now, while the majority (71%) of them are either not trying hard or at all.

MARCH 14
VICE PRESIDENT QUAYLE

Interviewing Date: 3/8–11/90
Survey #GO 922005

Based on what you know about Vice President Dan Quayle, do you think he is qualified to serve as president if it becomes necessary, or not?

Yes, qualified 31%
No, not qualified 54
No opinion 15

Selected National Trend

	Yes	No	No opinion
1989			
May	34%	52%	14%
1988			
October	46	42	12
September	34	47	19
August	41	40	19

Do you approve or disapprove of the way Dan Quayle is handling his job as vice president?

Approve 46%
Disapprove 27
No opinion 27

Selected National Trend

	Approve	Dis- approve	No opinion
November 1989	43%	29%	28%

If President Bush runs for reelection in 1992, do you think he should keep Dan Quayle as his vice presidential running mate or choose someone new?

Keep Quayle 35%
Choose someone new 49
No opinion 16

Will the issue of whether or not President Bush keeps Dan Quayle as his running mate in 1992 be very important, somewhat important, or not at all important in your vote for president in that election?

Very important 22%
Somewhat important 39
Not at all important 32
No opinion 7

If President Bush does choose someone new as his vice presidential running mate in 1992, would you favor appointing Dan Quayle to a cabinet post such as secretary of defense, or not?

Yes 30%
No 51
No opinion 19

I'd like you to rate Vice President Dan Quayle using a scale that goes from the highest possible rating of +5 for someone you have a very favorable opinion of, all the way down to the lowest position of −5 for someone you have a very unfavorable opinion of. How far up or down the scale would you rate Vice President Dan Quayle?

Highly favorable (+5, +4) 15%
Mildly favorable (+3, +2, +1) 31
Mildly unfavorable (−1, −2, −3) 12
Highly unfavorable (−4, −5) 15
No opinion 27

Note: The Dan Quayle factor could shape up to be one of the most significant issues of the 1992 presidential election campaign. The majority of Americans believes that Quayle is not qualified to be president, should it become necessary for him to step into that office. Additionally, almost one half says that Quayle should be replaced with another vice presidential candidate if President George Bush seeks reelection in 1992. And, for the most part, respondents are not particularly receptive to the idea that Bush gently move Quayle off the ticket into a cabinet post. The majority says that he should simply be dropped.

This public assessment of Quayle's capabilities for the presidency has gone down, not up. When Quayle was nominated in August 1988, he was largely unknown. At that time the public was slightly more likely to say that he was qualified than not. Perceptions of his qualifications rallied immediately before the 1988 election but dropped significantly by May 1989.

Now, more than one year after his inauguration, Americans' assessment of Quayle's ability to be president has dropped slightly more. Only 31% now think that Quayle is qualified, with a majority (54%) saying that he is not qualified. Moreover, almost one half (49%) says that Bush should get a new running mate in 1992, while only slightly more than one third (35%) think that Quayle should be retained.

The public apparently is looking beyond either its views of Quayle as a person or his job so far as vice president. His job approval, now at 46% (with 27% saying they disapprove), although significantly lower than Bush's, is still more positive than negative. And, in a measure of basic opinion, only 27% say that they have an unfavorable opinion of Quayle the man, with 46% saying they have a favorable opinion.

MARCH 21
U.S. CENSUS

Interviewing Date: 3/15–18/90
Survey #GO 922006

The U.S. government conducts a census, or a count, of this country's population on a regular basis. Can you tell me if the census is taken every year, every five years, every ten years, or every twenty years?

Every year 7%
Every five years 21
Every ten years (correct) 60
Every twenty years 2
Don't know 10

Would you happen to know when the next U.S. Census will be taken?

Right now/this month/next month/   %
    April 1/soon (correct) 36%
Later this year 30
Other 7
Don't know 27

The census by law collects social and economic information about people and their housing. Only grouped information is released by the Census Bureau. The law says that information on individuals must be kept confidential by the U.S. Census Bureau and not given out. How confident are you that the Census Bureau will not release an individual's census information to other government agencies?

Very confident 23%
Somewhat confident 44
Not at all confident 28
No opinion 5

It has been suggested that parts of certain groups in America, particularly minorities and the poor in inner cities, are missed and not counted by the census. The suggestion has been made that the government estimate how many people are missed and add these estimates into the final census count. Other people say that the census should only include the actual number of people counted. Which of these views comes closer to your own?

Include estimates in count 48%
Include only actual number counted 45
No opinion 7

The Census Bureau is required by law to conduct a count of this country's population. To the best of your knowledge, is your participation in the survey required by law, or not?

Yes, required (correct) 47%
No, not required 43
No opinion 10

Which state do you think has the largest population of all the states in the United States?

California (correct) 59%
New York 28
Texas 6
Florida 2
No opinion; other 5

What percent of the U.S. population today would you say is black?

Less than 10 percent 2%
Between 10 and 14 ⎫ correct 8
Between 15 and 19 ⎭ 7
Between 20 and 29 21
Between 30 and 39 22
Between 40 and 49 16
50 percent or more 13
No opinion 11

What percent of the U.S. population today would you say is Jewish?

Less than 5 percent (correct) 8%
Between 5 and 9 10
Between 10 and 19 25
Between 20 and 29 18
Between 30 and 49 12
50 percent or more 3
No opinion 24

What percent of the U.S. population today would you say is Hispanic?

Less than 5 percent 3%
Between 5 and 9 (correct) 12
Between 10 and 19 28
Between 20 and 29 20
Between 30 and 49 16
50 percent or more 5
No opinion 16

Again, just your best guess, about how many people currently live in the United States?

Under one million 1%
One million to less than 10 million 9
10 to less than 50 million 7
50 to less than 100 million 4
100 to less than 200 million 5
200 to less than 300 million (correct) 27

300 to less than 500 million 3
500 million people or more 15
No opinion 29

Note: On the eve of the 1990 decennial U.S. Census, Americans exhibit a generally low familiarity with the process, according to the Gallup Poll. Only about one fourth of respondents comes anywhere close to estimating the correct population of the United States, and the average person thinks that it is 32% black, 21% Hispanic, and 18% Jewish—although the actual figures are 12%, 8%, and less than 3%, respectively.

The 1989 estimate of the U.S. population from the Census Bureau is about 250 million, but only 27% select a very broad "correct" range, between 200 and 300 million. Another 26% guess that the total is less than 200 million, including 17% who say that the U.S. population is less than 50 million. On the other end of the scale, 15% think that our population is more than 500 million, while three out of ten do not even venture a guess.

There has been one controversial issue surrounding the census this year: whether the government should use estimates to add to its tallies in areas, mainly in the inner cities and among the poor and ethnic groups, where research shows that previous counts have missed population. Americans are evenly split on this issue.

MARCH 28
INCOME TAX

Interviewing Date: 3/8–11/90
Survey #GO 922005

Do you consider the amount of federal income tax which you have to pay as too high, about right, or too low?

Too high 63%
About right 31
Too low 2
No opinion 4

Selected National Trend

	Too high	About right	Too low	No opinion
1973	65%	28%	1%	6%
1969	69	25	*	6
1967	58	38	1	3
1961	46	45	1	8
1957	61	31	*	8
1953	59	37	*	4
1951	52	43	1	4
1948	57	38	1	4

*Less than 1%

Since the Tax Reform Act of 1986, has the amount of taxes you now pay gone down a lot, gone down a little, gone up a little, gone up a lot, or stayed about the same?

Down a lot 2%
Down a little 5
Up a little 34
Up a lot 22
Stayed the same 27
No opinion 10

Selected National Trend

	Down a lot, a little	Up a little, a lot	Stayed same	No opinion
1986*	18%	41%	30%	11%

*In a poll conducted in September 1986, this and the next three questions were asked in the context of the public's expectations of the changes that the Tax Reform Act of 1986 would bring about.

Do you think the Tax Reform Act of 1986 has made for a fairer distribution of the tax load among all taxpayers, one that's less fair, or hasn't it been much different from the previous system?

Fairer 9%
Less fair 37
No difference 40
No opinion 14

Selected National Trend

	Fairer	Less fair	No difference	No opinion
1986	27%	20%	36%	17%

Do you think the Tax Reform Act of 1986 has made it less complicated for you to pay your taxes, more complicated, or about the same as the previous system?

More complicated 31%
Less complicated 12
About the same 48
No opinion 9

Selected National Trend

	More	Less	Same	No opinion
1986	17%	19%	51%	13%

All things considered, do you think the Tax Reform Act of 1986 has had a positive effect on the nation's economy, a negative effect, or hasn't it made much difference one way or the other?

Positive effect 15%
Negative effect 20
No difference 56
No opinion 9

Selected National Trend

	Positive	Negative	No difference	No opinion
1986	28%	15%	41%	16%

Will you file your return early this year, will you wait until April 15 itself to mail it in, or will you file for an extension?

Will file early 69%
Will wait until April 15 19
Will file for extension 5
No opinion 7

Will you or your family pay for the help of an outside tax specialist or firm this year to help you do your taxes, or not?

Yes 54%
No 43
No opinion 3

Will you or your family buy or use a book to help you do your taxes this year, or not?

Yes 14%
No 82
No opinion 4

Will you or your family use a computer program to help you do your taxes this year, or not?

Yes 9%
No 87
No opinion 4

All in all, which of the following best describes how you feel about doing your income taxes:

I love it 2%
I like it 21
I dislike it 33
I hate it 30
Neither like nor dislike it 10
No opinion 4

Note: More than three years after the 1986 Tax Reform Act restructured the federal income tax, there is little evidence that Americans perceive the reform as having achieved its stated goals of creating a fairer and less complicated tax system. In fact, according to a new 1990 Gallup Poll, respondents say that since 1986 their taxes have gone up, not down; that the system is no fairer now than it used to be; and that it has not simplified paying taxes. Indeed, many believe that it

has made paying taxes more complicated. The Tax Reform Act is thought to have had little impact on the nation's economy, either positive or negative.

These opinions fulfill the public's generally low expectations for the Tax Reform Act when it became law. Gallup Polls in September 1986 indicated that respondents did not hold out much hope that the reforms would make taxes fairer, lower, or less complicated. Now, after three years of experience with the new system, they have become even more critical of it.

APRIL 2
SPORTS

Interviewing Date: 2/15–18/90
Survey #GO 922004

What is your favorite sport to watch?

Football 35%
Baseball 16
Basketball 15
Ice hockey 3
Tennis 3
Boxing 2
Golf 2
Ice skating, figure skating 2
Bowling 1
Wrestling 1
Soccer 1
Auto racing 1
Fishing 1
Horse racing 1
Other 3
None; don't watch sports 11
No opinion 2

Selected National Trend

	Football	Baseball	Basketball
1981	38%	16%	9%
1972	36	21	8
1960	21	34	9
1948	17	39	10

Overall, how interested are you in following professional and college sports such as football, baseball, basketball, and hockey?

Extremely interested 9%
Very interested 21
Somewhat interested 40
Not at all interested; no opinion 30

Those who responded that they are extremely, very, or somewhat interested in following professional and college sports were asked:

Thinking about the amount of time you personally spend watching, reading, and listening to sports events and programs, do you think you spend too much time, too little time, or about the right amount of time on sports?

Too much 11%
Too little 13
About right; no opinion 76

Which is your favorite NFL team?*

49ers 15%
Bears 7
Broncos 6
Giants 6
Cowboys 5
Redskins 5
Steelers 3
Vikings 3
Browns 3
Raiders 3
Packers 3

By Region

East

49ers 9%
Bears 2
Broncos 3
Giants 17
Cowboys 3
Redskins 8
Steelers 9
Vikings .... **

Browns 2
Raiders 4
Packers .... **

Midwest

49ers 10%
Bears 15
Broncos 5
Giants .... **
Cowboys 2
Redskins 1
Steelers 2
Vikings 9
Browns 7
Raiders 1
Packers 10

South

49ers 14%
Bears 7
Broncos 6
Giants 4
Cowboys 11
Redskins 6
Steelers 2
Vikings 1
Browns 1
Raiders 2
Packers 1

West

49ers 30%
Bears 3
Broncos 12
Giants 1
Cowboys 2
Redskins 4
Steelers .... **
Vikings 1
Browns 1
Raiders 6
Packers .... **

*In this and the next two questions, only teams named by at least 3% nationwide are included.
**Less than 1%

Which is your favorite major league baseball team?

Yankees	7%
Cubs	7
Mets	7
Dodgers	6
Cardinals	6
Red Sox	5
Giants	4
Tigers	4
Reds	4
Braves	3
Twins	3

By Region
East

Yankees	14%
Cubs	1
Mets	20
Dodgers	3
Cardinals	2
Red Sox	14
Giants	2
Tigers	*
Reds	2
Braves	*
Twins	*

Midwest

Yankees	2%
Cubs	15
Mets	*
Dodgers	1
Cardinals	10
Red Sox	2
Giants	2
Tigers	12
Reds	6
Braves	*
Twins	9

South

Yankees	7%
Cubs	6
Mets	3
Dodgers	6
Cardinals	8
Red Sox	2
Giants	3
Tigers	3
Reds	4
Braves	11
Twins	1

West

Yankees	5%
Cubs	4
Mets	4
Dodgers	17
Cardinals	2
Red Sox	3
Giants	11
Tigers	*
Reds	3
Braves	1
Twins	2

*Less than 1%

Which is your favorite NBA team?

Lakers	16%
Celtics	13
Bulls	6
Pistons	6
Knickerbockers	3
76ers	3

By Region
East

Lakers	14%
Celtics	21
Bulls	3
Pistons	1
Knickerbockers	11
76ers	8

Midwest

Lakers	6%
Celtics	11
Bulls	12
Pistons	14
Knickerbockers	*
76ers	1

Lakers	16%
Celtics	14
Bulls	6
Pistons	5
Knickerbockers	2
76ers	2

West

Lakers	32%
Celtics	6
Bulls	2
Pistons	2
Knickerbockers	1
76ers	*

*Less than 1%

All in all, which one of the following professional sports do you think requires its players to be the best athletes—that is, to have the highest level of athletic skill?

Football	34%
Basketball	29
Hockey	11
Baseball	9
Tennis	8
Golf	4
None of these	2
No opinion	3

During baseball season, roughly how many hours do you typically spend watching either professional or college baseball on television? (This question was also asked about in-season television viewing of football, basketball, and hockey.)

	Base-ball	Basket-ball	Foot-ball	Hockey
None	31%	27%	14%	70%
Up to 2 hours	30	36	26	16
3 to 4 hours	15	14	21	4
5 to 6 hours	7	7	16	1
7 hours or more	12	11	19	2
No opinion	5	5	4	7

In your opinion, are professional baseball players generally overpaid, underpaid, or are their salaries just about right? (This question was also asked about professional basketball, football, and hockey players.)

	Base-ball	Basket-ball	Foot-ball	Hockey
Overpaid	75%	59%	62%	27%
Underpaid	3	3	7	11
About right	19	29	27	25
No opinion	3	9	4	37

Now, please think for a moment about how major league baseball today compares with how major league baseball was played twenty or thirty years ago. As far as you are concerned, is major league baseball more fun to watch these days, less fun to watch, or has it really not changed over the past twenty or thirty years?

More fun	29%
Less fun	29
Not changed	35
No opinion	7

Compared to twenty or thirty years ago, would you say baseball players today care more about the game, care less about the game, or are about as concerned with the game as they were in the past?

Care more	16%
Care less	50
Concerned as in past	31
No opinion	3

I am going to name some changes major league baseball has seen over the past twenty or thirty years and want you to tell me whether you think each has been a change for the better, a change for the worse, or not made a difference:

Increases in the number of major league teams?

Better 65%
Worse 11
No difference 16
No opinion 8

Playoffs in each league to determine who goes to the World Series?

Better 65%
Worse 8
No difference 20
No opinion 7

The use of domed stadiums in some cities?

Better 62%
Worse 17
No difference 16
No opinion 5

The designated-hitter rule in the American League?

Better 36%
Worse 26
No difference 20
No opinion 18

Increases in the average salary paid to players?

Better 26%
Worse 53
No difference 15
No opinion 6

Increasing use of artificial turf in some ball parks?

Better 26%
Worse 50
No difference 17
No opinion 7

As I read a list of changes which could be made in major league baseball in the years to come, please tell me whether you favor or oppose each change:

Interleague play between American and National League teams during regular season?

Favor 61%
Oppose 30
No opinion 9

Adding two to four more teams to major league baseball?

Favor 60%
Oppose 31
No opinion 9

Use of a designated hitter in the National League as well as in the American League?

Favor 53%
Oppose 32
No opinion 15

Elimination of the designated hitter in both leagues?

Favor 44%
Oppose 40
No opinion 16

Allowing players to use aluminum bats?

Favor 30%
Oppose 56
No opinion 14

Note: Football continues to reign as America's favorite spectator sport, while basketball is gaining fan support and baseball's popularity remains static, according to a new Gallup Mirror of America survey.

The poll shows football winning across the board on most measures of fan popularity. It is the game that people enjoy watching the most and that sports fans spend the most time watching on television. It is also the most popular spectator sport at the college and high-school levels, although baseball continues to be the professional sport that attracts the highest total attendance, due to the large number of games played each season.

Baseball's impact on American fans has been slipping in general compared to thirty or forty years ago, when Gallup consistently found it to be the nation's favorite sport. In 1972 a Gallup Poll showed for the first time football replacing baseball as the favorite spectator event. Baseball's popularity has stayed about the same since then.

Today, more than one third (35%) of all adults name football as their favorite sport to watch. Less than one half cite baseball (16%) or basketball (15%) as their favorite, with ice hockey (3%) and tennis (3%) tied for a distant fourth.

APRIL 11
MOST IMPORTANT PROBLEM/
ENVIRONMENT

Interviewing Date: 4/5–8/90
Survey #GO 922007

What do you think is the most important problem facing this country today?

Economic Problems

Economy	7%
Federal budget deficit, failure to balance budget	6
Unemployment	3
Trade deficit, trade relations, balance of trade	2
High cost of living, inflation	1
High cost of borrowing, interest rates	**
Recession, depression	**
Other specific economic problems	3

Other Problems

Drugs, drug abuse	30%
Poverty, hunger, homelessness	11
Environment, pollution	8
Crime	2
Quality of education	1
Ethics in society, moral decline	1
Fear of war, nuclear war	1

International problems	1
AIDS	1
Dissatisfaction with government	1
Other noneconomic problems	11
No opinion	9

*Totals do not add to 100% due to rounding.
**Less than 1%

Do you consider yourself to be an environmentalist, or not?

	Yes
National	73%

Selected National Trend
May 1989

	Yes
National	76%

Asked of those who replied in the affirmative: Would you say you are a strong environmentalist, or not?

Yes, strong environmentalist	35%
Not strong	38
	73%

I'm going to read you a list of environmental problems. As I read each one, please tell me if you personally worry about this problem a great deal, a fair amount, only a little, or not at all. First, how much do you personally worry about:

Pollution of drinking water?

Great deal	65%
Fair amount	22
Only a little	9
Not at all	4
No opinion	*

*Less than 1%

Pollution of rivers, lakes, and reservoirs?

Great deal 64%
Fair amount 23
Only a little 9
Not at all 4
No opinion .... *

*Less than 1%

Selected National Trend
May 1989

Great deal 72%
Fair amount 19
Only a little 5
Not at all 3
No opinion 1

Contamination of soil and water by toxic waste?

Great deal 63%
Fair amount 22
Only a little 10
Not at all 5
No opinion .... *

Selected National Trend
May 1989

Great deal 69%
Fair amount 21
Only a little 7
Not at all 3
No opinion .... *

*Less than 1%

Air pollution?

Great deal 58%
Fair amount 29
Only a little 9
Not at all 4
No opinion .... *

Selected National Trend
May 1989

Great deal 63%
Fair amount 25
Only a little 8
Not at all 4
No opinion .... *

*Less than 1%

Ocean and beach pollution?

Great deal 52%
Fair amount 27
Only a little 12
Not at all 7
No opinion 2

Selected National Trend
May 1989

Great deal 60%
Fair amount 23
Only a little 11
Not at all 5
No opinion 1

Loss of natural habitats for wildlife?

Great deal 51%
Fair amount 30
Only a little 12
Not at all 7
No opinion .... *

*Less than 1%

Selected National Trend
May 1989

Great deal 58%
Fair amount 27
Only a little 9
Not at all 5
No opinion 1

Contamination of soil and water by radio-activity from nuclear facilities?

Great deal 48%
Fair amount 23
Only a little 17
Not at all 10
No opinion 2

Selected National Trend
May 1989

Great deal 54%
Fair amount 24
Only a little 14
Not at all 7
No opinion 1

Damage to the earth's ozone layer?

Great deal 43%
Fair amount 28
Only a little 15
Not at all 10
No opinion 4

Selected National Trend
May 1989

Great deal 51%
Fair amount 26
Only a little 13
Not at all 8
No opinion 2

Loss of tropical rain forests?

Great deal 40%
Fair amount 24
Only a little 19
Not at all 14
No opinion 3

Selected National Trend
May 1989

Great deal 42%
Fair amount 25
Only a little 18
Not at all 12
No opinion 3

Acid rain?

Great deal 34%
Fair amount 30
Only a little 18
Not at all 14
No opinion 4

Selected National Trend
May 1989

Great deal 41%
Fair amount 27
Only a little 18
Not at all 11
No opinion 3

The "greenhouse effect," or global warming?

Great deal 30%
Fair amount 27
Only a little 20
Not at all 16
No opinion 7

Selected National Trend
May 1989

Great deal 35%
Fair amount 28
Only a little 18
Not at all 12
No opinion 7

All in all, which of the following best describes how you feel about the environmental problems facing the earth: Life on earth will continue without major environmental disruptions only if:

We take additional, immediate, and drastic action concerning the environment? 54%
We take some additional actions concerning the environment? 33
We take just about the same actions we have been taking on the environment? .. 9
No opinion 4

Do you think that the American public today is too worried about the environment, not worried enough, or expresses about the right amount of concern about the environment?

Too worried 7%
Not worried enough 72
About right 19
No opinion 2

Do you think the government is too worried about the environment, not worried enough, or expresses about the right amount of concern about the environment?

Too worried 3%
Not worried enough 75
About right 18
No opinion 4

Do you think American business and industry is too worried about the environment, not worried enough, or expresses the right amount of concern about the environment?

Too worried 1%
Not worried enough 85
About right 11
No opinion 3

How much progress have we made in dealing with environmental problems in this country over the last twenty years—that is, since 1970? Would you say we have made a great deal of progress, only some progress, or hardly any progress at all?

Great deal 14%
Only some 63
Hardly any 21
No opinion 2

How much optimism do you have that we will have our environmental problems well under control in twenty years—that is, by the year 2010?

Great deal 18%
Only some 58
Hardly any 22
No opinion 2

It has been estimated that complying with current pollution laws and controls costs business and industry about $33 billion a year. Would you favor or oppose a new clean air law which would require the spending of an additional $20 billion a year by business and industry to clean up the air and reduce pollution?

Favor 78%
Oppose 15
No opinion 7

From what you have heard or read, would you say the United States does more to help solve environmental problems, less, or about the same amount as other countries?

More 40%
Less 18
About the same 32
No opinion 10

Which of the following things, if any, have you or other household members done in recent years to try to improve the quality of the environment:

Voluntarily recycled newspapers, glass, aluminum, motor oil, or other items?

                                                           Have done
National 85%

Avoided buying or using aerosol sprays?

                                                           Have done
National 63%

Contributed money to an environmental, conservation, or wildlife preservation group?

	Have done
National	49%

Specifically avoided buying a product because it was not recyclable?

	Have done
National	42%

Used cloth rather than disposable diapers?

	Have done
National	31%

Boycotted a company's products because of its record on the environment?

	Have done
National	28%

Did volunteer work for an environmental, conservation, or wildlife preservation group?

	Have done
National	18%

Are there any other things you have done in recent years to try and improve the quality of the environment?

Taken more care in the use of chemicals	5%
Kept car running clean, switched to unleaded gas, used car less	4
Planted a tree	4
Did not litter	3
Quit smoking	1
Quit burning trash, leaves	1
Other	13
Nothing	67
No opinion	2

Does your community require the sorting of glass, metal, and paper garbage so that materials can be reused or recycled, or not?

Yes	30%
No	67
No opinion	3

Here are two statements which people sometimes make when discussing the environment and economic growth. Which of these statements comes closer to your own point of view:

Protection of the environment should be given priority, even at the risk of curbing economic growth?	71%
Economic growth should be given priority, even if the environment suffers to some extent?	19
No opinion	10

Selected National Trend
September 1984

Protection of environment	61%
Economic growth	28
No opinion	11

Note: A new Gallup Poll shows that Americans are strongly in tune with Earth Day's avowed purpose of calling attention to the environmental problems of the world. A significant majority says that the public, government, business, and industry do not worry enough about the environment. However, large numbers claim that they themselves personally worry a great deal about environmental problems that could affect them directly.

These concerns notwithstanding, roughly the same number of Americans as in 1970 list the environment as a major problem facing the United States today. These concerns are overshadowed by the drug problem and economic considerations today, just as they were overshadowed by Vietnam in 1970. Even activist environmentalists who say that their issues are critically important do not list the environment as this country's most important problem.

Despite this, two thirds of Americans say that they are personally worrying a great deal about three environmental problems that could affect them directly: pollution of drinking water (65%); pollution of rivers, lakes, and reservoirs (64%); and contamination of soil and water by toxic waste (63%). There is slightly lower concern about air pollution (58%). About one half say that they personally worry a great deal about ocean and beach pollution (52%), the loss of natural habitats for wildlife (51%), and nuclear contamination (42%).

Concerns not so directly connected to the individual are less likely to be worrying respondents: damage to the earth's ozone layer (43%), loss of tropical rain forests (40%), acid rain (34%), and the greenhouse effect (30%). Indeed, personal worry about each of these issues (with the exception of concern about rain forest deforestation) has actually gone down slightly over the last year.

One Gallup Poll finding is of special relevance for participants in Earth Day: A significant majority of Americans says that hardly anyone—the public itself (72%), the government (75%), or business and industry (85%)—is concerned enough about the environment.

APRIL 18
SPORTS

Interviewing Date: Several between 11/10/89–1/15/90
Various Surveys

Which of these sports and activities, if any, have you, yourself, participated in within the last twelve months? [Respondents were handed a card listing more than fifty recreational activities.]

	1990	1989
Swimming	38%	36%
Fishing	29	29
Bicycling	28	24
Bowling	22	21
Camping	22	19
Hiking	20	19
Pool, billiards	20	17
Running, jogging	19	17
Weight training (NET)	16	19
Bicycle touring, racing	16	11
Softball	16	16
Volleyball	15	13
Motorboating	15	12
Aerobics, dancercize	13	14
Golf	13	12
Basketball	13	14
Weight lifting (free weights)	12	14
Darts	12	10
Ping-Pong, table tennis	11	9
Calisthenics	11	11
Hunting	10	12
Baseball	10	10
Canoeing, rowing	10	7
Tennis	9	8
Bodybuilding	9	10
Target shooting	9	9
Snow skiing	8	7
Rollerskating	8	7
Waterskiing	7	6
Flying disc (Frisbee)	7	5
Horseback riding	7	7
Badminton	6	3
Racquetball	5	4
Touch, flag football	5	4
Ice skating	5	4
Nautilus training	5	6
Archery	5	4
Snorkeling	4	3
Sailing	4	4
Soccer	4	2
Croquet	3	3
Skeet, trapshooting	3	3
Handball	2	2
Paddle, platform tennis	2	2
Scuba diving	2	1
Martial arts	2	2
Skateboarding	2	1
Distance, marathon running	2	1

Men's Top Activities

	1990	1989
Fishing	38%	41%
Swimming	36	38
Bicycling	27	24

Pool, billiards	27	26
Camping	25	22
Hiking	22	19
Bowling	22	23
Running, jogging	22	18
Softball	21	22
Basketball ⎱ tied	20	21
Motorboating ⎰	20	17

Women's Top Activities

	1990	1989
Swimming	39%	34%
Bicycling	29	25
Bowling	21	20
Fishing	21	17
Aerobics, dancercize	20	23
Camping	19	16
Hiking	18	13
Running, jogging	17	16
Bicycle touring, racing	15	9
Pool, billiards	14	9

Participation Changes by Decade

	1990	1980	1972	1959
Swimming	38%	37%	42%	33%
Fishing	29	24	24	32
Bicycling	28	27	28	–
Bowling	22	24	28	18
Softball	16	16	13	–
Pool, billiards	20	–	–	6
Volleyball	15	13	12	4
Hunting	10	13	12	16
Golf	13	8	14	8
Tennis	9	14	12	4
Horseback riding	7	7	9	5
Snow skiing	8	6	5	3

Frequency of Participation
(During Past Twelve Months)

Weight lifting	69%
Aerobics	61
Nautilus training	56
Bicycling	50
Swimming	34
Bowling	32
Tennis	31
Golf	29

Fishing	26
Hunting	24
Sailing	17
Horseback riding	12
Camping	11
Snow skiing	8

Note: The most common recreational activities pursued by Americans in their leisure hours have remained remarkably constant over the past thirty years, with swimming, fishing, bicycling, and bowling continuing to be the favorite pastimes. However, participation in a wide variety of other activities has risen over the years, with participation down in only a few.

The results are based on information gathered by Gallup from a random sample of 2,000 Americans who were interviewed about their participation in more than fifty leisure activities. Gallup has been conducting this leisure audit since 1959.

Respondents were particularly likely this past year to be engaging in back-to-nature sports such as bicycle touring and racing, camping, hiking, and boating. Pool, billiards, and badminton also have increased in popularity. Conversely, there have been slight declines in the popularity of more individually oriented body-image activities such as aerobics and weight lifting.

APRIL 25
U.S. CENSUS

Interviewing Date: 4/19–22/90
Survey #GO 922008

Has your household received your official 1990 U.S. Census form from the government yet?

Yes	89%
No	9
No opinion	2

Asked of those who had received a census form: Have you filled out the census form and sent it back yet?

Yes	90%
No	10

Asked of those who had received a form, filled it out, and returned it: How complicated was it to fill out your census form?

Very complicated 4%
Somewhat complicated 6
Not very complicated 19
Not at all complicated 67
No opinion 4

Note: According to the latest Gallup Poll, 89% of Americans say that they have received their 1990 census form, and nine in ten of those (90%) report that they have filled it out and returned it.

This high level of self-reported behavior stands in contrast to the low compliance reported by the Census Bureau. Recent estimates were that only about 60% of the forms distributed at the beginning of April had been returned. Census officials had earlier predicted a return rate of 70%.

As in all surveys, the Gallup Poll had more difficulty in measuring the responses of the urban and minority populations that many critics claim were missed by the census. Thus, to some degree, a higher reported rate of response would be expected from the Gallup survey than from Census Bureau estimates. Additionally, the latest Gallup Poll was conducted after extensive publicity about returning census forms; consequently, the poll may have measured last-minute returns sent after the bureau had made its compliance estimates.

APRIL 26
ABORTION

Interviewing Date: 4/5–8/90
Survey #GO 92207

As you may know, the state of New Hampshire recently considered a new law which would legalize abortion any time until fetal viability, and after that if the woman's physician determines if it is necessary for the woman's health or life, or if the fetus has a life-threatening abnormality. Would you favor or oppose the state where you live passing this law?

Favor 53%
Oppose 36
No opinion 11

As you may know, the state of Idaho recently considered a new law which would make it illegal for any woman to have an abortion except in four cases: 1) rape reported to the police within seven days of the rape; 2) incest where the woman is under eighteen; 3) where the fetus is deformed; and 4) where there is a physical threat to the health of the mother. Would you favor or oppose the state where you live passing this law?

Favor 42%
Oppose 52
No opinion 6

Interviewing Date: 4/5–8; 19–22/90
Survey #GO 92207; 92208

Do you think abortions should be legal under any circumstances, legal only under certain circumstances, or illegal in all circumstances?

Legal, any circumstances 31%
Legal, certain circumstances 53
Illegal, all circumstances 12
No opinion 4

Selected National Trend

	Legal, any	Legal, certain	Illegal, all	No opinion
1988	24%	57%	17%	2%
1983	23	58	16	3
1981	23	52	21	4
1980	25	53	18	4
1979	22	54	19	5
1977	22	55	19	4
1975	21	54	22	3

Note: The percentage of Americans who say that abortion should be legal under any circumstances has increased from 24% two years ago to 31% this month, representing the sharpest shift recorded by the Gallup Poll in its fifteen years of measuring opinions about abortion. At the same time, those who choose the other extreme on the scale—abortion should be illegal under all circumstances—has declined from 17% in 1988 to 12%, the lowest point to date. The percentage holding a middle position between these two extremes has not changed substantially since the question was first asked.

This 19-point margin of pro-choice over pro-life attitudes is significantly greater than Gallup's measures on this question between 1975 and 1988, when the margin was never more than 7 percentage points. However, the majority of Americans continue to say that they favor abortion under certain circumstances only.

The battleground of the abortion debate in the United States was effectively shifted back to the states by a 1989 Supreme Court decision that allowed state legislatures more latitude in enacting abortion laws than was previously the case. Consequently, Idaho passed a strongly pro-life bill making most abortions illegal except in rigidly specified situations. New Hampshire's legislature, on the other hand, passed a decidedly pro-choice bill, allowing abortions in most circumstances until fetal viability is reached, and even after that with a doctor's permission.

Neither bill will become law; each was vetoed by the respective state's governor. The proposed laws, however, provide an excellent measure of the potential support that such bills may be able to generate in various states in the months and years ahead.

APRIL 26
GREATEST BASEBALL PLAYER

Interviewing Date: 4/19–22/90
Survey #GO 922008

> Asked of those who follow major league baseball: Who would you say is the greatest baseball player of all time?*

Babe Ruth	31%
Mickey Mantle	7
Hank Aaron	7

Joe DiMaggio	7
Ted Williams	5
Willie Mays	4
Ty Cobb	4
Pete Rose	4
Lou Gehrig	4
Jackie Robinson	1

Selected National Trend
1949

Babe Ruth	30%
Ty Cobb	6
Lou Gehrig	5
Christy Mathewson	1
Honus Wagner	1
Grover Alexander	1
Rogers Hornsby	1
Carl Hubbell	1
Dizzy Dean	1
Charlie Gehringer	1

*Only the top ten players are listed here.

Note: Babe Ruth overwhelmingly is voted by American baseball fans as the greatest ball player of all time, according to a new Gallup Poll, just as he was forty years ago when Gallup last asked the question.

Six of the top ten players are still alive, but no active player is on the list. Ruth gets the vote of 31% of respondents who follow baseball, head and shoulders ahead of his nearest competitors—Mickey Mantle, Hank Aaron, and Joe DiMaggio, who rate 7% each.

Despite his recent troubles with the law, Pete Rose is eighth on the all-time greatest player list, thus suggesting that the public is willing to forgive him his transgressions and evaluate him on the basis of his playing ability.

MAY 1
VIETNAM WAR

Interviewing Date: 3/15–18/90
Survey #GO 922008

> Some people feel that war is an outmoded way of settling differences between nations.

*Others feel that wars are sometimes neces-
sary to settle differences. With which point
of view do you agree?*

Outmoded 49%
Sometimes necessary 48
No opinion 3

Selected National Trend

	Outmoded	Sometimes necessary	No opinion
1975	45%	46%	9%
1971	46	43	11

*Since World War II the policy of the United
States has been to maintain our military
strength throughout the world in order to help
governments that might be overthrown by
Communist-backed forces. Do you think we
should or should not continue to follow this
policy?*

Should continue 66%
Should not continue 29
No opinion 5

Selected National Trend

	Should continue	Should not continue	No opinion
1975	53%	37%	10%

*As I read a list of the major wars the United
States has been involved in during this century, please tell me, for each, whether you
think it was a just war, or not:*

World War I?

Yes, just 74%
No, not just 14
No opinion 12

World War II?

Yes, just 84%
No, not just 11
No opinion 5

Korean War?

Yes, just 47%
No, not just 41
No opinion 12

Vietnam War?

Yes, just 25%
No, not just 68
No opinion 7

*And in which of these wars do you think the
greatest number of American troops lost their
lives?*

World War I 9%
World War II (correct) 38
Korean War 3
Vietnam War 45
No opinion 5

*In the Vietnam War was the United States
fighting on the side of the North Vietnamese
or the South Vietnamese?*

North Vietnamese 19%
South Vietnamese (correct) 67
No opinion 14

*All in all, did the United States win or lose
the Vietnam War?*

Win 15%
Lose 70
No opinion 15

*Which one of the following American presi-
dents do you think was most responsible for
getting our country involved in the Vietnam
War?*

Dwight Eisenhower 13%
John F. Kennedy 23
Lyndon Johnson 36
Richard Nixon 17
Other (volunteered) 1
No opinion 10

And which one of the following American presidents was most responsible for getting our country out of the Vietnam War?

Lyndon Johnson 10%
Richard Nixon 48
Gerald Ford 31
Other (volunteered) 2
No opinion 9

Looking back, do you think the United States made a mistake sending troops to fight in Vietnam?

	Yes
National	74%

Selected National Trend

	Yes
1985*	63%
1973	60
1971	61
1970	56
1968	49
1967	46
1966	35

*Newsweek poll conducted by the Gallup Organization

Some people say that the United States should have cut its losses by accepting a negotiated withdrawal from Vietnam much earlier than it did. Others say the United States should have made an even greater military effort to try to win a victory there. Which comes closer to your view?

Withdrawn earlier 56%
Made greater military effort 38
No opinion 6

Do you think the United States and the South Vietnamese could have won the Vietnam War and kept communism out of South Vietnam if our country had made a stronger military effort to win the war, or not?

Yes 53%
No 37
No opinion 10

Some people say we should have gone all out to win a military victory in Vietnam using nuclear weapons. Do you agree or disagree with this view?

Agree 9%
Disagree 89
No opinion 2

Did either you, yourself, a relative, or a close friend serve in the military in Vietnam?

Yes 57%
No 42
No opinion 1

Did you, yourself, participate in any demonstrations for or against the Vietnam War during the time we were involved in fighting that war? If yes: Did you demonstrate against the war or in support of the war?

Yes, demonstrations against
the war 5%
Yes, demonstrations for the war 3
No, did not participate in any
demonstrations 91
No opinion 1

Looking back, do you wish that you had made a stronger effort to protest or demonstrate against the Vietnam War, or not?

Yes 25%
No 67
No opinion 8

As far as you know, are there any American prisoners of war still in captivity in Southeast Asia?

Yes 64%
No 24
No opinion 12

I am going to name some people and groups that played an active public role during the Vietnam War years. Looking back, please tell me, for each, whether you have a favorable or unfavorable opinion of this person's or group's role in the Vietnam War. If you don't know enough about a person or group to have an opinion, please tell me.

	Favorable	Unfavorable	No opinion
Antiwar protestors	39%	39%	22%
Henry Kissinger	55	18	27
Jane Fonda	23	52	25
George McGovern	24	26	50
Richard Nixon	43	38	19
Lyndon Johnson	34	40	26
American soldiers who served in Vietnam	87	5	8
Congress	22	48	30
American military leadership	36	39	25

Do you think our participation in the war in Southeast Asia strengthened America's position throughout the world, or do you think it weakened our position?

Strengthened position 23%
Weakened position 63
No opinion 14

Selected National Trend

	Strengthened	Weakened	No opinion
1972	12%	68%	20%

Now, I'm going to read several statements. As I read each one, please tell me whether you agree strongly, agree somewhat, disagree somewhat, or disagree strongly:

As a result of the Vietnam War, Americans now have less trust in their government leaders.

Agree strongly 38%
Agree somewhat 33
Disagree somewhat 16
Disagree strongly 9
No opinion 4

As a result of the Vietnam War, the United States is now more cautious about involvement in military conflicts abroad.

Agree strongly 42%
Agree somewhat 33
Disagree somewhat 11
Disagree strongly 10
No opinion 4

The pace of communism in Southeast Asia was slowed by the Vietnam War.

Agree strongly ....:........ 11%
Agree somewhat 35
Disagree somewhat 26
Disagree strongly 16
No opinion 12

The expense of the Vietnam War led to the growing American budget deficit.

Agree strongly 39%
Agree somewhat 31
Disagree somewhat 14
Disagree strongly 8
No opinion 8

As a result of the Vietnam War, the U.S. government became more responsive to the opinions of the American people.

Agree strongly 28%
Agree somewhat 40
Disagree somewhat 17
Disagree strongly 10
No opinion 5

America's commitment to fight communism in Vietnam helped bring about the current decline of communism around the world.

Agree strongly 16%
Agree somewhat 26
Disagree somewhat 29
Disagree strongly 22
No opinion 7

As a result of the Vietnam War, Congress became more assertive in limiting the ability to involve us in a foreign war.

Agree strongly 30%
Agree somewhat 39
Disagree somewhat 15
Disagree strongly 7
No opinion 9

Have you visited the Vietnam War Memorial in Washington, DC?

	Yes
National	16%

In your opinion, have Vietnam veterans been treated well by the people of the United States in the years since the Vietnam War, or not?

Yes 26%
No 69
No opinion 5

And have Vietnam veterans been treated well by the U.S. government in the years since the Vietnam War, or not?

Yes 24%
No 67
No opinion 9

Finally, thinking of the American soldiers who lost their lives in the Vietnam War, do you think they died in vain, or not?

Yes 51%
No 41
No opinion 8

Note: The number of Americans who believe that the U.S. involvement in the Vietnam War was a mistake has reached its highest level in nearly twenty-five years, with 74% now saying that it was wrong to send troops into the Southeast Asian nation. This opposition has risen steadily since Gallup's first poll on the subject in 1966. At that time, 35% said that it was a mistake to send troops.

A new Gallup Mirror of America survey, taken shortly before the fifteenth anniversary of the April 30, 1975, departure of the last U.S. troops from Vietnam, also shows that respondents overwhelmingly believe our country lost the war and that, unlike World War II or even the Korean conflict, it was not a "just war." However, although Americans think that our involvement did more harm than good for the image of the United States around the world, there is some willingness to concede that the war may have had some positive benefits in terms of stopping the spread of communism.

Americans, in retrospect, have a great deal of respect for soldiers who fought in the war, and for Henry Kissinger and Richard Nixon, whom they credit with getting the United States out of the conflict. They blame Lyndon Johnson for getting the nation into Vietnam. They have mixed feelings about antiwar protesters, do not think that Congress acquitted itself well during the Vietnam years, and have a very low opinion of Jane Fonda, who was a focal figure in the antiwar effort.

MAY 16
1992 PRESIDENTIAL CANDIDATES

Interviewing Date: 3/8–11/90 (Telephone interviews);
3/16–29/90 (Personal interviews)
Survey #GO 922005; 922025

Asked of Democrats and Democratic-leaning independents: Thinking of all the Democratic political leaders you are familiar with, which one, if any, would you like to see nominated as the Democratic party's candidate for president in 1992?* [Names were not read.] And who would be your second choice?**

	First choice*	First choice**	First & second choices**
Bruce Babbitt	†%	1%	3%
Lloyd Bentsen	1	9	16
Joseph Biden	†	†	1
Bill Bradley	1	4	8

Dale Bumpers	†	1	2
Mario Cuomo	7	15	22
Michael Dukakis	2	13	23
Dianne Feinstein	†	1	4
Richard Gephardt	1	3	8
Gary Hart	†	4	12
Jesse Jackson	7	14	23
Bob Kerrey	1	1	3
Sam Nunn	1	2	4
Charles Robb	†	2	3
Jay Rockefeller	1	2	2
Patricia Schroeder ...	†	2	5
Paul Simon	†	2	3
Other	15	–	–
None of the above ...	5	15	14
No opinion	57	10	11

*Telephone interviews
**Personal interviews
†Less than 1%

*Asked of Democrats and Democratic-leaning independents: Will you please look over this list and tell me which of these persons, if any, you have heard of?**

Jesse Jackson	95%
Michael Dukakis	90
Gary Hart	84
Lloyd Bentsen	61
Richard Gephardt	58
Mario Cuomo	56
Paul Simon	47
Patricia Schroeder	41
Jay Rockefeller	40
Bill Bradley	38
Sam Nunn	37
Bruce Babbitt	36
Dianne Feinstein	36
Joseph Biden	31
Charles Robb	28
Dale Bumpers	15
Bob Kerrey	15
None of the above	1
No opinion	**

*Personal interviews
**Less than 1%

*Asked of Republicans and Republican-leaning independents: Which one would you like to see nominated as the Republican party's candidate for president in 1992? And who would be your second choice?**

	First choice	First & second choices
George Bush	65%	73%
Robert Dole	7	29
Elizabeth Dole	4	10
Pierre du Pont	1	3
Alexander Haig	1	6
Jack Kemp	4	18
Jeane Kirkpatrick	1	6
Dan Quayle	5	19
Pat Robertson	2	5
None of the above	6	6
No opinion	3	3

*Personal interviews

*Asked of Republicans and Republican-leaning independents: Will you please look over this list and tell me which of these persons, if any, you have heard of?**

George Bush	98%
Dan Quayle	95
Robert Dole	84
Elizabeth Dole	80
Pat Robertson	79
Alexander Haig	74
Jack Kemp	71
Jeane Kirkpatrick	60
Pierre du Pont	36
None of the above	**
No opinion	2

*Personal interviews
**Less than 1%

*Asked of the entire sample: In politics, as of today, do you consider yourself a Republican, a Democrat, or an independent?**

Republican	35%
Democrat	39
Independent	26

*Those who said "don't know" or "other" are omitted.

Selected National Trend

	Repub- lican	Demo- crat	Inde- pendent
1989 4th Quarter	31%	41%	28%
3d Quarter	32	40	28
2d Quarter	34	38	28
1st Quarter	33	42	25
1988	30	42	28
1987	30	41	29
1986	32	39	29
1985	33	38	29
1984	31	40	29
1983	25	44	31
1982	26	45	29
1981	28	42	30
1980	24	46	30
1979	22	45	33
1976	23	47	30
1975	22	45	33
1972	28	43	29
1968	27	46	27
1964	25	53	22
1960	30	47	23
1954	34	46	20
1950	33	45	22
1946	40	39	21
1937	34	50	16

Note: With two years to go before the 1992 presidential campaign, the Gallup Poll has found no clear front-runner for the Democratic nomination. In sharp contrast, Gallup Polls taken two years before the four previous presidential elections found one Democrat (first Edward Kennedy, then Gary Hart) leading the rest of the field by a significant margin.

For the 1992 contest a nationwide sample of Democrats chooses three close competitors for the lead from a list of seventeen possible presidential candidates. New York Governor Mario Cuomo is the choice of only 15%, Jesse Jackson of 14%, and the Democrats' 1988 nominee, Massachusetts Governor Michael Dukakis, of 13%. These three are followed by 1988 vice presidential nominee Senator Lloyd Bentsen (9%), New Jersey Senator William (Bill) Bradley (4%), and Hart (4%).

Furthermore, in a separate telephone interview (without prompting or lists), as many as six out of ten Democrats did not choose anyone as their favorite to run in 1992. The two top candidates (Jackson and Cuomo) were mentioned by only 7% each.

Cuomo's potential 1992 strength at this juncture may be underestimated. He is tied with Jackson and Dukakis as first choice despite his low name recognition (Cuomo is recognized by only 56% of all Democrats). This contrasts with the much higher name identification of the three best-known Democratic contenders: Jackson, known by 95%; Dukakis (90%); and Hart (84%). Cuomo is about as well known as two other possible contenders: Senator Bentsen at 61% and Representative Richard Gephardt at 58%.

Other past presidential hopefuls, such as Senator Paul Simon (47%), Governor Bruce Babbitt (36%), and Senator Joseph Biden (31%), are recognized by far fewer Democrats. One potential candidate for the 1992 nomination—Senator Bradley—is recognized by only 38% of Democrats, and frequently discussed potential candidate Bob Kerrey, the senator from Nebraska, is recognized by only 15%.

Cuomo, in other words, "overperforms"; although first choice in the poll, he is only sixth in recognition. Bradley also does better in terms of candidate preference (tied for fifth) than name recognition (tenth). On the other hand, Hart underperforms; he is third in recognition but fifth as choice for the nominee.

About two thirds of all Republicans surveyed opt for the renomination of President George Bush in 1992. Other Republicans who receive some support from party members include Senator Robert Dole (7%), Vice President Dan Quayle (5%), and two cabinet members: Secretary of Labor Elizabeth Dole and Secretary of Housing and Urban Development Jack Kemp, both with 4%.

Bush (98%) and Quayle (95%) have nearly universal recognition among Republicans. Several others who ran for the nomination in 1988 have retained substantial name recognition among Republicans: Dole (84%), General Alexander Haig

(74%), television evangelist Pat Robertson (79%), and Kemp (71%). Former Governor Pierre (Pete) du Pont of Delaware, however, is recognized by only 36% of Republicans surveyed.

MAY 23
U.S.-SOVIET RELATIONS

Interviewing Date: 5/17–20/90
Survey #GO 922010

I'd like your overall opinion of Mikhail Gorbachev. Is your overall opinion of him very favorable, mostly favorable, mostly unfavorable, or very unfavorable?

Very favorable 14%
Mostly favorable 54
Mostly unfavorable 15
Very unfavorable 6
No opinion 11

Selected National Trend

	Very, mostly favorable	Mostly, very unfavorable	No opinion
1989	77%	15%	8%
1988	72	21	7

How about the Soviet Union? Is your overall opinion of it very favorable, mostly favorable, mostly unfavorable, or very unfavorable?

Very favorable 7%
Mostly favorable 48
Mostly unfavorable 24
Very unfavorable 8
No opinion 13

Selected National Trend

	Very, mostly favorable	Mostly, very unfavorable	No opinion
1989			
August	51%	40%	9%
Feb.-March	62	29	9
1988			
December	44	46	10

Do you think the Western countries can continue to live more or less peacefully with the Russians, or do you think there is bound to be a major war sooner or later?

Can live peacefully 63%
Bound to be war 31
No opinion 6

Selected National Trend

	Peace	War	No opinion
1955	35%	49%	16%
1954	23	64	13

Do you believe it is possible or impossible to reach a peaceful settlement of differences between Russia and the West?

Possible 84%
Impossible 13
No opinion 3

Selected National Trend

	Possible	Impossible	No opinion
1962	53%	34%	13%
1961	50	27	23
1960	66	23	11

As you may know, the Soviet Union was our ally in World War II but has been our enemy during the Cold War in the years since the war. What about today—would you say the Soviet Union is an ally or an enemy of the United States?

Ally 39%
Enemy 31
Neither (volunteered) 21
No opinion 9

In general, do you approve or disapprove of the policy Russia is following in world affairs?

Approve 41%
Disapprove 40
No opinion 19

Selected National Trend

	Approve	Disapprove	No opinion
1946	7%	71%	22%

Do you think the Soviet Union is doing all it can to keep peace in the world?

Yes 31%
No 63
No opinion 6

Selected National Trend

	Yes	No	No opinion
1987	21%	68%	11%
1985	10	81	9
1983	8	81	11
1981	7	84	9

Do you think the United States is doing all it can to keep peace in the world?

Yes 48%
No 49
No opinion 3

As far as you know, is there still a "cold war" between the United States and the Soviet Union, or is the "cold war" over?

Still exists 52%
Over 40
No opinion 8

Do you trust what Soviet President Gorbachev says, or not?

Yes 43%
No 49
No opinion 8

How likely do you think we are to get into a nuclear war within the next ten years—very likely, fairly likely, fairly unlikely, or very unlikely?

Very likely 8%
Fairly likely 13
Fairly unlikely 33
Very unlikely 42
No opinion 4

Selected National Trend

	Very, fairly likely	Fairly, very unlikely	No opinion
1983	44%	51%	5%
1982	47	45	8
1981	47	49	4

As you may know, there will be a summit meeting in Washington at the end of this month between President Bush and President Gorbachev of the Soviet Union. One agenda item will be an agreement which would further reduce U.S. and Soviet conventional and short-range forces in Europe. Do you favor or oppose the United States agreeing to reduce forces in Europe?

Yes 59%
No 34
No opinion 7

It has been suggested that the United States loan money to the Soviet Union in order to help it through troubled times in its internal economy. Do you favor this action, or not?

Favor 23%
Oppose 73
No opinion 4

Note: A new Gallup Poll shows that attitudes toward the Soviet Union have softened significantly, but the "us versus them" mentality that has prevailed since the end of World War II remains strong. A substantial number of Americans thinks that the Cold War still continues, that Soviet President Mikhail Gorbachev is not to be trusted, and that the Soviet Union is not doing all it can to keep peace in the world. Additionally, few respondents want to lend the Soviet Union money to help it internally, and four out of ten are hesitant to endorse the type of arms reduction agreement scheduled to be the centerpiece of the Washington summit in May between the two countries.

It is clear, however, that American attitudes toward the Soviet Union and its intentions have become more conciliatory. Overall opinions are up from the depths of the 1950s and 1960s, but the favorable ratings of the Soviet Union are down somewhat from Gallup's measurement in February of this year, at the height of the collapse of communism in Eastern Europe. These ratings are apparently very event specific. Now fifty-five percent of Americans have a favorable attitude toward the Soviet Union, while 32% have an unfavorable opinion.

Moreover, President Gorbachev gets strongly favorable ratings from Americans: 68% have a favorable opinion of him, 21% an unfavorable one. This is down slightly from Gorbachev's December 1988 (72%) and December 1989 (77%) ratings.

Americans also are more likely now to think that we can live peacefully with the Soviet Union than they were at the height of the Cold War. In 1960, 66% thought that it would be possible to reach a peaceful settlement of differences; the figure now is 84%. Additionally, 63% say we can live in peace with the Soviet Union without a major war, compared to 23% in 1954.

And Americans are much more sanguine now that the world can avoid a nuclear war within the next ten years. In 1981 almost one half (47%) thought that it was very or fairly likely that a nuclear war would occur. Now that figure is down to 21%, a dramatic change.

MAY 24
PRESIDENT BUSH/VICE PRESIDENT QUAYLE

Interviewing Date: 5/17–20/90
Survey #GO 922010

Do you approve or disapprove of the way George Bush is handling his job as president?

Approve 65%
Disapprove 20
No opinion 15

Selected National Trend

	Approve	Dis-approve	No opinion
1990			
April 19–22	67%	17%	16%
April 5–8	68	16	16
March 15–18	74	15	11
March 8–11	68	18	14
Feb. 15–18	73	16	11
Feb. 8–11	73	16	11
Jan. 4–7	80	11	9
1989			
Dec. 7–10	71%	20%	9%
Nov. 2–5	70	17	13
Oct. 5–8	68	20	12
Sept. 7–10	70	17	13
August 10–13	69	19	12
July 6–9	66	19	15
June 8–11	70	14	16
May 4–7	56	22	22
April 10–16	58	16	26
March 10–13	56	16	28
Feb. 28–March 2	63	13	24
Jan. 24–26	51	6	43

Do you approve or disapprove of the way Dan Quayle is handling his job as vice president?

Approve 48%
Disapprove 27
No opinion 25

Selected National Trend

	Approve	Dis-approve	No opinion
1990			
February	46%	27%	27%
1989			
November	43	29	28

Note: The latest Gallup Poll shows a significant drop since January in Americans' approval of the way President George Bush is handling his job. According to the survey, 65% approve of the job he is doing as president, while 20% disapprove and 15% have no opinion.

In January, Bush's approval rating was 80%. It fell to the mid-70s in February and March and has hovered in the upper 60s since April.

Vice President Dan Quayle's job performance rating is statistically unchanged since February, when Gallup last asked Americans how well they thought he was doing. Nearly one half (48%) approves of the way he is handling his job, while 27% disapprove. Quayle's approval rating has shown a 5 percentage-point increase since November 1989.

MAY 30
FEDERAL BUDGET DEFICIT

Interviewing Date: 5/17–20/90
Survey #GO 922010

How important is reducing the federal budget deficit? Would you say it is very important, somewhat important, not too important, or not at all important?

Very important	70%
Somewhat important	20
Not too important	3
Not at all important	3
No opinion	4

Which of these would you most favor to reduce the deficit—reducing spending, raising or creating taxes, or a combination of both?

Reducing spending	43%
Raising or creating taxes	4
Combination of both	50
No opinion	3

If taxes were raised to reduce the deficit, which one of the following would be your first choice to help reduce the deficit? And which one would be your second choice?

	First choice	Second choice
Increasing taxes on alcohol and cigarettes	42%	30%
Increasing income taxes for very high-income households	32	25
Increasing energy, gas, or oil import taxes	11	18
Creating a national sales tax ..	10	15
None	3	9
No opinion	2	3

Regardless of what you want to happen, do you think it is very likely, somewhat likely, not very likely, or not at all likely that:

Taxes will be raised next year?

Very likely	58%
Somewhat likely	30
Not very likely	7
Not at all likely	3
No opinion	2

Federal government spending will be reduced next year?

Very likely	9%
Somewhat likely	17
Not very likely	40
Not at all likely	31
No opinion	3

If your senator or congressman voted for a tax increase this year, would that make you more likely to vote for him or her in the election in November, less likely, or wouldn't it make any difference?

More likely 7%
Less likely 36
No difference 52
No opinion 5

George Bush said in his campaign, "Read my lips: No new taxes." As far as you are concerned, should President Bush keep his pledge not to raise taxes, or should he now consider new taxes to help reduce the federal budget deficit?

Keep pledge 56%
Consider taxes to reduce deficit 40
No opinion 4

Do you think President Bush will be able to keep his pledge of no new taxes, or not?

Yes 20%
No 74
No opinion 6

Note: The reduction of the federal deficit has emerged as one of the most talked-about issues on the national agenda for the 1990s. However, analyses of recent Gallup Poll questions indicate that Americans' attitudes about the deficit are not always as straightforward as might be imagined. They clearly have reacted to the enormous amount of attention given to the deficit by their leaders and the press by citing it as an important problem for the country.

The public has a fairly clear-cut and perhaps cynical perception of what is going to happen in the attempt to reduce the deficit: The government will raise taxes and will be unable to reduce its own spending. Fifty-eight percent think that it is very likely that taxes will be raised in the next year, with only 10% saying that it is not likely. On the other hand, only 9% think it is very likely that the federal government will be able to reduce its own spending in the next year, while 71% say it is not likely. The public also thinks that President George Bush will not be of much help in all of this—the majority (74%) says that he will break his campaign pledge and advocate some new form of taxation.

This cynicism about the inevitability of new taxes is not new, but Americans are not so opposed to raising new taxes as might be thought. Apparently, fear of deficit has convinced a substantial percentage of the population that raising taxes might be acceptable.

Forty percent of them say that President Bush should break his "read my lips" promise and raise new taxes if it would help reduce the deficit; 56% think that he should stand firm. And, while very few Americans advocate that the government raise taxes exclusively, 50% say that they are willing to live with a combination of raising taxes and reducing federal spending. (Forty-three percent would choose to reduce federal spending without any new taxes.)

Asked about the types of taxes they prefer, respondents usually take the path of least resistance and pick those that would affect them the least personally; so it is in the latest Gallup Poll. Given a choice among a nationwide sales tax, some form of gasoline or energy tax, "sin taxes" on alcohol and cigarettes, or a tax of the very rich, most Americans opt for the sin taxes and taxes on the rich. Seventy-two percent choose sin taxes as first or second choice; 57% choose increased taxes for the rich. Only 29% favor energy or gas taxes, and only 25% choose a national sales tax.

Incumbent congressmen and senators seeking reelection this fall may not have as much to fear from being involved with this issue as they may think. Fifty-two percent of respondents say that a congressman's or senator's vote in favor of a tax increase would make no difference in how they would cast their ballots in November. Thirty-six percent say that they would be less likely to vote for a tax-increasing congressman or senator, but 7% say that such a vote would make them more likely to vote for him or her.

JUNE 4
CHILDREN

Interviewing Date: 4/19–22/90
Survey #GO 922008

What do you think is the ideal number of children for a family to have?

None 3%
One 3
Two 57
Three 18
Four 8
Five or more 3
No opinion 8

Selected National Trend

	1980	1973
None	1%	1%
One	3	1
Two	51	46
Three	21	23
Four	12	14
Five or more	4	6
No opinion	8	9

Do you think being an only child is an advantage or a disadvantage?

Advantage 17%
Disadvantage 70
No opinion 13

Selected National Trend

	Advantage	Disadvantage	No opinion
1950	20%	71%	9%

Do you think raising children today is easier, more difficult, or about the same as when your parents were raising you?

Easier 5%
More difficult 81
About the same 12
No opinion 2

Which of the following would be the ideal family situation for children as far as you are concerned:

A family in which the father has a job
and the mother stays home and cares
for the children? 63%

A family in which both parents have
jobs and both take care of the children
when they are home? 33

A family in which the mother has a
job and the father stays home and
cares for the children? 1

No opinion 3

Which do you, yourself, think is easier to raise—a boy or a girl?

Boy 43%
Girl 27
No difference (volunteered) 23
No opinion 7

Selected National Trend

	Boy	Girl	No difference	No opinion
1947	42%	23%	24%	11%

If you had another child, would you rather have a boy or a girl?

Boy 38%
Girl 34
No difference (volunteered) 24
No opinion 4

Selected National Trend

	Boy	Girl	No difference	No opinion
1947	40%	25%	27%	8%

During childhood, at what age do you think girls are usually at their best—that is, are the most fun to be around?

1 to 4 .... 23%
5 to 8 27
9 to 12 19
13 to 14 6
15 to 17 6
No age 2

Other age 3
No opinion 14

Mean age 8

And at what age during childhood do you think girls are usually at their worst—that is, are the most difficult to be around?

1 to 4 .... 5%
5 to 8 3
9 to 12 11
13 to 14 36
15 to 17 31
No age 1
Other age 4
No opinion 9

Mean age 13

During childhood, at what age do you think boys are usually at their best—that is, are the most fun to be around?

1 to 4 .... 19%
5 to 8 28
9 to 12 23
13 to 14 5
15 to 17 7
No age 2
Other age 5
No opinion 11

Mean age 9

And at what age during childhood do you think boys are usually at their worst—that is, are the most difficult to be around?

1 to 4 .... 6%
5 to 8 4
9 to 12 11
13 to 14 21
15 to 17 41
No age 1
Other age 8
No opinion 8

Mean age 14

How many children, if any, have you had?

None 26%
One 14
Two 26
Three 16
Four 8
Five or more 10

Mean: 2.1 children

In general, do you think parents today are too strict with their children, not strict enough, or just about right?

Too strict 2%
Not strict enough 81
About right 14
No opinion 3

Do you approve or disapprove of spanking children?

Approve 65%
Disapprove 25
No opinion 10

The following questions were asked of parents with children living at home:

What grade would you give yourself for the job you are doing in bringing up your children—A, B, C, D, or Fail?

A 31%
B 54
C 13
D 1
Fail .... *
No opinion 1

*Less than 1%

Thinking of your oldest child, I want you to estimate roughly how much time he/she spends on a variety of activities on a typical weekday, during the school year:

Watching television?

No time	7%
Less than 1/2 hour	7
More than 1/2 hr., up to 1 hr.	19
More than 1 hr., up to 2 hrs.	26
More than 2 hrs., up to 3 hrs.	15
More than 3 hrs., up to 4 hrs.	9
More than 4 hours	8
No opinion	3
Doesn't apply/child too young	6

Doing homework?

No time	6%
Less than 1/2 hour	11
More than 1/2 hr., up to 1 hr.	23
More than 1 hr., up to 2 hrs.	22
More than 2 hrs., up to 3 hrs.	6
More than 3 hrs., up to 4 hrs.	4
More than 4 hours	4
No opinion	2
Doesn't apply/child too young	22

Playing with friends?

No time	8%
Less than 1/2 hour	8
More than 1/2 hr., up to 1 hr.	20
More than 1 hr., up to 2 hrs.	20
More than 2 hrs., up to 3 hrs.	9
More than 3 hrs., up to 4 hrs.	4
More than 4 hours	18
No opinion	3
Doesn't apply/child too young	10

Playing video games?

No time	46%
Less than 1/2 hour	17
More than 1/2 hr., up to 1 hr.	11
More than 1 hr., up to 2 hrs.	3
More than 2 hrs., up to 3 hrs.	2
More than 3 hrs., up to 4 hrs.	2
More than 4 hours	2
No opinion	2
Doesn't apply/child too young	15

Playing outside?

No time	7%
Less than 1/2 hour	5
More than 1/2 hr., up to 1 hr.	17
More than 1 hr., up to 2 hrs.	26
More than 2 hrs., up to 3 hrs.	16
More than 3 hrs., up to 4 hrs.	6
More than 4 hours	11
No opinion	4
Doesn't apply/child too young	8

Talking to you?

No time	1%
Less than 1/2 hour	12
More than 1/2 hr., up to 1 hr.	24
More than 1 hr., up to 2 hrs.	21
More than 2 hrs., up to 3 hrs.	8
More than 3 hrs., up to 4 hrs.	6
More than 4 hours	18
No opinion	3
Doesn't apply/child too young	7

Doing chores?

No time	10%
Less than 1/2 hour	27
More than 1/2 hr., up to 1 hr.	29
More than 1 hr., up to 2 hrs.	12
More than 2 hrs., up to 3 hrs.	3
More than 3 hrs., up to 4 hrs.	2
More than 4 hours	2
No opinion	3
Doesn't apply/child too young	12

Do you think your oldest/only child watches too much television, not enough television, or is the amount of television he/she watches about right?

Too much	25%
Not enough	2
About right	68
No opinion	1
Doesn't apply/child too young	4

Do you place a definite limit on the amount of time your oldest child spends viewing television during the school week?

Yes 47%
No 43
No opinion 1
Doesn't apply/child too young 9

Do you allow your children to watch any type of television program they want, or do you restrict the types of program they watch?

Allow them to watch any type 21%
Restrict types they watch 69
Restrict for some/leave it to other
   children to decide (volunteered) 5
No opinion .... *
Doesn't apply/child too young 5

*Less than 1%

Do you think you, yourself, are too strict with your children, not strict enough, or about right?

Too strict 12%
Not strict enough 25
About right 62
No opinion 1

How often, if at all, do you spank your children?

Every day 6%
Every couple of days 8
Several times a month 7
Once a month 7
Once every few months 5
Less often than every few months 15
Never 49
No opinion 3

Asked of those with children at home and working mothers in the household: All things considered, do you think your child/children would be better off if (your wife/you) were

home and didn't work, or is your child/children just as well off even though (your wife/you) work?

Better off if mother did not work 32%
As well off with mother working 64
No opinion 4

If money were not an issue, would you want (your wife/self) to continue to work, or would you want (your wife/self) to stay home?

Want wife/self to work 44%
Want wife/self to stay home 50
No opinion 6

Asked of those with children at home and a mother who does not have a job: Do you think children today are better off if their mother is home and doesn't hold a job, or are children just as well off if the mother works?

Better off if mother is home 73%
As well off if mother works 24
No opinion 3

Note: The average American adult is fairly clear on what constitutes the "ideal" family today: two children and a father who works while the mother stays home and cares for the kids. Fifty-seven percent of respondents think that two children are just about perfect, 18% think three are ideal, while 3% say one child. Only 11% opt for four or more children. The Gallup Poll has been asking this question since 1936. The biggest change over time is that the number of Americans who think big families are the ideal has been steadily shrinking.

All overwhelmingly agree that parenthood is tougher than ever today; 81% say that it is more difficult raising kids now than it was for their parents. And beware the teenage years—clearly the period in childrens' lives that adults dread most. According to the current Gallup survey, respondents overwhelmingly agree that children are at their worst and most difficult to be around as teen-agers. For girls, the early teen years—13 and 14—seem to present the most problems. The median worst year for girls is perceived to be 14. For boys, it is the later teen years, 15 to 17; the median worst year for boys is 15. Moreover, according to the Gallup Poll sample, eight out of ten (81%) think that parents today are not strict enough in disciplining children, with only 2% saying that parents are too strict.

All in all, it is a difficult time today for working mothers in America, not only because of the practical problems they face in rearing children and working but also because they are to a significant degree fighting the disapproval of society itself. There is a clear perception among Americans that children are better off when the mother stays home and does not work.

JUNE 13
RACIAL TOLERANCE

Interviewing Date: 6/7–10/90
Survey #GO 922011

Do you think there is likely to be any serious racial trouble in this community in the next two or three years?

Likely 18%
Not likely 75
Trouble exists now (volunteered) 2
No opinion 5

Selected National Trend
1963

Likely 22%
Not likely 69
Trouble exists now (volunteered) 1
No opinion 8

Over the past year or so, how much progress do you think has been made in the area of civil rights in this country—a lot of progress, some progress, not very much progress, or no progress at all?

A lot 16%
Some 48
Not very much 23
No progress at all 9
No opinion 4

Selected National Trend
1989

A lot 11%
Some 44
Not very much 30
No progress at all 12
No opinion 3

In your opinion, how well do you think blacks are treated in your community—the same as whites are, not very well, or badly?

Same as whites 63%
Not very well 21
Badly 3
No blacks in this community
(volunteered) 8
No opinion 5

By Ethnic Background
White

Same as whites 66%
Not very well 18
Badly 2
No blacks in this community
(volunteered) 8
No opinion 6

Black

Same as whites 37%
Not very well 43
Badly 14
No blacks in this community
(volunteered) 1
No opinion 5

Selected National Trend

	Same as whites	Not very well	Badly	No opinion
1987	61%	24%	3%	12%
1981	63	20	5	12
1980	66	19	4	11
1978	65	18	4	13

For the next few questions I'd like you to think about your own community. In general, do you think blacks have as good a chance as white people in your community to get any kind of job for which they are qualified, or don't you think they have as good a chance?

Blacks have as good a chance 70%
Blacks do not have as good a chance 23
No blacks/whites in this community
   (volunteered) 3
No opinion 4

By Ethnic Background
White

Blacks have as good a chance 73%
Blacks do not have as good a chance 20
No blacks/whites in this community
   (volunteered) 4
No opinion 3

Black

Blacks have as good a chance 43%
Blacks do not have as good a chance 54
No blacks/whites in this community
   (volunteered) .... *
No opinion 3

*Less than 1%

Do you think blacks have as good a chance as white people in your community to get any kind of housing they can afford, or don't you think they have as good a chance?

Blacks have as good a chance 72%
Blacks do not have as good a chance 19
No blacks/whites in this community
   (volunteered) 3
No opinion 6

By Ethnic Background
White

Blacks have as good a chance 75%
Blacks do not have as good a chance 16
No blacks/whites in this community
   (volunteered) 4
No opinion 5

Black

Blacks have as good a chance 47%
Blacks do not have as good a chance 46
No blacks/whites in this community
   (volunteered) .... *
No opinion 7

*Less than 1%

Do you think black children have as good a chance as white children in your community to get a good education, or don't you think they have as good a chance?

Black children have as good a chance 83%
Black children do not have as good
   a chance 11
No blacks/whites in this community
   (volunteered) 3
No opinion 3

By Ethnic Background
White

Black children have as good a chance 85%
Black children do not have as good
   a chance 9
No blacks/whites in this community
   (volunteered) 4
No opinion 2

Black

Black children have as good a chance 68%
Black children do not have as good
   a chance 29
No blacks/whites in this community
   (volunteered) 1
No opinion 2

Selected National Trend

	As good a chance	Not as good a chance	No blacks/ whites	No opinion
1989	80%	15%	4%	1%

Looking back over the last ten years, do you think the quality of life of blacks has gotten better, stayed about the same, or gotten worse?

Better 61%
Stayed the same 24
Worse 8
No opinion 7

By Ethnic Background

White

Better 62%
Stayed the same 25
Worse 6
No opinion 7

Black

Better 46%
Stayed the same 25
Worse 23
No opinion 6

Selected National Trend

	Better	Same	Worse	No opinion
1981	77%	13%	6%	4%
1980	71	17	8	4

Asked of whites: If colored people/black people came to live next door, would you move?

Yes, definitely 1%
Yes, might move 4
No 93
No opinion 2

Selected National Trend

	Yes, definitely	Yes, might move	No	No opinion
1978	4%	9%	84%	3%
1967	12	23	65	*
1966	13	21	66	*
1965	13	22	65	*
1963	20	25	55	*

*Less than 1%

Also asked of whites: Would you move if colored people/black people came to live in great numbers in your neighborhood?

Yes, definitely 8%
Yes, might move 18
No 68
No opinion 6

Selected National Trend

	Yes, definitely	Yes, might move	No	No opinion
1978	20%	31%	45%	4%
1967	40	31	29	*
1966	39	31	30	*
1965	40	29	31	*
1963	49	29	22	*

*Less than 1%

Asked of whites with children in school: Would you, yourself, have any objection to sending your children to school where a few of the children are black?

	Yes
National	1%

Also asked of whites with children in school: Would you, yourself, have any objection to sending your children to a school where half of the children are black?

	Yes
National	10%

Also asked of whites with children in school: Would you, yourself, have any objection to sending your children to a school where more than half of the children are black?

	Yes
National	31%

Think for a moment about racial comments, jokes, criticisms, and so forth that you might hear from friends, relatives, and the people you work with. Has the number of these types of negative racial comments and remarks been increasing lately, decreasing, or has it not changed?

Increasing	7%
Decreasing	30
Not changed	55
No opinion	8

Thinking just about yourself for the moment, do you think you have become more tolerant of people of different colors and races lately, less tolerant, or has there been no change?

More tolerant	34%
Less tolerant	6
No change	58
No opinion	2

Now, thinking about American society as a whole, do you think society has become more tolerant of people of different colors and races lately, less tolerant, or has it not changed?

More tolerant	51%
Less tolerant	17
Not changed	26
No opinion	6

By Ethnic Background

White

More tolerant	54%
Less tolerant	16
Not changed	24
No opinion	6

Black

More tolerant	29%
Less tolerant	29
Not changed	36
No opinion	6

Note: Americans generally believe that the United States is more racially tolerant now than in the recent past, according to a new Gallup Poll. While racial attitudes have changed for the better, however, this shift has not been accompanied by a change in opinion about the state of racial equality. And there remain sharp differences of opinion between whites and blacks about the equitability of job opportunities, availability of housing for blacks, and racial views in general.

While the new poll also shows a continuation of the long-term downtrend in expression of hostile views by whites toward blacks, Americans' views of how blacks are treated in their own communities have not improved since the late 1970s. One in five (20%) sees serious racial trouble in their community on the horizon or already occurring. The percentage who say that, in their community, blacks have the same job opportunities as whites has not increased over the past decade. A smaller majority today (61%) than in 1980 (71%) says that the quality of life for blacks has improved over the past ten years.

Public attitudes toward race were dramatically different during the civil rights era of the 1960s. The belief that blacks lacked equal opportunities was certainly more pervasive at that time than it is today. In a 1963 Gallup Poll, fewer than one half (43%) said that blacks had job opportunities equal to similarly qualified whites living in the same community; now, the figure is 70%.

The biggest shift in racial attitudes is the decrease in public expression of overtly racist views. Only 5% of whites surveyed today say that they would be inclined to move out of their neighborhood if a black family moved next door. When Gallup first posed this question in 1963, almost one half of whites (45%) said that a black neighbor would spur them to move. In 1978, the last time the question was asked, those saying that they would move out had declined to 13%.

Responses to a similar question, asking whites whether large numbers of blacks moving into their neighborhood would prompt them to leave, show the same shift in attitudes over time. In 1963, 78% of whites say that they would move out rather than live in a neighborhood with a large increase in black families. That proportion had declined to 51% in 1978, and to 26% in the current poll.

In contrast, the Gallup Poll finds no significant change since the late 1970s in public opinion about blacks' success in achieving equal opportunities. People's perceptions of how well blacks

are treated in their communities have not improved since that time. While a majority (63%)
believes that blacks are treated the same as whites,
24% say that they are treated not very well or
badly.

Since blacks make up a relatively small percentage of the country's population—less than
10% of the poll respondents are black—the overall poll results tend to reflect the views of the
white majority. Even within the limitations of the
small size of the poll's subsample, however, it is
evident that blacks' views on racial issues are
often less optimistic than, and sharply divergent
from, those of the white majority.

JUNE 20
FLAG BURNING

Interview Date: 6/15–17/90
Survey #GO 922012

*There has been discussion lately about a con-
stitutional amendment which would make it
illegal to burn or desecrate the U.S. flag.
Some people favor a flag-burning amendment
because they say the flag is America's unique
symbol and deserves constitutional protection
from desecration. Others oppose a flag-
burning amendment because they say burning the flag is a form of freedom of speech,
no matter how offensive, which is protected
by the Bill of Rights. Which of these two
opinions comes closest to your own?*

Favor amendment 66%
Oppose amendment 29
No opinion 5

*Do you think we should pass a constitutional
amendment to make flag burning illegal, or
not?**

Yes 68%
No 27
No opinion 5

Selected National Trend

	Yes	No	No opinion
1989			
October**	65%	31%	4%
June*	71	24	5

Newsweek survey conducted by the Gallup
Organization
**In October the question was phrased: Do you
favor or oppose a constitutional amendment that
would allow federal and state governments to
make flag burning illegal?

Note: President George Bush is strongly in tune
with Americans when it comes to passing an
amendment to ban flag burning, a recent Gallup
Poll finds. The will of the public on making flag
burning illegal appears to be both straightforward
and remarkably stable. In two different studies in
1989, Gallup found that 65% to 71% of Americans supported a constitutional ban on flag burning. The response was the same when the question
was asked recently in a Gallup survey for *Newsweek* magazine.

Opponents of the flag-burning amendment ar-
gue that the public may be missing the First
Amendment free-speech implications of limiting
this kind of expression. To test this view, Gallup
respondents in the most recent poll were read
representative arguments for favoring and oppos-
ing the amendment.

The pro argument was expressed as "The flag
is America's unique symbol and deserves constitutional protection," the "con" argument as
"Burning the flag is a form of freedom of speech
. . . protected by the Bill of Rights." Those ques-
tioned were thus reminded of the most salient
arguments used by those on both sides of the
controversy.

The results showed no change from previous
polls. Sixty-six percent favor an amendment pro-
hibiting flag burning, and 29% oppose it—essentially the same results obtained with the more
basic measurement procedure.

JUNE 20
PARENTAL LEAVE LEGISLATION

Interviewing Date: 6/7–10/90
Survey #GO 922012

Congress is considering a new law which would require companies to allow employees to take up to twelve weeks unpaid leave if they had a new baby, or if there was a serious illness in the employee's immediate family. Would you favor or oppose Congress passing this type of law?

Favor 69%
Oppose 26
No opinion 5

Note: Americans do not support President George Bush in his threatened veto of the parental leave bill recently passed by the Senate. The legislation would require large businesses to grant twelve weeks in unpaid leave to employees with newborn or adopted babies, or in cases of serious family illness. Bush has said that such decisions should be left up to businesses without government interference.

Slightly more than two thirds of respondents do not agree with the president, as 69% favor this type of law. Support for the parental leave is remarkably constant across groups, although slightly lower among older Americans. There is no significant difference between men and women.

JUNE 27
RELIGION

Interviewing Date: 6/15–17/90
Survey #GO 922012

At the present time, do you think religion as a whole is increasing its influence on American life or losing its influence?

Increasing 33%
Losing 48
No difference; no opinion 19

Selected National Trend

	Increasing	Losing	No difference; no opinion
1988	36%	48%	16%
1986	48	39	13
1984	42	39	19
1980	35	46	19
1978	37	48	15
1976	44	45	11
1974	31	56	13
1970	14	75	11
1968	18	67	15
1965	33	45	22
1962	45	31	24
1957	69	14	17

Do you believe that religion can answer all or most of today's problems, or that religion is largely old-fashioned and out of date?

Can answer 63%
Out of date 18
Neither; no opinion 19

Selected National Trend

	Can answer	Out of date	Neither; no opinion
1988	57%	20%	23%
1986	58	23	19
1985	61	22	17
1984	56	24	20
1982	60	22	18
1981	65	15	20
1974	62	20	18
1957	81	7	12

How important would you say religion is in your life—very important, fairly important, or not very important?

Very important 58%
Fairly important 29
Not very important 13
No opinion .... *

*Less than 1%

Do you happen to be a member of a church or synagogue?

	Yes
National	69%

Did you, yourself, happen to attend church or synagogue in the last seven days?

	Yes
National	40%

Did you receive any religious training as a child?

	Yes
National	85%

Have you ever been aware of or influenced by a presence or a power—whether you call it God or not—which is different from your everyday self?

Yes	54%
No	42
No opinion	4

Would you say you have made a commitment to Jesus Christ, or not?

Yes	74%
No	24
No opinion	2

Do you believe in life after death?

Yes	71%
No	19
No opinion	10

Please tell me how much you agree or disagree with this statement: "There are clear guidelines about what's good or evil that apply to everyone regardless of their situation." Do you completely agree, mostly agree, mostly disagree, or completely disagree?

Completely agree	33%
Mostly agree	52
Mostly disagree	8
Completely disagree	3
No opinion	4

Note: A new Gallup Poll shows that Americans continue their traditionally strong belief in the transcendent—that which is beyond human experience and knowledge. The percentage who believe in life after death (71%) has held steady for almost half a century, but a growing number (54%) say that they have felt the presence of a power, whether they call it God or not, that was different from their everyday selves. The percentage saying they have felt an outside presence is 10 points more than in 1985, possibly reflecting a greater willingness to talk about such experiences.

That Americans remain strongly attached to religion is seen in the finding that 63% believe that it can answer all or most of today's problems. Religion is very important for 58%; 69% are members of a church or synagogue; and 40% attended church or synagogue in the week before the survey. These figures are generally the same as those found by Gallup over the past several years.

Almost one half (48%) believes that religion is losing its influence in society, a proportion that has held steady since 1988. One in three (33%) believes that religion is increasing in influence. In 1988, 36% held this view. Three in four (74%) say that they have made a commitment to Jesus Christ.

JULY 2
FINANCIAL SITUATION

Interviewing Date: 5/17–20/90
Survey #GO 922010

First of all, thinking just about your own financial situation, do you consider yourself to be rich, upper income, middle income, lower income, or poor?

Rich .... *%
Upper income 7
Middle income 59
Lower income 23
Poor 10
No opinion 1

*Less than 1%

Do you feel that the distribution of money and wealth in this country today is fair, or do you feel that the money and wealth in this country should be more evenly distributed among a larger percentage of the people?

Distribution is fair 28%
Should be more evenly distributed 66
No opinion 6

Selected National Trend

	Fair	More evenly distributed	No opinion
1984	31%	60%	9%

Would you say that the percentage of Americans living below the poverty line is increasing from year to year or decreasing from year to year?

Increasing 79%
Decreasing 15
No opinion 6

Selected National Trend

	Increasing	Decreasing	No opinion
1984	70%	18%	12%

Just your opinion: Which is more often to blame if a person is poor—lack of effort on his or her own part or circumstances beyond his or her control?

Lack of effort 35%
Circumstances 45
Both (volunteered) 17
No opinion 3

Selected National Trend

	Lack of effort	Circumstances	Both	No opinion
1984	33%	34%	31%	2%

Would you say that the percentage of Americans who are rich is increasing from year to year or decreasing from year to year?

Increasing 65%
Decreasing 26
No opinion 9

Just your opinion, which is more often the cause if a person is rich—strong effort to succeed on his or her part or luck or circumstances beyond his or her control?

Strong effort 50%
Luck or circumstances 33
Both (volunteered) 12
No opinion 5

The following three questions were asked of those who said they were not rich:

Looking ahead, how likely is it that you ever will be rich?

Very likely 9%
Somewhat likely 23
Not very likely 32
Not at all likely 35
No opinion 1

All in all, if you had your choice, would you want to be rich, or not?

Yes 59%
No 38
No opinion 3

Do you think that rich people in America today are happier than you, less happy, or about the same?

Happier 11%
Less happy 36
About the same 50
No opinion 3

The remaining questions were asked of the entire sample:

How good a chance do you think a person has to become rich today, if the person is willing to work hard?

Very good chance 18%
Good chance 33
Some chance 36
Little chance 10
No chance at all 2
No opinion 1

Do you envy rich people, or not?

Yes 17%
No 82
No opinion 1

Do you respect and admire rich people, or not?

Yes 52%
No 41
No opinion 7

Is it easier to get rich in America today than it used to be, harder, or no different than it used to be?

Easier today 31%
Harder 41
No different 24
No opinion 4

Being rich means that you are able to do things or own things that other people can't. How important is each of the following as a reason for wanting to be rich:

To be able to own an expensive car?

Very important 10%
Somewhat important 25
Not very important 64
No opinion 1

To be able to own a big house?

Very important 16%
Somewhat important 36
Not very important 47
No opinion 1

To be able to have a maid or other servants to do household work?

Very important 10%
Somewhat important 19
Not very important 71
No opinion .... *

*Less than 1%

To be able to travel around the world?

Very important 22%
Somewhat important 36
Not very important 41
No opinion 1

To be able to own expensive clothes?

Very important 8%
Somewhat important 24
Not very important 68
No opinion .... *

*Less than 1%

Not having to worry about affording unexpected expenses such as illnesses or emergencies?

Very important 81%
Somewhat important 14
Not very important 4
No opinion 1

To be able to entertain lavishly?

Very important 6%
Somewhat important 17
Not very important 77
No opinion .... *

*Less than 1%

To be able to pass money on to your children?

Very important 55%
Somewhat important 32
Not very important 12
No opinion 1

To be able to contribute generously to charities and help people in need?

Very important 63%
Somewhat important 31
Not very important 5
No opinion 1

To gain recognition and respect in the community?

Very important 19%
Somewhat important 32
Not very important 48
No opinion 1

To be able to quit working and worrying about losing your job?

Very important 46%
Somewhat important 29
Not very important 23
No opinion 2

To be able to send your children through college without financial strain?

Very important 79%
Somewhat important 15
Not very important 5
No opinion 1

To be free to do anything you want to when you want to?

Very important 43%
Somewhat important 39
Not very important 17
No opinion 1

Think for a moment about some sacrifices you could make which would enable you to become rich. How willing would you be to do each of the following if it were guaranteed to make you rich:

Work between twelve and fourteen hours per day year round?

Very willing 25%
Somewhat willing 27
Not very willing 47
No opinion 1

Work at a job you hated?

Very willing 8%
Somewhat willing 20
Not very willing 72
No opinion .... *

*Less than 1%

Do something illegal?

Very willing 1%
Somewhat willing 3
Not very willing 96
No opinion .... *

*Less than 1%

Marry a rich person you did not love?

Very willing 2%
Somewhat willing 7
Not very willing 90
No opinion 1

Not see much of your family?

Very willing 4%
Somewhat willing 15
Not very willing 80
No opinion 1

Do you think there is too much, too little, or about the right amount of emphasis and attention on the rich and trying to become rich in America today?

Too much 70%
Too little 6
About right 18
No opinion 6

As far as you are concerned, do we have too many rich people in this country, too few, or about the right amount?

Too many 21%
Too few 15
About right 55
No opinion 9

Does America benefit from having a class of rich people, or not?

Yes 62%
No 32
No opinion 6

How good a job do the rich in America do in terms of contributing back to society by charitable contributions, donations, and the like?

Excellent job 6%
Good job 27
Fair job 42
Poor job 19
No opinion 6

Is it more difficult for a rich person than a poor person to love God and one's neighbors, less difficult, or is there no difference?

More difficult 19%
Less difficult 6
No difference 71
No opinion 4

Note: Most Americans would like to be rich, but only one third think there is a chance that they ever will be. Yet, despite this desire, very few admit that they would marry a rich person whom they did not love or sacrifice time with their family in order to make a fortune, and few would work at a lucrative job that they hated. They do not think that the way income and wealth are distributed in the country is particularly fair, but most believe that those who are rich clearly benefit society.

In a new Gallup Mirror of America survey, less than 1% identify themselves as rich, while another 7% say that they are in the upper-income group. Another 59% put themselves into a middle-income category, 23% into a lower-income bracket, and only 10% consider themselves poor.

Whatever it takes to be affluent, the number of Americans who qualify is thought to be getting larger rather than smaller; almost two thirds (65%) of those surveyed say that the number of rich people in this country is increasing. (At the same time, however, 79% say that the number of poor people also is increasing.)

Moreover, the American dream of becoming rich is apparently alive and well in the hearts of many. When asked point-blank, 59% say that if they had their choice, they would want to be wealthy, while only 38% say that they would not.

Despite this general interest in being rich, there is some evidence that reality intrudes when respondents survey their own chances. Only 32% think that it is likely that they themselves will ever be wealthy, and the rest (68%) apparently accept the fact that great wealth is an elusive dream.

In a very broad sense, respondents agree that the way riches in our society are distributed today is unjust. A sizable percentage (66%) told the Gallup Poll that the allocation of money in the country is not fair and needs to be more evenly divided among a larger percentage of people. Paradoxically, however, almost two thirds (62%) say that the country actually benefits from having rich people in its midst; only one third (32%) says that it does not.

Many believe that America is the land of opportunity, and 51% say that a person has a good chance to become rich today if only he or she is willing to work hard. Only 12% say that a person would have only little chance or none at all. In fact, Americans tend to give substantial credit to hard work—usually considered to be a "legitimate" reason—as an explanation for why rich people have gotten where they are. One half (50%) believes that a strong effort to succeed is most often the cause, as opposed to luck or circumstance. This compares to 33% who think that the lack of hard work is responsible for people being poor.

However, the door to riches is perceived to be a little less wide open now than before: 41% say that it is harder now than it used to be to become rich, while 31% see it as easier.

JULY 11
PRESIDENT BUSH/VICE PRESIDENT QUAYLE

Interviewing Date: 7/6–8/90
Survey #GO 922013

Do you approve or disapprove of the way George Bush is handling his job as president?

Approve 63%
Disapprove 24
No opinion 13

Selected National Trend

	Approve	Dis-approve	No opinion
1990			
June	67%	18%	15%
May	65	20	15
April	68	16	16
March	74	15	11
February	73	16	11
January	80	11	9

1989			
December	71%	20%	9%
November	70	17	13
October	68	20	12
September	70	17	13
August	69	19	12
July	66	19	15
June	70	14	16
May	56	22	22
April	58	16	26
March	56	16	28
February	63	13	24
January	51	6	43

Now, let me ask you about some specific problems facing the country. As I read off each one, would you tell me whether you approve or disapprove of the way President Bush is handling that problem:

Economic conditions in this country?

Approve 40%
Disapprove 53
No opinion 7

Selected National Trend

	Approve	Dis-approve	No opinion
1989			
November	40%	51%	9%
March	52	27	21

Federal budget deficit?

Approve 26%
Disapprove 64
No opinion 10

Selected National Trend

	Approve	Dis-approve	No opinion
1989			
November	32%	53%	15%
March	40	36	24

Abortion issue?

Approve 36%
Disapprove 44
No opinion 20

Selected National Trend

1989	Approve	Dis-approve	No opinion
November	38%	45%	17%
July	43	35	22

Drug problem?

Approve 46%
Disapprove 48
No opinion 6

Selected National Trend

1989	Approve	Dis-approve	No opinion
November	53%	41%	6%
September	72	18	10

Environmental issues?

Approve 42%
Disapprove 46
No opinion 12

Selected National Trend

1989	Approve	Dis-approve	No opinion
September	46%	40%	14%

Poverty and homelessness?

Approve 30%
Disapprove 62
No opinion 8

Selected National Trend

1989	Approve	Dis-approve	No opinion
November	30%	59%	11%
August	33	53	14

Education policy?

Approve 46%
Disapprove 41
No opinion 13

Selected National Trend

1989	Approve	Dis-approve	No opinion
November	53%	35%	12%

Foreign policy?

Approve 62%
Disapprove 26
No opinion 12

Selected National Trend

1989	Approve	Dis-approve	No opinion
November	65%	21%	14%
March	62	15	23

Relations with the Soviet Union?

Approve 82%
Disapprove 12
No opinion 6

Selected National Trend

1989	Approve	Dis-approve	No opinion
November	81%	11%	8%
March	70	10	20

Situation in Eastern Europe?

Approve 63%
Disapprove 20
No opinion 17

Selected National Trend

1989	Approve	Dis-approve	No opinion
November	63%	16%	21%

Situation in Central America?

Approve 42%
Disapprove 39
No opinion 19

Selected National Trend

1989	Approve	Dis-approve	No opinion
November	40%	39%	21%
March	37	33	30

Savings and Loan crisis?

Approve 22%
Disapprove 58
No opinion 20

At this point, would you say George Bush is doing a better job as president than you expected or not as good a job as you expected?

Better job 50%
Not as good a job 30
As well as expected (volunteered) 17
No opinion 3

Selected National Trend

1989	Better	Not as good	As well as expected	No opinion
November	44%	21%	28%	7%
March*	32	26	30	12

*Survey conducted for *Newsweek* by the Gallup Organization

What do you think is President Bush's greatest achievement to date?

Panama invasion, Noriega capture 3%
Drug war, fighting drugs 4
Changes in USSR; getting along
  with Gorbachev 24
General foreign policy; foreign
  affairs; peace in world 9
Getting elected 1

Leadership qualities 1
Changes in Eastern Europe; Berlin
  Wall 4
Abortion stand 1
Economy; budget 1
Taxes .... *
Other 12
Nothing 13
No opinion 27

*Less than 1%

How would you rate President George Bush on the following questions, after a year and a half in office? Would you say his performance has been excellent, good, only fair, or poor on:

Making good appointments to cabinet and other positions?

Excellent 5%
Good 40
Fair 36
Poor 7
No opinion 12

Selected National Trend

1990	Excellent	Good	Fair	Poor	No opinion
Feb.	7%	42%	32%	6%	13%

Being an efficient manager of government?

Excellent 7%
Good 45
Fair 33
Poor 11
No opinion 4

Selected National Trend

1990	Excellent	Good	Fair	Poor	No opinion
Feb.	10%	52%	28%	5%	5%

Developing programs to address the pressing problems America faces?

Excellent 4%
Good 31
Fair 42
Poor 19
No opinion 4

Selected National Trend

	Excellent	Good	Fair	Poor	No opinion
1990					
Feb.	8%	39%	35%	13%	5%

Communicating his ideas to the American public?

Excellent 9%
Good 46
Fair 30
Poor 13
No opinion 2

Selected National Trend

	Excellent	Good	Fair	Poor	No opinion
1990					
Feb.	16%	49%	26%	7%	2%

Following through on his ideas and initiatives?

Excellent 4%
Good 36
Fair 38
Poor 18
No opinion 4

Selected National Trend

	Excellent	Good	Fair	Poor	No opinion
1990					
Feb.	10%	45%	32%	7%	6%

Working effectively with Congress?

Excellent 5%
Good 46
Fair 35
Poor 7
No opinion 7

Selected National Trend

	Excellent	Good	Fair	Poor	No opinion
1990					
Feb.	7%	46%	34%	6%	7%

Being a good representative or symbol of the United States?

Excellent 22%
Good 49
Fair 22
Poor 6
No opinion 1

Selected National Trend

	Excellent	Good	Fair	Poor	No opinion
1990					
Feb.	24%	52%	18%	4%	2%

Being an inspirational leader to the American people?

Excellent 10%
Good 45
Fair 30
Poor 13
No opinion 2

Selected National Trend

	Excellent	Good	Fair	Poor	No opinion
1990					
Feb.	17%	47%	27%	8%	1%

Please tell me which word or phrase better describes your impression of George Bush. If you feel neither phrase describes Bush, please say so.

Sincere 75%
Insincere 18
Neither; no opinion 7

Selected National Trend

	Sincere	Insin-cere	Neither; no opinion
1990			
Feb.	85%	9%	6%
1988			
Aug. 19–21	74	15	11
Aug. 5–7	59	26	15

Steady, reliable 72%
Undependable 19
Neither; no opinion 9

Selected National Trend

	Steady, reliable	Unde-pendable	Neither; no opinion
1990			
Feb.	83%	8%	9%
1988			
Aug. 19–21	73	19	8
Aug. 5–7	59	27	14

Intelligent 66%
Only average 31
Neither; no opinion 3

Selected National Trend

	Intel-ligent	Only average	Neither; no opinion
1990			
Feb.	72%	25%	3%
1988			
Aug. 19–21	70	27	3
Aug. 5–7	61	33	6

Confident 76%
Insecure 18
Neither; no opinion 6

Selected National Trend

	Confident	Insecure	Nei-ther; no opinion
1990			
Feb.	82%	12%	6%
1988			
Aug. 19–21	67	25	8
Aug. 5–7	56	32	12

Warm, friendly 84%
Cold, unfriendly 7
Neither; no opinion 9

Selected National Trend

	Warm, friendly	Cold, un-friendly	Nei-ther; no opinion
1990			
Feb.	86%	5%	9%
1988			
Aug. 19–21	65	18	17
Aug. 5–7	49	28	23

Strong 63%
Weak 21
Neither; no opinion 16

Selected National Trend

	Strong	Weak	Nei-ther; no opinion
1990			
Feb.	73%	14%	13%
1988			
Aug. 19–21	57	28	15
Aug. 5–7	42	39	19

A leader 67%
A follower 24
Neither; no opinion 9

Selected National Trend

	A leader	A fol- lower	Nei- ther; no opinion
1990			
Feb.	75%	18%	7%
1988			
Aug. 19–21	50	39	11
Aug. 5–7	37	52	11

An active president 70%
A passive president 22
Neither; no opinion 8

Do you approve or disapprove of President Bush's recent announcement that he would consider increasing taxes, if necessary, to reduce the deficit?

Approve 41%
Disapprove 54
No opinion 5

Do you approve or disapprove of the way Dan Quayle is handling his job as vice president?

Approve 44%
Disapprove 30
No opinion 26

Selected National Trend

	Approve	Dis- approve	No opinion
1990			
May	48%	27%	25%
February	46	27	27
1989			
November	43	29	28

Note: A new Gallup Poll shows President George Bush's job approval at its lowest level since May 1989. In the latest survey his approval is 63%, continuing a downward trend from the 80% in January following the U.S. invasion of Panama. Twenty-four percent now disapprove of Bush's performance in office.

Gallup Poll data suggest several reasons for the drop in approval. First, Americans are now significantly less positive than earlier about the president's handling of several key elements of the national agenda: the federal budget deficit (26% approval), education (46%), and the environment (42%). On each of these, Bush's approval levels are down from Gallup's previous measurements, and disapproval ratings are up. Additionally, respondents give him low marks for his handling of the Savings and Loan crisis (22%).

These decreases in approval stand in contrast to several other areas of Bush's administration where his approval levels have not changed significantly. He continues to get high marks for foreign policy in general (62%), relations with the Soviet Union (82%), and the situation in Eastern Europe (63%).

On several other issues on which Bush previously has not scored so well, ratings have not changed substantively from past measurements. These include the problems of poverty and the homeless (30%), abortion (36%), and the nation's general economic conditions (40%).

Second, there is evidence of increasing doubts about Bush's ability to follow through on his programs and to inspire the public. Respondents give him almost as much credit as they did in February for his development of government programs (35%), working effectively with Congress (51%), and being a good symbol or representative of this country (71%).

Bush has lost ground since February, however, in terms of following through on his ideas and initiatives (40%). He also gets lower marks for his skills as an efficient manager (52%), communicating his ideas to the public (55%), and being an inspirational leader (55%).

Third, Bush's recent breaking of his "read my lips" promise on taxation does not sit well with many Americans. Fifty-four percent disapprove, with 41% approving.

And fourth, the impact of the Panama invasion in January 1990 has diminished. The invasion was seen as Bush's greatest achievement in February of this year (cited by 18%, twice as many as mentioned anything else) but is cited by only 3% now. Instead, improved relations with the Soviet Union are now seen as Bush's greatest achievement, cited by 24%.

By contrast, Vice President Dan Quayle's approval ratings have remained relatively constant. Now, 44% approve and 30% disapprove—measurements similar to those taken in the last three surveys.

JULY 12
DONALD TRUMP

Interviewing Date: 7/6–8/90
Survey #GO 922013

As you may have heard or read, Donald Trump is now in financial difficulty and has been put on a monthly personal spending allowance by his financial backers. Do you feel sorry for him, or do you feel he is getting what he deserves?

Sorry for Trump 13%
Trump is getting what he deserves 64
No opinion; have not heard 23

Note: Donald Trump's latest financial problems generate little sympathy with the public, according to a new Gallup Poll. With the hard-pressed entrepreneur put on a (albeit hefty) monthly allowance by his creditors, Americans were asked if they felt sorry for him or if Trump was getting what he deserved. By a margin of nearly 2 to 1, they think that he brought his troubles on himself. Sixty-four percent say that he deserves it, while 23% have no opinion and only 13% feel sorry for him.

JULY 18
CIGARETTE SMOKING

Interviewing Date: 7/6–8/90
Survey #GO 922013

Have you, yourself, smoked any cigarettes in the past week?

	Yes
National	27%

Selected National Trend

	Yes
1989	27%
1988	32
1987	30
1986	31
1985	35
1983	38
1981	35
1978	36
1977	38
1974	40
1972	43
1971	42
1969	40
1957	42
1954	45
1949	44
1944	41

Asked of those who replied in the affirmative: About how many cigarettes do you smoke each day?

Less than one pack 51%
One pack 32
More than one pack 14
No opinion 3

Selected National Trend

	Less than one pack	One pack	More than one pack	No opinion
1989	39%	39%	20%	2%
1988	40	38	20	2
1987	48	32	18	2
1981	38	37	24	1
1977	41	31	27	1

Asked of cigarette smokers: All things considered, would you like to give up smoking, or not?

Yes 74%
No 24
No opinion 2

Selected National Trend

	Yes	No	No opinion
1989	63%	33%	4%
1988	68	27	5
1987	77	20	3
1986	75	22	3
1981	66	30	4
1977	66	29	5

Also asked of smokers: Have you ever made a really serious effort to stop smoking, or not?

Yes 50%
No 25
Don't want to quit; no opinion 25

Selected National Trend

	Yes	No	Don't want to quit; no opinion
1989	38%	25%	37%
1988	48	20	32

Also asked of smokers: Do you feel you would be able to quit smoking if you made the decision to do so, or not?

Yes 78%
No 16
No opinion 6

Selected National Trend

	Yes	No	No opinion
1980	66%	27%	7%

Also asked of smokers: Do you consider your-self addicted to cigarettes, or not?

Yes 61%
No; no opinion 39

Also asked of smokers: If you had it to do over again, would you start smoking, or not?

Yes 13%
No 83
No opinion 4

Do you think that cigarette smoking is or is not harmful to your health?

Harmful 96%
Not harmful 3
No opinion 1

Selected National Trend

	Harmful	Not harmful	No opinion
1987	94%	4%	2%
1981	91	7	2
1977	90	7	3

What is your opinion—do you think cigarette smoking is one of the causes of heart disease?

Yes 85%
No 9
No opinion 6

Selected National Trend

	Yes	No	No opinion
1981	74%	14%	12%
1977	68	17	15
1969	60	15	25
1960	34	38	28
1958	33	37	30

What is your opinion—do you think cigarette smoking is one of the causes of lung cancer?

Yes 94%
No 4
No opinion 2

Selected National Trend

	Yes	No	No opinion
1987	87%	7%	6%
1981	83	10	7

1977	81	11	8
1972	70	13	17
1971	71	16	13
1969	70	11	19
1960	50	28	22
1958	44	30	26
1957	47	32	21
1954	39	29	32

What is your opinion—do you think that cigarette smoking is one of the causes of birth defects?

Yes 68%
No 16
No opinion 16

Selected National Trend

	Yes	No	No opinion
1987	63%	12%	25%
1981	54	23	23
1977	41	30	29

Do you agree with the new law that completely bans cigarette smoking on domestic flights on commercial airplanes, or not?

Yes 78%
No 20
No opinion 2

Smokers Only

Yes 57%
No 40
No opinion 3

What is your opinion regarding smoking in these public places? First, should they set aside certain areas, totally ban smoking, or should there be no restrictions on smoking in:

Hotels and motels?

Set aside areas 73%
Totally ban smoking 18
No restrictions 8
No opinion 1

Selected National Trend

	Set aside areas	Totally ban smoking	No restrictions	No opinion
1987	67%	10%	20%	3%

Workplaces?

Set aside areas 69%
Totally ban smoking 25
No restrictions 5
No opinion 1

Selected National Trend

	Set aside areas	Totally ban smoking	No restrictions	No opinion
1987	70%	17%	11%	2%

Restaurants?

Set aside areas 66%
Totally ban smoking 30
No restrictions 4
No opinion .... *

*Less than 1%

Selected National Trend

	Set aside areas	Totally ban smoking	No restrictions	No opinion
1987	74%	17%	8%	1%

Should smokers refrain from smoking in the presence of nonsmokers?

Yes 77%
No 18
No opinion 5

Selected National Trend

	Yes	No	No opinion
1987	77%	19%	4%

Would you favor or oppose a complete ban on smoking in all public places?

Favor 51%
Oppose 46
No opinion 3

Selected National Trend

	Favor	Oppose	No opinion
1988	60%	38%	2%
1987	55	43	2

Should smoking in this country be made totally illegal, or not?

Yes 14%
No 84
No opinion 2

Smokers Only

Yes 8%
No 90
No opinion 2

Do you think there should or should not be a complete ban on cigarette advertising?

Should 49%
Should not 48
No opinion 3

Selected National Trend

	Should	Should not	No opinion
1988	55%	40%	5%
1987	49	47	4
1981	43	51	6
1977	36	54	10

As far as you are concerned, is the advertising and promotion paid for by the tobacco companies an active attempt to get teenagers and young people to start smoking, or are the tobacco companies just trying to get those people who already smoke to switch brands?

Attempt to get young people to start 49%
Trying to get people to switch brands 38
No opinion 13

Smokers Only

Attempt to get young people to start 30%
Trying to get people to switch brands 55
No opinion 15

From what you know and have read, what percentage of the American population do you think smokes?*

0 to 24% 8%
25 to 35% 22
36 to 50% 30
51 to 75% 23
76 to 100% 6
No opinion 11

*Approximately 27% smoke, according to the latest Gallup survey.

If someone is sitting with you in a restaurant and asks if you mind if he or she smokes, would you allow them to smoke or say that you would prefer that they did not smoke at your table?

Allow them to smoke 52%
Prefer that they did not smoke 44
Not allow them to smoke at all
  (volunteered) 2
No opinion 2

Smokers Only

Allow them to smoke 86%
Prefer that they did not smoke 12
Not allow them to smoke at all .... *
No opinion 2

*Less than 1%

If someone comes to vist you in your home and asks if you mind if he or she smokes, would you allow them to smoke or say that you prefer that they did not smoke in your home?

Allow them to smoke 53%
Prefer that they did not smoke 37
Not allow them to smoke at all
    (volunteered) 9
No opinion 1

Smokers Only

Allow them to smoke 90%
Prefer that they did not smoke 8
Not allow them to smoke at all 2
No opinion .... *

*Less than 1%

If you were in a position to hire someone for a job and you learned that the person smoked, would it make you more likely to hire that person, less likely, or would it make no difference?

More likely 1%
Less likely 23
No difference 75
No opinion 1

Smokers Only

More likely 2%
Less likely 5
No difference 92
No opinion 1

All in all, does the fact that a person smokes make you respect them more, respect them less, or does it make no difference to you?

Respect them more 1%
Respect them less 17
No difference; no opinion 82

Smokers Only

Respect them more 1%
Respect them less 2
No difference; no opinion 97

Note: The latest 1990 Gallup audit of cigarette smoking reveals growing antismoking sentiment in the United States. Almost all Americans now favor some type of restriction on smoking in public places, up slightly over the past year.

Restaurants are the most sensitive area tested: 30% say that they want a total ban, up from 17% in 1987. Still, the significant majority (66%) say that they just want certain areas in restaurants set aside for smokers and nonsmokers. Only 4% want no restrictions whatever.

Those who want a total ban on smoking in the workplace is now at 25%, with 69% desiring some restrictions; only 5% want no restrictions. Furthermore, 18% want a total ban in hotels while 73% want designated areas and 8% opt for no restrictions. However, there has been an actual decline in the percentage who favor a complete ban on smoking in all public places—now at 51%, compared to 60% in 1988 and 55% in 1987. Similarly, the number of Americans who want a complete ban on cigarette advertising is now 49%, down from 55% in 1988 but still up from earlier measurements in 1977 and 1981.

It is clear from the Gallup Poll data that smokers face an inhospitable world in which to indulge their habit. About 37% of respondents say they would prefer that guests in their home not smoke. Similarly, 44% would object if a person asked to smoke at their table while dining.

More important, there is apparently now an economic consequence to smoking in the workplace: 23% say that they would be less likely to hire a person if they found that he or she smoked—one of the highest expressions of antismoking sentiment measured by Gallup in recent years.

The new poll also shows that smokers do not describe their behavior as something they are happy to be doing: 83% say that they wish they had never started smoking, and 74% would like to give it up. More surprisingly, 61% of smokers agree that they are addicted to cigarettes.

Among the public there continues to be almost universal agreement (96%) that smoking is harmful to one's health. Moreover, there have been significant increases in recent years in those who say that smoking is a causal factor in several different health problems, perhaps as a result of the warnings now required on packages of cigarettes and in print advertisements. Belief that smoking causes lung cancer has been high for the past ten to fifteen years. In the latest Gallup Poll, 94% agree. Now, 85% agree with the heart disease link, up from 74% in 1981. And those who think that smoking is a cause of birth defects is now up to 68%.

The new Gallup audit also finds that the percentage of Americans who smoke has not changed over the past year but has held steady at the same 27% measured in 1989 (thus still tied for the lowest levels in Gallup history and down from the historic high of 45% in 1954).

The number of cigarettes smoked each day has declined; now 50% of smokers claim that they smoke less than one pack per day. Also, those who say that they smoke more than one pack per day has dropped dramatically, from 27% in 1977 to the current 14%.

Although there is some disagreement, more respondents (49%) believe that tobacco companies are actively using their advertising to get young people to begin smoking than those who say that the companies are only trying to get smokers to change brands (38%). Smokers disagree with the prevailing view, by 55% to 30%.

The prevalence of smoking in this country is exaggerated by smokers and nonsmokers alike. The average person believes that about one half of the public smokes. This may reflect two factors: the enormous presence and power of the promotion and advertising of cigarettes and the amount of discussion generated in recent years by various antismoking measures.

JULY 25
MOST IMPORTANT PROBLEM/ SATISFACTION INDEX

Interviewing Date: 7/19–22/90
Survey #GO 922014

What do you think is the most important problem facing this country today?

Economy 7%
High cost of living, inflation 1
Federal budget deficit, failure to
    balance budget 21

Trade deficit 1
Unemployment 3
Other economic problems 2
Drugs, drug abuse 18
Crime 1
Poverty, homelessness 7
Environment 5
Education 2
Ethics in society, moral decline 2
Fear of war 1
AIDS 2
Dissatisfaction with government 1
Other noneconomic problems 6
Taxes 1
Savings and Loan crisis 1
No opinion 5

Selected National Trend

1990 ......Budget deficit; drugs
1989 ......Drugs; poverty and homelessness
1988 ......Budget deficit; drug abuse
1987 ......Fear of war; unemployment
1986 ......Unemployment; fear of war
1985 ......Unemployment; recession; fear of
        war
1984 ......Fear of war; unemployment
1983 ......Unemployment; high cost of living
1982 ......Unemployment; high cost of living
1981 ......High cost of living; unemployment
1980 ......High cost of living; unemployment

Do you approve or disapprove of the way George Bush is handling his job as president?

                      Approve
National 60%

Selected National Trend

                      Approve
February 1990 .... 73%

In general, are you satisfied or dissatisfied with the way things are going in the United States at this time?

                      Satisfied
National 45%

Selected National Trend

	Satisfied
February 1990	55%
September 1988	56
August 1987	45
March 1986	66
November 1985	51
February 1984	50
August 1983	35
April 1982	25
January 1981	17
February 1979	26

In general, are you satisfied or dissatisfied with the way things are going in your own personal life?

	Satisfied
National	81%

Selected National Trend

	Satisfied
February 1990	83%
September 1988	87
August 1987	83
March 1986	84
November 1985	82
February 1984	79
August 1983	77
April 1982	76
January 1981	81
February 1979	77

We are interested in how people's financial situation may have changed. Would you say that you are financially better off now than you were a year ago, or are you financially worse off now?

Better	44%
Worse	28
Same (volunteered)	27
No opinion	1

Selected National Trend

	Better	Worse	Same	No opinion
Feb. 1990	49%	24%	26%	1%
June 1989	42	25	31	2
May 1988	47	24	28	1

June 1987	43	32	24	1
June 1986	46	30	24	*
June 1985	43	29	26	2
July 1984	40	25	34	1
June 1983	28	39	32	1
Aug. 1982	25	46	26	3
June 1981	33	35	30	2
March 1980	30	45	24	1
June 1979	30	41	27	2
June 1978	35	32	31	2
June 1977	39	31	28	2
Sept. 1976	33	30	36	1

*Less than 1%

Now, looking ahead, do you expect that at this time next year you will be financially better off than now, or worse off than now?

Better	58%
Worse	17
Same (volunteered)	18
No opinion	7

Selected National Trend

	Better	Worse	Same	No opinion
Feb. 1990	65%	13%	16%	6%
June 1989	58	13	20	9
May 1988	63	9	17	11
June 1987	57	17	18	8
June 1986	57	20	17	6
June 1985	52	19	19	10
July 1984	52	12	28	8
June 1983	43	19	28	10
Aug. 1982	37	29	24	10
June 1981	41	26	25	8
March 1980	36	31	24	9
June 1979	33	30	27	10
June 1978	38	20	30	12
June 1977	47	17	27	9
Sept. 1976	44	12	31	13

How would you describe business conditions in your community—would you say they are very good, good, not too good, or bad?

Very good	10%
Good	47
Not too good	30
Bad	11
No opinion	2

Selected National Trend

	Very good, good	Not too good, bad	No opinion
January 1975	41%	56%	3%

Asked of those who are employed: Thinking about the next twelve months, how likely do you think it is that you will lose your job or be laid off—very likely, fairly likely, not too likely, or not at all likely?

Very likely	6%
Fairly likely	6
Not too likely	24
Not at all likely	62
No opinion	2

Selected National Trend

	Very, fairly likely	Not too, not at all likely	No opinion
1982			
Nov.	19%	77%	4%
June	15	81	4
Jan.	15	82	3
1980			
May	14	84	2
1975			
April	12	85	3
Jan.	15	81	4

How familiar are you with the Savings and Loan crisis and the government rescue plans—are you very familiar, somewhat familiar, not too familiar, or not at all familiar?

Very familiar	14%
Somewhat familiar	42
Not too familiar	25
Not at all familiar	19
No opinion	*

*Less than 1%

Selected National Trend

	Very, somewhat familiar	Not too, not at all familiar	No opinion
June 1990	59%	40%	1%

How serious is the Savings and Loan crisis for the United States—is it very serious, somewhat serious, not too serious, or not at all serious?

Very serious	56%
Somewhat serious	28
Not too serious	5
Not at all serious	1
No opinion	10

Selected National Trend

	Very, somewhat serious	Not too, not at all serious	No opinion
June 1990	85%	6%	9%

And if you had to say—who would you say is most to blame for the Savings and Loan crisis?

	July	June
President Reagan	7%	6%
President Bush	2	1
Congress	6	3
Government	13	18
Savings and Loan management	21	27
Regulatory agencies	3	2
American people	1	3
Political leaders	2	1
Other	9	7
No opinion	36	32

Note: A new Gallup Poll shows that the number of Americans who say that they are dissatisfied with the way things are going in the country has jumped significantly over the past five months and is now larger than the number who say that they are satisfied. This is a sharp reversal from sentiments of five months ago and may suggest the beginning of a period of national insecurity, possibly related to recent, highly publicized government crises. At the same time, however, respondents on the whole appear to be satisfied with their personal lives, with only a slight increase in the number who say that they worry about their personal financial situations.

Less than one half (45%) now say that they are satisfied with the way things are going in this country, while slightly more than one half (51%) say that they are dissatisfied. This contrasts with the 55% satisfied, 39% dissatisfied measure taken in February 1990. The current satisfaction levels are down compared with those recorded during the last years of the Reagan administration but are still higher than the very low satisfaction levels measured during the Carter administration and the recession years of Ronald Reagan's first term.

Satisfaction with the nation is often related to presidential approval. President George Bush's popularity rating dropped recently from the high levels he enjoyed in early 1990 to the current 60%, with 25% disapproving.

An increasing public awareness of the implications of the federal budget deficit may be a contributing factor to the rise in dissatisfaction. For example, in 1987 there was national consensus that drugs were the number one problem facing the country. Today, however, drugs have been supplanted by the deficit, followed by more general economic concerns. (The drug problem remains the second most important problem cited.)

There is no clear evidence that the Savings and Loan crisis is the cause of general dissatisfaction or of the declines in Bush's approval ratings, as few Americans lay the blame for it on specific individuals or political parties. Only 6% say that President Reagan is to blame, and only 2% mention President Bush—numbers essentially unchanged from early June. In addition, there is little direct criticism of either political party.

Respondents point to Savings and Loan management and the government for the cause.

Despite the sharp drop in the public's satisfaction with the way things are going in the country, 81% remain satisfied with the way things are going in their personal lives. The poll also shows only slight signs of an increase in respondents' concerns about their personal financial situation. Forty-four percent think that they are better off today than one year ago, and 28% say that they are worse off. These measures are down slightly from February, when 49% thought that they were better off and 24% worse off. At the same time, the levels are roughly in line with those measured by Gallup from 1984 through 1989 and significantly above those obtained in the late 1970s and early 1980s.

Perhaps more important is the fact that while 58% think that they will be better off financially one year from now and 17% say that they will be worse off, those who think they will be worse off rank 4 percentage points higher than the two previous measures taken during the Bush administration (13% in February 1990 and 13% in June 1989). However, the number who thought that they would be worse off rose to as high as 31% in March 1980 in the waning months of the Carter administration.

Overall, most American workers think that they will be holding onto their jobs over the next year—only 12% say that they are very or fairly likely to lose their jobs or be laid off.

AUGUST 6
PSYCHIC AND PARANORMAL PHENOMENA

Interviewing Date: 6/14–17/90
Survey #GO 922012

Some people are superstitious and try to behave in such a way as to avoid bad luck or "jinxing" themselves, and others are not. How superstitious are you? Would you say you are:

Very superstitious 3%
Somewhat superstitious 15
Not very superstitious 26
Not at all superstitious 56
No opinion .... *

*Less than 1%

*And what one or two superstitions affect you most?**

Black cat crossing path 14%
Walking under a ladder 12
Numbers; Friday the 13th; bad
   things happening in threes 9
Breaking a mirror 5
Wearing special or lucky clothing;
   dressing in a certain order;
   avoiding some colors 2
Speaking ill or good about a person
   or event makes it happen 2
Picking up pennies, coins 1
Following horoscope 1
Knocking on wood 1
Evil; the Devil 1
Telepathy; ESP 1
Other 11
None 4
No opinion 52

*Total adds to more than 100% due to multiple responses.

For each of the following items I am going to read you, please tell me whether it is something you believe in, something you're not sure about, or something you don't believe in:

Déjà vu, or the feeling that you have been somewhere or done something before?

Believe 55%
Not sure 13
Don't believe; no opinion 32

The Devil?

Believe 55%
Not sure 8
Don't believe; no opinion 37

ESP or extrasensory perception?

Believe 49%
Not sure 22
Don't believe; no opinion 29

That people on this Earth are sometimes possessed by the Devil?

Believe 49%
Not sure 16
Don't believe; no opinion 35

Psychic or spiritual healing, or the power of the human mind to heal the body?

Believe 46%
Not sure 20
Don't believe; no opinion 34

Telepathy, or communication between minds without using the traditional five senses?

Believe 36%
Not sure 25
Don't believe; no opinion 39

That houses can be haunted?

Believe 29%
Not sure 17
Don't believe; no opinion 54

That extraterrestrial beings have visited Earth at some time in the past?

Believe 27%
Not sure 32
Don't believe; no opinion 41

Clairvoyance, or the power of the mind to know the past and predict the future?

Believe 26%
Not sure 23
Don't believe; no opinion 51

Astrology, or that the position of the stars and planets can affect people's lives?

Believe 25%
Not sure 22
Don't believe; no opinion 54

Ghosts, or that spirits of dead people can come back in certain places and situations?

Believe 25%
Not sure 19
Don't believe; no opinion 56

Reincarnation, or the rebirth of the soul in a new body after death?

Believe 21%
Not sure 22
Don't believe; no opinion 57

That people can hear from or communicate mentally with someone who has died?

Believe 18%
Not sure 20
Don't believe; no opinion 62

Telekinesis, or the ability of the mind to move or bend objects using just mental energy?

Believe 17%
Not·sure 24
Don't believe; no opinion 59

Witches?

Believe 14%
Not sure 8
Don't believe; no opinion 78

Channeling, or allowing a "spirit-being" to temporarily assume control of a human body during a trance?

Believe 11%
Not sure 22
Don't believe; no opinion 67

That pyramids have a special healing power?

Believe 7%
Not sure 26
Don't believe; no opinion 67

That rock crystals have a special healing power?

Believe 4%
Not sure 20
Don't believe; no opinion 76

Selected National Trend
Those Who Believe

	1978
ESP	51%
The Devil	39
Déjà vu	30
Astrology	29
Clairvoyance	24
Ghosts	11
Witches	10

Now, as I read another list, I want you to tell me whether or not you have ever had each of these types of experiences. First, have you ever:

	Yes
Had the feeling of déjà vu and felt you had been somewhere or done something before?	56%
Felt that you were in touch with or getting a message from someone who was far away without using the traditional five senses?	25
Been able to heal your body using the power of your mind without traditional medicine?	25
Felt that you were in touch with someone who has already died?	17
Consulted a fortune-teller or psychic?	14
Been in a house you felt was haunted?	14
Felt you were talking to or being talked to by the Devil?	10
Seen or been in the presence of a ghost?	9

Felt that you were here on Earth in
a previous life or existence in another
body? 8
Personally seen someone moving or
bending an object using just mental
energy? 7
Consulted an astrologer? 6
Bought or used a rock crystal for
its special healing powers? 3
Been personally involved in channeling,
by participating in a trance during
which a "spirit-being" temporarily
assumed control of your body? 2
Bought or used a pyramid for its
special healing powers? 1

*Asked of those who read their horoscope in
a newspaper or magazine: Do you read it
every day, a couple of times each week, once
a week, once a month, or just every once in
a while?*

Yes, every day 10%
Yes, a couple of times each week 10
Yes, once a week 6
Yes, once a month 5
Yes, just every once in a while 43
No, do not read 26
No opinion .... *

*Less than 1%

*Have you heard or read about unidentified
flying objects—UFOs?*

	Yes
National	90%

Selected National Trend

	Yes
1978	93%
1973	95

*Have you, yourself, ever seen anything you
thought was a UFO?*

	Yes
National	14%

Selected National Trend

	Yes
1978	9%
1973	11

*In your opinion, are UFOs something real or
just people's imagination?*

Real	47%
Imagination	31
No opinion	22

Selected National Trend

	Real	Imagi-nation	No opinion
1978	57%	27%	16%
1973	54	30	16

*Do you think there are people somewhat like
ourselves living on other planets in the uni-
verse, or not?*

	Yes
National	46%

Selected National Trend

	Yes
1989	41%
1978	51
1973	46

*Have you heard or read about the New Age
movement?*

	Yes
National	29%

The following three questions were asked only
of those who had heard of the New Age
movement:

*Do you have a favorable or unfavorable opin-
ion of it?*

Favorable	18%
Unfavorable	49
No opinion	33

Do you think the New Age movement is good for traditional religions, a threat to traditional religions, or does it not affect traditional religions either way?

Good for traditional religions 7%
A threat to traditional religions 35
Does not affect traditional religions 36
No opinion 22

Do you think the New Age movement is good for U.S. society, a threat to society, or does it not affect society either way?

Good for society 13%
A threat to society 34
Does not affect society 33
No opinion 20

Note: Americans always have been fascinated by the idea that there is something beyond the traditional world of experience. These "out of the normal" experiences can involve many different types of occurrences. Some, called psychic phenomena, include such unusual mental experiences as telepathy, clairvoyance, precognition, déjà vu, telekinesis, and the ability of the mind to control and heal the physical body.

Other such experiences involve the belief that our lives can be controlled by superstitious occurrences or, in the case of believers in astrology, by the positions of the planets and stars. Still others involve the mysterious realm of death. And there is the unknown beyond our planet, including UFOs, visits by extraterrestrials, and the possibility of life on other planets.

The results of a new Gallup Mirror of America survey support the fact that respondents are very much aware of psychic and paranormal phenomena. All in all, only 7% deny believing in any of a list of eighteen paranormal experiences asked by Gallup. Almost one half say that they believe in five or more. And, even though actual experience is less frequent than belief, three of four have experienced at least one such occurrence, with about one half claiming experience with more than three.

AUGUST 6
ATOMIC BOMB

Interviewing Date: 7/19–22/90
Survey #GO 922014

To your knowledge, has an atomic or nuclear weapon ever been used on an enemy in wartime, or not?

	Yes
National	75%

Asked of the aware group: Where was it used?

Hiroshima, Nagasaki; World War II;
   Japan   91%
Other 3
No opinion 6

As you may know, the United States dropped atomic bombs on the Japanese cities of Hiroshima and Nagasaki in August 1945 near the end of World War II. Looking back, would you say you approve or disapprove of using the atomic bomb on Japanese cities in 1945?

Approve 53%
Disapprove 41
No opinion 6

By Age
18–29 Years

Approve 38%
Disapprove 56
No opinion 6

30–49 Years

Approve 50%
Disapprove 45
No opinion 5

50 Years and Over

Approve 66%
Disapprove 27
No opinion 7

55 Years and Over

Approve 67%
Disapprove 26
No opinion 7

Selected National Trend

	Approve	Dis- approve	No opinion
August 1945*	85%	10%	5%

*The wording of the question differed.

Do you think it was a good thing or bad thing that the atomic bomb was developed?

Good thing 37%
Bad thing 56
No opinion 7

Selected National Trend

	Good thing	Bad thing	No opinion
February 1949	59%	29%	12%
October 1947	55	38	7
August 1945	69	17	14

What is your own opinion about our using the atom bomb or nuclear weapons if the United States gets into another world war— do you think we should use it, or not?

Yes, use 17%
Yes, qualified 18
No 58
No opinion 7

Selected National Trend

	Yes, use	Yes, qualified	No	No opinion
July 1950	61%	16%	16%	7%

Note: On the forty-fifth anniversary of the U.S. destruction of the Japanese cities of Hiroshima and Nagasaki with atomic bombs, one in four Americans does not recall that such bombs have ever been used in wartime. A recent Gallup Poll also found that in the years since 1945 there has been a big shift in the level of approval of the use of the bomb. In a Gallup survey conducted immediately after the first atomic bomb was dropped on August 6, 1945, 85% of respondents approved of its use. Now, a bare majority (53%) approves of the decision to drop the bomb.

However, those persons now 55 years or older, who were at least 10 years old in 1945 during the waning months of the war, strongly approve of the bomb's use on Japan. These Americans presumably remember the circumstances in the final months of World War II: the mounting death toll from assaults on such Japanese-held islands as Guam, Tarawa, Iwo Jima, and Okinawa, and the massive casualties predicted as the United States prepared to invade Japan's home islands.

Two thirds of these older Americans (67%) now approve of the use of the bomb at Hiroshima and Nagasaki, compared to only 38% of those 18 to 29 years of age.

Opinion also has changed over the past forty-five years on the issue of nuclear weapons in general. In the era immediately following World War II, from 55% to 69% thought that the development of the bomb was a good thing. Today, only 36% view its development in a positive light, while 56% view it negatively.

Now, 58% think that we should not use nuclear weapons in a future war. Interestingly, in 1950 the same percentage thought that we should use nuclear weapons if there were another war.

AUGUST 6
PERSIAN GULF SITUATION

Interviewing Date: 8/3–4/90
Survey #GO 122002

How closely have you followed news about the situation involving the invasion of Kuwait by Iraq? Would you say you have followed it very closely, fairly closely, not too closely, or not at all closely?

Very closely 18%
Fairly closely 39
Not too closely 25
Not at all closely 18
No opinion .... *

*Less than 1%

Do you approve or disapprove of the way George Bush is handling this current situation in the Middle East involving Iraq and Kuwait?

Approve 52%
Disapprove 16
No opinion 32

In your opinion, what, if anything, should the United States do concerning the current situation involving Iraq and Kuwait?*

Do nothing 14%
Wait and see; wait for further
developments 13
Send in troops to actively fight
against Iraq 6
Bomb, airplane strikes 2
Impose economic sanctions, embar-
goes, boycotts; freeze assets 9
Send U.S. troops, ships to the area
but don't use them 3
Other 19
No opinion 36

*Multiple responses were given.

As a result of the Iraqi invasion of Kuwait, would you favor or oppose the following actions the United States has taken or could take:

Freeze Kuwait's assets so that Iraq can't spend them?

Favor 80%
Oppose 10
No opinion 10

Ban all imports from Iraq into the United States, including oil?

Favor 72%
Oppose 17
No opinion 11

Move U.S. naval vessels to the Persian Gulf as a show of force?

Favor 68%
Oppose 22
No opinion 10

Use U.S. naval airplanes to bomb Iraqi military targets?

Favor 31%
Oppose 57
No opinion 12

Send in U.S. Marines and Army ground troops to defend Kuwait?

Favor 32%
Oppose 56
No opinion 12

Encourage all U.S. allies to boycott Iraqi oil imports?

Favor 76%
Oppose 13
No opinion 11

Do you favor or oppose direct U.S. military action against Iraq at this time?

Favor 23%
Oppose 68
No opinion 9

If Iraq invades Saudi Arabia in addition to Kuwait, would you favor or oppose direct U.S. military action against Iraq?

Favor 60%
Oppose 26
No opinion 14

If there is another gasoline crisis in the United States as a result of the Iraq/Kuwait situation, with long lines and higher gas prices, would you favor or oppose direct U.S. military action against Iraq?

Favor 44%
Oppose 45
No opinion 11

If the Iraqis take U.S. citizens as hostages or prisoners, would you favor or oppose direct U.S. military action against Iraq?

Favor 77%
Oppose 16
No opinion 7

Note: Three days after the invasion of Kuwait by Iraqi troops, a majority of Americans favors direct U.S. military intervention if Iraq invades Saudi Arabia or if Americans are taken prisoners or held as hostages. Significantly less than a majority, however, favors immediate intervention.

At the same time, Americans strongly favor economic sanctions against Iraq, including an embargo on oil imports. About four out of ten opt for direct U.S. military involvement if a gasoline crisis is created as a result of Iraqi actions, a scenario seen as at least somewhat likely by two thirds of the public. However, despite the invasion's banner headline status, only about six out of ten claim to have been following the situation in Kuwait closely; thus, it may be too early for the public to form opinions about the crisis.

Asked to make a spontaneous suggestion about what the United States should do, a majority either say that they have no opinion (36%) or that we should do nothing now and/or wait and see (27%). Only 8% spontaneously recommend active U.S. military intervention, while another 3% say that we should send troops to the area as a show of force.

When direct military intervention is posed as a specific option, most offer conditional responses. Slightly more than one fifth (23%) favor direct military action against Iraq at this time, although one third favors two very specific actions: the bombing of Iraqi military targets (31%) and sending in troops to defend Kuwait (32%). Six out of ten (60%) favor U.S. military intervention if Saudi Arabia is invaded, and almost eight out of ten (77%) favor direct U.S. intervention if Iraq takes American citizens as hostages or prisoners. Moreover, slightly more than four out of ten (44%) favor U.S. military intervention if a gasoline crisis, including long lines with higher gas prices, is created as a result of the Iraqi actions.

Approval for the economic sanctions already imposed or encouraged by the United States is high: 80% favor freezing Kuwait's assets so that Iraq cannot spend them; 72% favor banning all Iraqi imports, including oil; and 76% favor encouraging all U.S. allies to boycott Iraqi oil imports.

Many Americans apparently are still making up their minds about how well President George Bush is handling the Iraqi crisis. In the current poll, 52% approve, 16% disapprove, and 32% have no opinion.

AUGUST 15
PERSIAN GULF SITUATION

Interviewing Date: 8/9–12/90
Survey #GO 922015

How closely have you followed news about the situation involving the invasion of Kuwait by Iraq? Would you say you have followed it very closely, fairly closely, not too closely, or not at all closely?

Very closely 40%
Fairly closely 43
Not too closely 12
Not at all closely 5
No opinion .... *

Selected National Trend

	Very, fairly closely	Not too, not at all closely	No opinion
August 3–4	57%	43%	*

*Less than 1%

Do you approve or disapprove of the way George Bush is handling this current situation in the Middle East involving Iraq and Kuwait?

Approve 80%
Disapprove 12
No opinion 8

Selected National Trend

	Approve	Dis- approve	No opinion
August 3–4	52%	16%	22%

In your opinion, what, if anything, should the United States do concerning the current situation involving Iraq and Kuwait?*

	Aug. 3–4	Aug. 9–12
Do nothing	14%	8%
Wait and see; wait for further developments	13	15
Send in troops to actively fight against Iraq	6	6
Bomb, airplane strikes	2	3
Impose economic sanctions, embargoes, boycotts; freeze assets	9	4
Send U.S. troops, ships to the area but don't use them	3	5
Impose a naval blockade on Iraq's imports and exports ...	–	1
Bomb Iraq's oil pipelines through Turkey and Saudi Arabia	–	**
Other	19	32
No opinion	36	27

*Multiple responses were given.
**Less than 1%

Would you approve or disapprove of using U.S. troops to force the Iraqis to leave Kuwait?

Approve 58%
Disapprove 32
No opinion 10

Do you approve or disapprove of the U.S. decision to send U.S. troops to Saudi Arabia as a defense against Iraq?

Approve 78%
Disapprove 17
No opinion 5

If Iraq invades Saudi Arabia, would you favor or oppose the United States sending as many more U.S. troops and weapons as necessary to stop Iraq?

Favor 75%
Oppose 18
No opinion 17

Do you favor or oppose leaving U.S. troops in Saudi Arabia if it becomes a long, drawn-out military conflict?

Favor 49%
Oppose 39
No opinion 12

How likely do you think it is that the U.S. involvement in Saudi Arabia could turn into another situation like Vietnam—that is, that the United States could become more and more deeply involved as time goes on? Would you say this is very likely, fairly likely, fairly unlikely, or very unlikely?

Very likely 22%
Fairly likely 26
Fairly unlikely 28
Very unlikely 18
No opinion 6

Do you think America's allies are doing all they should to support the U.S. efforts in the Iraqi-Kuwait situation?

Yes 45%
No 44
No opinion 11

How serious would you say the energy situation is in the United States—very serious, fairly serious, or not at all serious?

Very serious 28%
Fairly serious 45
Not at all serious 23
No opinion 4

Has the price of gasoline in your area gone up within the last week or two, or not?

Yes 95%
No 2
No opinion 3

Asked of those who replied that the price of gasoline has gone up: By how many cents have gasoline prices gone up in your area?

1 to 5 cents 9%
6 to 9 cents 12
10 cents 16
11 to 14 cents 10
15 cents 10
16 to 20 cents 18
21 to 25 cents 8
26 cents or more 9
No opinion 8

Do you think that the price increase by the oil companies was necessary because of the Iraqi situation, or do you think the oil companies only raised prices to take advantage of the situation?

Necessary to raise prices because of
  Iraqi situation 5%
Oil companies take advantage of
  situation 91
No opinion 4

Do you happen to be doing anything to reduce your use of energy—that is, your use of gasoline, electricity, or natural gas?

	Yes
National	66%

Selected National Trend

	Yes
February 1979	85%
August 1977	85

Asked of those who replied in the affirmative: What is that?

None; not doing anything 34%
Driving less 25
Turning off lights in home 10
Conserving (in general) 16
Turning down thermostat 3
Reducing use of appliances 3
Minimum use of air
  conditioner 7
Bought gas-saving car 2
Insulated home 1
Limit use of hot water 2
Participate in car pool 3
Using wood to heat 1
Ride bicycle; walk 2
Other 11
No opinion 1

Do you approve or disapprove of the way George Bush is handling his job as president?

Approve 74%
Disapprove 16
No opinion 10

Selected National Trend

	Approve	Disapprove	No opinion
July 19–22	60%	25%	15%
July 6–8	63	24	13
June 15–17	69	17	14

Note: More than three in four Americans (78%) approve of sending U.S. troops to defend Saudi Arabia; similar numbers (75%) also approve of sending as many more troops and weapons as necessary to stop Iraq.

Far fewer, however, favor our continued involvement in a lengthy military operation, according to a Gallup Poll conducted August 9–12. Only 49% would favor leaving U.S. troops in Saudi Arabia for a long, drawn-out military conflict, and equal numbers (48%) fear that our current involvement in the Middle East is very or fairly likely to turn into another situation like Vietnam; the same percentage (45%) says that America's allies have not done all they should to support our efforts.

President George Bush's job approval rating has increased 14 percentage points from the 60% measured in July, before the Iraqi invasion of Kuwait. Historically, there is a strong tendency for Americans to rally around a president whenever military action is taken. The current 74% approval level is nearly as high as Bush's record levels measured in the weeks after the invasion of Panama earlier this year.

Approval of the way President Bush is handling the Iraqi crisis is even higher, currently at 80%—an increase from the first weekend of the crisis, when up to one third of respondents had yet to form their opinions of how he was handling the situation.

Respondents so far do not express as high a level of economic anxiety as some analysts had predicted, but nearly everyone (95%) reports that the price of gasoline has gone up in their area in the past week or two, an average of about 15 cents per gallon. Nevertheless, they are not yet convinced that the current energy situation is as serious as was experienced in the late 1970s. In August 1979 as many as 47% said that our energy situation was very serious. Now, only 28% see it that way.

One reason for this lower level of concern may be that respondents think that the increase in the price of gas is more a case of oil company profiteering than a direct result of the crisis. More than nine in ten (91%) say that oil companies have raised prices to take advantage of the situation.

AUGUST 22
PERSIAN GULF SITUATION

Interviewing Date: 8/16–19/90
Survey #GO 922016

How closely have you followed news about the situation involving the invasion of Kuwait by Iraq?* Would you say you have followed it very closely, fairly closely, not too closely, or not at all closely?

Very closely 45%
Fairly closely 42
Not too closely 11
Not at all closely 2
No opinion .... **

Selected National Trend

	Very, fairly closely	Not too, not at all closely	No opinion
August 3–4	57%	43%	**
August 9–12	83	17	**

*The August 16–19 question included the words: "and the sending of U.S. troops to Saudi Arabia."
**Less than 1%

Do you approve or disapprove of the way George Bush is handling this current situation in the Middle East involving Iraq and Kuwait?

Approve 79%
Disapprove 14
No opinion 7

Selected National Trend

	Approve	Disapprove	No opinion
August 3–4	52%	16%	32%
August 9–12	80	12	8

Do you approve or disapprove of the U.S. decision to send U.S. troops to Saudi Arabia as a defense against Iraq?

Approve 76%
Disapprove 19
No opinion 5

Selected National Trend

	Approve	Dis-approve	No opinion
August 9–12	78%	17%	5%

Do you approve or disapprove of the U.S. embargo on all supplies and food coming into and out of Kuwait and Iraq?

Approve 83%
Disapprove 12
No opinion 5

Do you feel you have a clear idea of what the U.S. military involvement in the Iraqi situation is all about—that is, why our troops are in Saudi Arabia?

Yes 74%
No 24
No opinion 2

Why do you think we are involved in the Iraqi situation and why are our troops in Saudi Arabia?

Defend oil interests 49%
We should be; have to defend
  other countries 17
Stop Iraqi aggression 11
Defend Saudi Arabia 6
Protect U.S. citizens 4
Get Iraq out of Kuwait 1
Other 6
None 1
No opinion 5

In view of the developments since we first sent our troops to Saudi Arabia, do you think the United States made a mistake in sending troops to Saudi Arabia, or not?

Yes 17%
No 75
No opinion 8

Some people say we should go all out to win a military victory over Iraq and force Iraq to leave Kuwait, using whatever force is necessary. Do you agree or disagree with this view?

Agree 39%
Disagree 52
No opinion 9

Just your impression, do you think the United States and its allies are losing ground in the Iraqi situation in the Persian Gulf, standing still, or making progress?

Losing ground 6%
Standing still 45
Making progress 42
No opinion 7

In terms of time—that is, months or years—how long do you think U.S. forces will remain in the Mideast?

Less than 1 month 1%
1 to less than 2 months 5
2 to less than 3 months 6
3 to less than 6 months 12
6 months to less than 1 year 23
1 to less than 2 years 14
2 to less than 3 years 7
3 years and more 11
No opinion 21

Just from what you have heard, read, or seen, which of these statements comes closer to how you, yourself, feel about the U.S. presence in the Mideast:

United States should begin to withdraw
  its troops 12%
United States should continue with its
  present level of troop presence 49

United States should increase the
level of its troops to force Iraq to
leave Kuwait 35
No opinion 4

*How likely do you think it is that the U.S.
involvement in Saudi Arabia could turn into
another situation like Vietnam—that is, that
the United States could become more and
more deeply involved as time goes on? Would
you say this is very likely, fairly likely, fairly
unlikely, or very unlikely?*

Very likely 28%
Fairly likely 29
Fairly unlikely 23
Very unlikely 17
No opinion 3

Selected National Trend

	Very, fairly likely	Fairly, very unlikely	No opinion
1990			
August 9–12	48%	46%	6%
1985			
March*	59	38	3
1983			
October**	64	28	8

*Asked of the U.S. involvement in Nicaragua
**Asked of the U.S. involvement in Lebanon

*If Iraq uses chemical weapons against U.S.
forces, should the United States retaliate by
using chemical weapons against Iraq, or
not?*

Yes 44%
No 48
No opinion 8

*There is much discussion as to the amount
of money the government in Washington
should spend for national defense and military purposes. How do you feel about this?
Do you think we are spending too little, about
the right amount, or too much?*

Too little 15%
About right 40
Too much 41
No opinion 4

Selected National Trend

	Too little	About right	Too much	No opinion
Jan. 1990	10%	35%	50%	5%
1987	14	36	44	6
1986	13	36	47	4
1985	11	36	46	4
1983	21	36	37	6
1982	16	31	41	12
1981	51	22	15	12
1976	22	32	36	10
1973	13	30	46	11
1971	11	31	50	8
1969	8	31	52	9

*Do you approve or disapprove of the way
George Bush is handling his job as
president?*

Approve 75%
Disapprove 16
No opinion 9

Selected National Trend

	Approve	Dis- approve	No opinion
Aug. 9–12	74%	16%	10%
July 19–22	60	25	15
July 6–8	63	24	13
June 15–17	69	17	14
June 7–10	67	18	15
May 17–20	65	20	15

Note: Support for the U.S. military intervention
in the Middle East remains strong as the nation
enters its third week of active involvement. Most,
but not all, Americans claim to have a clear idea

of why the United States is involved in the Middle East, thus suggesting that President George Bush has done a good job of explaining his policy to the public.

Basic support for the U.S. involvement stands firm, with no significant signs of erosion. About three quarters (76%) approve of the decision to send U.S. troops to Saudi Arabia as a defense against Iraq, down only 2 percentage points from last week's measure. More than eight out of ten (83%) support the embargo on all supplies and food coming into and out of Kuwait and Iraq.

President Bush's job approval remains very high at 75%, the second highest level of his tenure in office (Bush received an 80% approval rating in January 1990). Seventy-nine percent approve of the way he is handling the situation in the Middle East involving Iraq and Kuwait.

Three quarters (74%) now say that they have a clear idea of what the U.S. military involvement in the Iraqi situation is all about. (By way of comparison, when this question was asked about the U.S. involvement in Vietnam in 1967, only 48% said yes.)

The most frequent justification offered for U.S. intervention by those polled is that it is necessary to protect our economic interests, including the free flow of oil. Smaller numbers justify our involvement in broader terms, saying that the United States has an obligation to defend other countries or to stop Iraqi aggression. About 4% say that we are involved to protect U.S. citizens.

The continuing strong support for this involvement comes despite the fact that most Americans apparently are settling down for a relatively long stay by the U.S. military in the Middle East. The most frequently occurring estimate is that we will be involved six months to one year, but fully one third (32%) thinks that U.S. troops will be involved for more than one year.

There is a good deal of support for an even more aggressive posture in the Middle East. A little more than one third (35%) believe that the United States should increase the level of its troops to force Iraq to leave Kuwait, and 39% agree that we should go all out to win a military victory over Iraq and force it to leave Kuwait. Forty-four percent go so far as to say that we

should use chemical weapons against Iraq if they are used by that country against the United States first.

The potential for military conflict with Iraq apparently has led to some increased support for additional defense spending, up 5 percentage points over Gallup's last measure in January. More significant, perhaps, is the 9 percentage-point decline among those who think that we are spending too much for military purposes.

AUGUST 22
CONFIDENCE IN INSTITUTIONS

Interviewing Date: 8/16–19/90
Survey #GO 922016

I am going to read you a list of institutions in American society. Please tell me how much confidence you, yourself, have in each one—a great deal, quite a lot, some, or very little:

The military?

Great deal	37%
Quite a lot	31
Some	22
Very little	7
None (volunteered)	1
No opinion	2

Selected National Trend

	Those saying "great deal" or "quite a lot"
1989	63%
1988	58
1987	61
1986	63
1985	61
1984*	58
1983	53
1981	50

1979	54
1977	57
1975	58

*In this and the following trends, the 1984 survey was conducted for *Newsweek* by the Gallup Organization.

Church or organized religion?

Great deal	33%
Quite a lot	23
Some	26
Very little	14
None (volunteered)	2
No opinion	2

Selected National Trend

Those saying "great deal" or "quite a lot"

1989	52%
1988	59
1987	61
1986	57
1985	66
1984	64
1983	62
1981	64
1979	65
1977	64
1975	68
1973	66

U.S. Supreme Court?

Great deal	19%
Quite a lot	28
Some	31
Very little	16
None (volunteered)	2
No opinion	4

Selected National Trend

Those saying "great deal" or "quite a lot"

1989	46%
1988	56
1987	52
1986	54
1985	56
1984	51
1983	42
1981	46
1979	45
1977	46
1975	49
1973	44

Public schools?

Great deal	21%
Quite a lot	24
Some	34
Very little	18
None (volunteered)	1
No opinion	2

Selected National Trend

Those saying "great deal" or "quite a lot"

1989	43%
1988	49
1987	50
1986	49
1985	48
1984	47
1983	39
1981	42
1979	53
1977	54
1973	58

Newspapers?

Great deal	15%
Quite a lot	24
Some	42

Very little 16	Very little 30
None (volunteered) 2	None (volunteered) 3
No opinion 1	No opinion 1

Selected National Trend

	Those saying "great deal" or "quite a lot"
1988	36%
1987	31
1986	37
1985	35
1984	34
1983	38
1981	35
1979	51
1973	39

Selected National Trend

	Those saying "great deal" or "quite a lot"
1988	27%
1987	28
1986	27
1985	29
1984	25
1983	25
1981	25
1979	38
1973	37

Banks?

Great deal	13%
Quite a lot	23
Some	40
Very little	21
None (volunteered)	2
No opinion	1

Organized labor?

Great deal	11%
Quite a lot	16
Some	40
Very little	25
None (volunteered)	3
No opinion	5

Selected National Trend

	Those saying "great deal" or "quite a lot"
1989	42%
1988	49
1987	51
1986	49
1985	51
1984	51
1983	51
1981	46
1979	60

Selected National Trend

	Those saying "great deal" or "quite a lot"
1988	26%
1987	26
1986	29
1985	28
1984	30
1983	26
1981	28
1979	36
1977	39
1975	38
1973	30

Television?

Great deal	12%
Quite a lot	13
Some	41

Congress?

Great deal	9%
Quite a lot	15
Some	43

Very little 28
None (volunteered) 2
No opinion 3

Selected National Trend

	Those saying "great deal" or "quite a lot"
1989	32%
1988	35
1986	41
1985	39
1984	29
1983	28
1981	29
1979	34
1977	40
1975	40
1973	42

Big business?

Great deal 9%
Quite a lot 16
Some 40
Very little 28
None (volunteered) 3
No opinion 4

Selected National Trend

	Those saying "great deal" or "quite a lot"
1988	26%
1987	26
1986	29
1985	28
1984	30
1983	26
1981	28
1979	36
1977	39
1975	38
1973	30

Note: The situation in the Middle East has had a positive effect on Americans' perceptions of the military. For the second year in a row of the eighteen years that the Gallup Poll has tracked public confidence in ten major institutions, the military ranks alone in the number one spot, and by a substantially larger margin than last year.

At the same time, confidence in two other institutions has dropped sharply. The most notable decrease is in banks; only 36% now profess either a great deal or quite a lot of confidence in banks, off 6 points from Gallup's measurement last year, and 24 points below the confidence in banks recorded in 1979, the first year they were included on the list. The other institution showing a sharp decline in confidence is Congress, at 24% (down 8 points from its 1989 rating of 32%).

At one point in time, church and organized religion consistently engendered the most confidence of any institution tested by Gallup; over the past several years, however, such confidence had steadily declined. This year showed a small upswing (from 52% to 56%) in the number who express a great deal or quite a lot of confidence in religious institutions.

AUGUST 26
HOME OWNERSHIP

Interviewing Date: 4/19–22; 8/16–19/90
Survey #GO 922008; 922016

Thinking back to ten years ago, if you had bought a house in your neighborhood then, do you think it would now be worth a lot more than you paid for it, a little more, a little less, or would it be worth a lot less than you paid for it ten years ago?

	Worth a lot more	Worth a lot less	Point difference
National*	62%	13%	+49

By Region

	Worth a lot more	Worth a lot less	Point difference
Pacific	82%	4%	+78
New England	80	5	+75
Middle Atlantic	71	9	+62
Southeast	68	11	+57
East Central	59	14	+45

Rocky Mountain ...	50	15	+35
West Central	45	20	+25
Southwest	34	29	+ 5

*In this and the next question the following responses have been omitted: "worth a little more," "worth the same," "worth a little less," and "don't know."

Now, thinking ahead to the next ten years, if you bought a house in your neighborhood now, do you think it would be worth a lot more money ten years from now, a little more, a little less, or would it be worth a lot less ten years from now?

	Worth a lot more	Worth a lot less
National	38%	13%

By Region

Pacific	52%	8%
Southeast	46	13
Middle Atlantic	43	11
East Central	40	16
Rocky Mountain	36	16
Southwest	32	15
West Central	29	19
New England	28	9

Note: Many Americans believe that owning a house will not be as good an investment during the 1990s as it had been during the 1980s. A nationwide Gallup Business Poll found only 38% expecting houses in their neighborhood to be worth a lot more ten years from now. That is far below the 62% who believe that these same houses are now worth a lot more than they were ten years ago.

AUGUST 29
PERSIAN GULF SITUATION

Interviewing Date: 8/23–26/90
Survey #GO 122003

Do you approve or disapprove of the way George Bush is handling this current situation in the Middle East involving Iraq and Kuwait?

Approve	76%
Disapprove	17
No opinion	7

Selected National Trend

	Approve	Dis-approve	No opinion
August 16–19	79%	14%	7%
August 9–12	80	12	8
August 3–4	52	16	32

Do you feel you have a clear idea of what the U.S. military involvement in the Iraqi situation is all about—that is, why our troops are in Saudi Arabia?

Yes	70%
No	28
No opinion	2

Selected National Trend

	Yes	No	No opinion
August 16–19	74%	24%	2%

How closely have you followed news about the situation involving the invasion of Kuwait by Iraq? Would you say you have followed it very closely, fairly closely, not too closely, or not at all closely?*

Very closely	44%
Fairly closely	42
Not too closely	12
Not at all closely	2
No opinion	**

Selected National Trend

	Very, fairly closely	Not too, not at all closely	No opinion
August 16–19	87%	13%	**
August 9–12	83	17	**
August 3–4	57	43	**

*August 16–19, 23–26: "and the sending of U.S. troops to Saudi Arabia."
**Less than 1%

*In your opinion, what, if anything, should the United States do concerning the current situation involving Iraq and Kuwait?**

Do nothing	3%
Wait and see; wait for further developments	10
Send in troops to actively fight against Iraq	4
Bomb, airplane strikes	4
Impose economic sanctions, embargoes, boycotts; freeze assets	4
Send U.S. troops, ships to the area but don't use them	2
Impose a naval blockade on Iraq's imports and exports	1
Bomb Iraq's oil pipelines through Turkey and Saudi Arabia	**
Keep things as they are now	10
Pull out; don't get involved; stay neutral; let Arabs do it	5
Talk, negotiate, use diplomatic process or the United Nations	6
Do all we can to prevent war	3
Do whatever it takes	3
Stay strong; show our force; be firm	10
Get American civilians out, protect them .	6
Assassinate Hussein	2
Get the Iraqis out of Kuwait	1
Take action quickly, get it over with	1
Other	6
No opinion	25

*Multiple responses were given.
**Less than 1%

Do you approve or disapprove of the U.S. decision to send U.S. troops to Saudi Arabia as a defense against Iraq?

Approve	80%
Disapprove	16
No opinion	4

Selected National Trend

	Approve	Disapprove	No opinion
August 16–19	76%	19%	5%
August 9–12	78	17	5

Asked of those who approve of the decision: Why do you approve of the U.S. decision to send U.S. troops to Saudia Arabia?

Protect our allies from aggression; they asked for our help	14%
Show force; presence; our responsibility, duty	17
Protect oil, our economy, our freedom, interests in region	25
Protect civilians, hostages	5
Right thing to do	3
Prevent war and keep peace; maintain world balance; stop Hussein's aggression	24
Other	9
No opinion	3

Asked of those who disapprove of the decision: Why do you disapprove of the U.S. decision to send U.S. troops to Saudi Arabia?

We have no business being there	18%
Boys might get killed for nothing	9
There are other ways to solve crisis	9
Being there might start a war	7
It is costing us too much money	2
We went in too fast; should have waited and seen what happens	6
It is another Vietnam situation	4
Sending in too many troops	2
Other	29
No opinion	14

Do you approve or disapprove of calling up Army, Navy, and Air Force reservists to active duty because of the current Mideast situation?

Approve	68%
Disapprove	26
No opinion	6

Just from what you have heard, read, or seen, which of these statements comes closer to how you, yourself, feel about the U.S. presence in the Mideast:

	Aug. 16–19	Aug. 23–26
United States should begin to withdraw its troops	12%	11%
United States should continue with its present level of troop presence	49	51
United States should increase the level of its troops to force Iraq to leave Kuwait	35	34
No opinion	4	4

In view of the developments since we first sent our troops to Saudi Arabia, do you think the United States made a mistake in sending troops to Saudi Arabia, or not?

	Aug. 16–19	Aug. 23–26
Yes	17%	18%
No	75	76
No opinion	8	6

All in all, is the current situation in the Mideast worth going to war over, or not?

Yes	49%
No	41
No opinion	10

Do you favor or oppose leaving U.S. troops in Saudi Arabia if it becomes a long, drawn-out military conflict?

Favor	46%
Oppose	41
No opinion	13

How likely do you think it is that the U.S. involvement in Saudi Arabia could turn into another situation like Vietnam—that is, that the United States could become more and more deeply involved as time goes on? Would you say this is very likely, fairly likely, fairly unlikely, or very unlikely?

Very likely	30%
Fairly likely	28
Not too likely	22
Not at all likely	17
No opinion	3

Selected National Trend

	Very, fairly likely	Not too, not at all likely	No opinion
August 16–19	57%	40%	3%
August 9–12	48	46	6

How likely do you think it is that there will be a recession in the country during the next twelve months—very likely, fairly likely, not too likely, or not at all likely?

Very likely	31%
Fairly likely	38
Not too likely	17
Not at all likely	6
No opinion	8

Selected National Trend

	Very, fairly likely	Not too, not at all likely	No opinion
Aug. 9–12, 1990	65%	28%	7%
Jan. 1979	62	31	7

Note: While eight out of ten Americans continue to approve of the U.S. decision to send troops to Saudi Arabia, only one half thinks that the current situation in the Middle East is worth going to war over. The predominant response is that the United

States should wait and see before taking further actions. These and other findings are based on the Gallup Poll's fourth weekly tracking of public opinion since the August 2 invasion of Kuwait by Iraqi troops.

Overall approval of President George Bush's actions in the Persian Gulf remains positive: 76% approve of the way he is handling the situation in Iraq and Kuwait, with 17% disapproving. Although these numbers are very high, they mark a slight decrease in approval from the August 9–12 poll, when 80% approved Bush's handling of the situation, with 12% disapproving. (Bush's overall job approval is now 76%.) There has also been a slight decrease in the percentage who claim that they have a clear idea of what U.S. military involvement is all about—70%, down from the 74% of August 16–19.

There are substantial indications that the public is cautious about getting much further involved in the Middle East, pending further developments. When asked what the United States should do about the current situation, the most frequently occurring responses center on wait-and-see actions: 10% say that we should wait for further developments; 10% want to keep things just as they are now; 6% say that we should talk, negotiate, or use the diplomatic process or the United Nations; 4% advocate sanctions; and 3% say that we should do whatever it takes to prevent war. When asked point-blank whether the current situation is worth going to war over, only 49% say yes.

Americans who favor the U.S. actions in Saudi Arabia are basing their approval now more on generic or general principles than on specific benefits to the United States. About six out of ten (65%) justify their approval by saying that it is necessary to prevent war or keep peace, to stop Saddam Hussein's aggression; to show force, that it is our responsibility, that it is our duty; or to protect our allies from aggression when they ask for help. Only about one out of four (25%) justify their approval of our involvement in terms of protecting our own oil supply, our economy, or U.S. interests in the region, with another 5% saying that they approve in order to protect our civilians in Kuwait.

In two other related developments, two thirds (68%) approve of President Bush's recent decision to call up U.S. Army, Navy, and Air Force reservists to active duty; 26% disapprove. And a national economic recession continues to loom large for respondents. Now, 69% think it is very or fairly likely that we will have a recession during the next twelve months—already up 4 percentage points from the last survey taken two weeks ago.

SEPTEMBER 3
PETS

Interviewing Date: 7/19–22/90
Survey #GO 922014

Do you or any other household members have any pets in your home, such as dogs, cats, birds, and the like?

	Yes
National	58%

Asked of those who replied in the affirmative: What kinds of pets do you have? *

Any pet	58%
Dog	40
Cat	27
Fish	8
Bird	5
Hamster	1
Rabbit	1
Turtle	1
Mouse	1
Snake	1
Guinea pig	1
Other	2

*Multiple responses were given.

Asked of pet owners: For each of the following reasons people give for having pets, please tell me whether it applies to you, or not:

For someone to pet or play with?

	Yes
National	89%

By Pet Owner

Dog owner	90%
Cat owner	93
Other pet	73

To help children learn responsibility?

	Yes
National	81%

By Pet Owner

Dog owner	82%
Cat owner	78
Other pet	88

For companionship?

	Yes
National	81%

By Pet Owner

Dog owner	83%
Cat owner	84
Other pet	61

For security?

	Yes
National	69%

By Pet Owner

Dog owner	79%
Cat owner	51
Other pet	53

For someone to communicate with?

	Yes
National	57%

By Pet Owner

Dog owner	57%
Cat owner	62
Other pet	45

In your opinion, do people who have household pets such as dogs, cats, birds, etc., lead a more satisfying life or a less satisfying life than people who do not have pets, or is there no difference?

More satisfying	61%
Less satisfying	2
No difference	32
No opinion	5

As I read off the names of some different groups of people, please tell me if having pets would provide them with a more satisfying life, a less satisfying life, or wouldn't pets make any difference:

Senior citizens or the elderly?

More satisfying	89%
Less satisfying	3
No difference	6
No opinion	2

Young children?

More satisfying	85%
Less satisfying	5
No difference	7
No opinion	3

Retarded people?

More satisfying	78%
Less satisfying	6
No difference	9
No opinion	7

People with mental health problems?

More satisfying	63%
Less satisfying	12
No difference	15
No opinion	10

Handicapped people?

More satisfying	89%
Less satisfying	3
No difference	5
No opinion	3

People who are sick or ill?

More satisfying 59%
Less satisfying 19
No difference 16
No opinion 6

People living alone?

More satisfying 91%
Less satisfying 2
No difference 5
No opinion 2

The average person?

More satisfying 63%
Less satisfying 5
No difference 27
No opinion 5

In your opinion, do you think pets can sense natural disasters such as earthquakes, hurricanes, or violent storms before they occur, or not?

Yes 74%
No 18
No opinion 8

By Pet Owner

	Yes	No	No opinion
All owners	78%	17%	5%
Dog owner	79	17	4
Cat owner	79	16	5
Other pet	80	15	5

Some people say that dog owners sometimes look like their dogs. Thinking about all your dog-owning friends, neighbors, and business associates, do you think any of them resemble their dogs, or not?

Yes 39%
No 58
No opinion 3

By Pet Owner

	Yes	No	No opinion
All owners	42%	56%	2%
Dog owner	40	58	2
Cat owner	42	56	2
Other pet	49	50	1

When you are alone with your pet, how often, if at all, do you talk or converse with him/her—all of the time, most of the time, occasionally, or never?

	All or most of the time
All owners	46%
Dog owner	50
Cat owner	44
Other pet	28

How would you grade your pet for the following, using the standard school grading system of A, B, C, D, or Fail:

For displaying affection?

	Grade of A or B
All owners	88%
Dog owner	96
Cat owner	87
Other pet	49

For intelligence?

	Grade of A or B
All owners	87%
Dog owner	91
Cat owner	85
Other pet	66

As companion for children?

	Grade of A or B
All owners	85%
Dog owner	91
Cat owner	80
Other pet	59

For cleanliness?

	Grade of A or B
All owners	85%
Dog owner	85
Cat owner	89
Other pet	69

As personal companion?

	Grade of A or B
All owners	83%
Dog owner	90
Cat owner	76
Other pet	59

For trying to please?

	Grade of A or B
All owners	73%
Dog owner	86
Cat owner	57
Other pet	43

For obedience?

	Grade of A or B
All owners	66%
Dog owner	78
Cat owner	52
Other pet	33

As watchpet?

	Grade of A or B
All owners	56%
Dog owner	79
Cat owner	20
Other pet	22

Do you sometimes turn on the television, radio, or stereo at home when you leave your pet alone?

	Yes
All owners	30%
Dog owner	33
Cat owner	25
Other pet	24

Do you ever celebrate your pet(s)' birthdays or the anniversary of the day it (they) came to live with you?

	Yes
All owners	24%
Dog owner	26
Cat owner	23
Other pet	14

Do you ever give toys or presents to your pet(s) on Christmas?

	Yes
All owners	65%
Dog owner	69
Cat owner	64
Other pet	46

Do you happen to have pictures of any of your pets in any of the following places: on the wall or furniture at home; at work; in your wallet or purse?

	Yes, home	Yes, work	Yes, wallet or purse
All owners	41%	8%	17%
Dog owner	45	8	21
Cat owner	36	10	11
Other pet	28	7	7

Which of the following, if any, is your pet allowed to do:

Ride in the family car?

	Allowed to do
All owners	60%
Dog owner	76
Cat owner	39
Other pet	28

Lie on the furniture?

	Allowed to do
All owners	48%
Dog owner	36
Cat owner	79
Other pet	28

Sleep on some family member's bed?

	Allowed to do
All owners	43%
Dog owner	37
Cat owner	67
Other pet	17

Go along on visits to your friends' homes?

	Allowed to do
All owners	32%
Dog owner	43
Cat owner	13
Other pet	18

Go along on family vacations?

	Allowed to do
All owners	27%
Dog owner	36
Cat owner	13
Other pet	18

Be fed at the table by hand?

	Allowed to do
All owners	20%
Dog owner	23
Cat owner	19
Other pet	10

By any chance has your pet ever done any of the following:

Gone to a veterinarian?

	Yes
All owners	86%
Dog owner	94
Cat owner	86
Other pet	37

Gone to a pet groomer?

	Yes
All owners	29%
Dog owner	43
Cat owner	7
Other pet	14

Gone to a pet boarding place?

	Yes
All owners	16%
Dog owner	21
Cat owner	8
Other pet	8

Gone to an obedience training class or school?

	Yes
All owners	9%
Dog owner	15
Cat owner	*
Other pet	1

Been included in somebody's will?

	Yes
All owners	1%
Dog owner	2
Cat owner	1
Other pet	2

Gone to a pet counselor or psychiatrist?

	Yes
All owners	*%
Dog owner	*
Cat owner	*
Other pet	1

*Less than 1%

Do you consider your pet a member of the family, or not?

	Yes	No
All owners	88%	12%
Dog owner	93	7
Cat owner	86	14
Other pet	72	28

Just off hand, would you consider your pet to be spoiled, or not?

	Yes	No
All owners	62%	38%
Dog owner	65	35
Cat owner	62	38
Other pet	45	55

Do you ever feed your pet the following:

Dry food?

	Yes
All owners	88%
Dog owner	90
Cat owner	88
Other pet	74

Table scraps?

	Yes
All owners	60%
Dog owner	72
Cat owner	48
Other pet	22

Canned food?

	Yes
All owners	56%
Dog owner	54
Cat owner	71
Other pet	23

Special food for young pets, older pets, etc.?

	Yes
All owners	39%
Dog owner	48
Cat owner	28
Other pet	23

Special dietary food, i.e., low fat, low sodium, low ash?

	Yes
All owners	24%
Dog owner	26
Cat owner	20
Other pet	25

Food cooked and prepared at home especially for him/her?

	Yes
All owners	22%
Dog owner	29
Cat owner	13
Other pet	7

Where does your pet usually sleep at night— inside your home or out of doors?

	Kept outdoors	Put outdoors at night	Indoors
All owners	23%	8%	69%
Dog owner	30	6	64
Cat owner	11	16	73
Other pet	11	5	84

Asked of those who replied "indoors": Where does he/she sleep—on the floor; in a pet bed, basket, or cage; or on some family member's bed?

	Floor	Pet bed	Family bed	Other
All owners	21%	22%	22%	4%
Dog owner	25	20	18	1
Cat owner	17	14	36	6
Other pet	9	59	5	11

Which best describes your pet's living arrangement in your household? Is he/she kept indoors all the time, indoors except when being walked or exercised, allowed to come in or go out at will, or is he/she kept outside?

	Kept indoors	Allowed in and out	Kept outside
All owners	12%	65%	23%
Dog owner	3	67	30
Cat owner	18	71	11
Other pet	49	40	11

Asked of dog owners: What breed or breeds of dog do you have?

Mixed, mutt	22%
German shepherd	9
Lab/retriever	9
Poodle	7
Cocker spaniel	6
Beagle	4
Dachshund	3
Collie	3
Chow	3
Chihuahua	3
Husky	3
Doberman	2
Pit bull	2
Shih Tzu	2
Rottweiler	2
Other	20

Asked of cat owners: What breed or breeds of cat do you have?

Mixed, American shorthair, alley cat	65%
Siamese	6
Himalaya	4
Persian	4
Manx	1
Angora	1
Other	19

Note: Americans today reveal an extraordinary attachment to their pets. In nine out of every ten households with animals—and most homes have them—owners regard their pets as family members. They talk to them, reward them with Christmas presents, birthday parties, and home-cooked meals; allow them to sleep on family members' beds; and even carry their pictures in a wallet or purse. These are some of the findings of a Gallup Mirror of America survey to determine the attitudes and behavior of pet owners and the general public on a wide range of topics relating to household animals.

About six in ten households (58%) have pets today. All told, Americans own about 170 million household animals of various species, with dogs and cats the favorites. Contrary to some other estimates, the Gallup survey shows dogs to be substantially more numerous than cats. Four in ten households (40%) have one or more dogs, while 27% have one or more cats. Next in order of popularity are fish and birds, which are found in 8% and 5% of households, respectively. Hamsters, rabbits, turtles, mice, snakes, and guinea pigs each are found in about 1% of homes.

Most respondents—those with pets and those without—believe that pets play a positive role in people's lives. Six in ten (61%) think that people with animals lead a more satisfying life than those without them, whereas only 2% think that pets detract from life. The remaining 32% say that while pets may not contribute to a more satisfying life, they have no negative effect.

The public's view regarding the influence of pets is even more positive in the case of some of the more vulnerable or disadvantaged groups in society. For example, large majorities believe that the following lead a more satisfying life if they have pets: people living alone (91%), senior citizens (89%), disabled people (89%), young children (85%), and retarded people (78%).

Indeed, owners' interactions with pets sometimes approximate a human relationship. Almost one half (46%) admit that they talk often to their pets.

Americans reward their pets handsomely for their contribution to family life but also imply that they probably overdo it. Six in ten (62%) say that they consider their pet spoiled. And in contrast to primitive societies, where animals are never allowed in the home, only 30% of American households with dogs treat them as totally outdoor animals, forced to live full-time out of doors. In cat households, even fewer (11%) are kept outside permanently.

SEPTEMBER 5
PERSIAN GULF SITUATION

Interviewing Date: 8/30–9/2/90
Survey #GO 122004

How closely have you followed news about the situation involving the invasion of Kuwait by Iraq?* Would you say you have followed it very closely, fairly closely, not too closely, or not at all closely?

Very closely 18%
Fairly closely 39
Not too closely 25
Not at all closely 18
No opinion .... **

Selected National Trend

	Very, fairly closely	Not too, not at all closely	No opinion
August 23–26	86%	14%	**
August 16–19	87	13	**

August 9–12	83	17	**
August 3–4	57	43	**

*August 16–19, 23–26; August 30–September 2: "and the sending of U.S. troops to Saudia Arabia."
**Less than 1%

Do you approve or disapprove of the way George Bush is handling this current situation in the Middle East involving Iraq and Kuwait?

Approve 74%
Disapprove 18
No opinion 8

Selected National Trend

	Approve	Disapprove	No opinion
August 23–26	76%	17%	7%
August 16–19	79	14	7
August 9–12	80	12	8
August 3–4	52	16	32

In your opinion, what, if anything, should the United States do concerning the current situation involving Iraq and Kuwait?*

Do nothing 4%
Wait and see; wait for further
    developments 9
Send in troops to actively fight
    against Iraq 3
Bomb, airplane strikes 2
Impose economic sanctions,
    embargoes, boycotts; freeze assets 2
Send U.S. troops, ships to the area
    but don't use them 1
Impose a naval blockade on Iraq's
    imports and exports .... **
Bomb Iraq's oil pipelines through
    Turkey and Saudi Arabia 1
Keep things as they are now 7
Pull out; don't get involved; stay
    neutral; let Arabs do it 6
Talk, negotiate, use diplomatic
    process or the United Nations 8

Do all we can to prevent war 2
Do whatever it takes 2
Stay strong; show our force; be firm 6
Get American civilians out, protect
  them 3
Assassinate Hussein 2
Get the Iraqis out of Kuwait 1
Take action quickly, get it over with 4
Other 20
No opinion 24

*Multiple responses were given.
**Less than 1%

*Do you approve or disapprove of the U.S.
decision to send U.S. troops to Saudi Arabia
as a defense against Iraq?*

Approve 74%
Disapprove 20
No opinion 6

Selected National Trend

	Approve	Dis- approve	No opinion
August 23–26	80%	16%	4%
August 16–19	76	19	5
August 9–12	78	17	5

*Do you feel you have a clear idea of what
the U.S. military involvement in the Iraqi
situation is all about—that is, why our troops
are in Saudi Arabia?*

Yes 76%
No 23
No opinion 1

Selected National Trend

	Yes	No	No opinion
August 23–26	70%	28%	2%
August 16–19	74	24	1

*In view of the developments since we first
sent our troops to Saudi Arabia, do you think
the United States made a mistake in sending
troops to Saudi Arabia, or not?*

Yes 16%
No 76
No opinion 8

Selected National Trend

	Yes	No	No opinion
August 23–26	18%	76%	6%
August 16–19	17	75	8

*Just from what you have heard, read, or
seen, which of these statements comes closer
to how you, yourself, feel about the U.S. presence in the Mideast?*

United States should begin to
  withdraw its troops 12%
United States should continue with
  its present level of troop presence 51
United States should increase the
  level of its troops to force Iraq to
  leave Kuwait 31
No opinion 6

*All in all, is the current situation in the
Mideast worth going to war over, or not?*

Yes 35%
No 56
No opinion 9

Selected National Trend

	Yes	No	No opinion
August 23–26	49%	41%	10%

*Do you think America's allies are doing all
they should to support the U.S. efforts in the
Iraqi-Kuwait situation?*

Yes 35%
No 56
No opinion 9

Selected National Trend

	Yes	No	No opinion
August 9–12	45%	44%	11%

Just your impression, do you think the United States and its allies are losing ground in the Iraqi situation in the Persian Gulf, standing still, or making progress?

Losing ground 6%
Standing still 47
Making progress 41
No opinion 6

Selected National Trend

	Losing ground	Stand-ing still	Making progress	No opinion
Aug. 16–19	6%	45%	42%	7%

In terms of time—that is, months or years—how long do you think U.S. forces will remain in the Mideast?

	Aug. 16–19	Aug. 30–Sept. 2
Less than 1 month	1%	1%
1 to less than 2 months	5	3
2 to less than 3 months	6	6
3 to less than 6 months	12	11
6 months to less than 1 year ..	23	25
1 to less than 2 years	14	15
2 to less than 3 years	7	7
3 years and more	11	7
No opinion	21	25

Here are some conditions under which the United States might consider withdrawing its troops from the Mideast. For each, please tell me if you favor or oppose the United States withdrawing its troops if that condition is met:

If Iraq allows all U.S. and other foreign citizens to leave Kuwait but Iraqi troops remain in Kuwait and Saddam Hussein remains in power?

Favor 21%
Oppose 72
No opinion 7

If Iraq pulls all of its troops out of Kuwait but Saddam Hussein remains in power in Iraq?

Favor 45%
Oppose 46
No opinion 9

If Iraq pulls all of its troops out of Kuwait and Saddam Hussein is removed from power in Iraq?

Favor 86%
Oppose 9
No opinion 5

In general, how would you rate the job the press in this country has done in covering the situation in the Mideast concerning Iraq and Kuwait? Would you say it has been excellent, good, only fair, or poor?

Excellent 29%
Good 47
Fair 16
Poor 6
No opinion 2

As far as you are concerned, has there been too much media coverage of the Mideast crisis, not enough, or has the amount of coverage of the Mideast crisis been about right?

Too much 18%
Not enough 10
About right 70
No opinion 2

Has the media in this country been too critical of President Bush's action in the current Mideast situation, not critical enough, or has it been about right?

Too critical 13%
Not critical enough 10
About right 71
No opinion 6

As you may know, several television networks have gone to a great deal of trouble and expense to send their well-known news anchors to the Mideast to cover the current situation. As far as you are concerned, would you rather watch a newscast with the lead anchor on the scene in the Mideast, or with the lead anchor home in New York coordinating the coverage of other reporters?

Watch anchor on the scene 48%
Watch anchor coordinating coverage 31
Neither (volunteered) 17
No opinion 4

Should women in the U.S. military serve in actual combat roles if it becomes necessary in the current situation in the Mideast, or not?

Yes 60%
No 37
No opinion 3

Do you favor or oppose reinstating the military draft to provide soldiers for the current Mideast situation?

Favor 40%
Oppose 56
No opinion 4

Note: Nearly one month after the arrival of American troops on Saudi Arabian soil, most respondents continue to support U.S. involvement there and appear ready to maintain that support until Iraqi leader Saddam Hussein is ousted. The public clearly thinks that Iraq must withdraw from Kuwait and that President Hussein must be removed from power before U.S. troops should be withdrawn.

Only one in five (21%) supports withdrawing our troops in the current situation, where Iraqi forces occupy Kuwait and Hussein is in power in Iraq, even if all foreign citizens are allowed to leave. Opinion is more evenly divided on whether our troops should remain in Saudi Arabia if Iraq's forces do withdraw from Kuwait but Hussein remains in power. Forty-five percent would favor a

withdrawal under those conditions, and 46% would oppose. A substantial majority (86%), however, favors withdrawing U.S. troops if Iraq pulls out of Kuwait and Hussein also is removed from power.

A majority of Americans (60%) supports the idea of women assuming combat roles in the Middle East if it becomes necessary. Additionally, more than one half (56%) would oppose reinstating the draft to provide troops for the situation in Saudi Arabia. Only four in ten (40%) support reinstating a draft at this time.

Overall, Americans still support the actions their country has taken in the Middle East. Over the past month, some Gallup measurements have shown a slight decline and some a slight increase, but the typical rally-round-the-flag reaction in a foreign policy crisis has yet to subside. President George Bush's handling of the situation and the deployment of troops to Saudi Arabia continue to enjoy high levels of support from three quarters of all respondents (74%). Moreover, similar proportions do not think that sending troops to Saudi Arabia was a mistake (76%) and say that they have a clear understanding of why our troops were sent there (76%).

SEPTEMBER 12
PARTY BETTER FOR PEACE AND PROSPERITY/CONGRESSIONAL ELECTIONS

Interviewing Date: 8/9–12; 16–19/90
Survey #GO 122004; 922015; 922016

Asked of registered voters: Looking ahead for the next few years, which political party do you think would be more likely to keep the United States out of World War III—the Republican or the Democratic party?

Republican 37%
Democratic 34
No difference; no opinion 29

Selected National Trend

	Repub-lican	Demo-cratic	No difference; no opinion
Sept. 1988	43%	33%	24%
July 1988	39	36	25
May 1988	31	39	30
Jan. 1988	36	35	29
Aug. 1984	36	40	24
April 1984	30	42	28
Sept. 1983	26	39	35
Oct. 1982	29	38	33
April 1981	29	34	27
Sept. 1980	25	42	33
Aug. 1976	29	32	39
Sept. 1972	32	28	40
Oct. 1968	37	24	39
Oct. 1960	40	25	35
Oct. 1956	46	16	38
Jan. 1952	36	15	49
Sept. 1951	28	21	51

Asked of registered voters: Which political party—the Republican or the Democratic—do you think will do a better job of keeping the country prosperous?

Republican 46%
Democratic 30
No difference; no opinion 24

Selected National Trend

	Repub-lican	Demo-cratic	No difference; no opinion
Sept. 1988	52%	34%	14%
July 1988	46	39	15
May 1988	41	39	20
Jan. 1988	42	35	23
Aug. 1984	48	36	24
April 1984	44	36	20
Sept. 1983	33	40	27
Oct. 1982	34	43	23
April 1981	41	28	31
Sept. 1980	35	36	29
Aug. 1976	23	47	30
Sept. 1972	38	35	27
Oct. 1968	34	37	29

Oct. 1960	31	46	23
Oct. 1956	39	39	22
Jan. 1952	31	35	34
Sept. 1951	29	37	34

Asked of registered voters: If the elections for Congress were being held today, which party's candidate would you like to see win in your congressional district—the Democratic party's candidate or the Republican party's candidate?

Democratic candidate 51%*
Republican candidate 49

Selected National Trend

	Democratic candidate	Republican candidate
April 1990	53%	47%
July 1986	57	43
October 1985	53	47
July 1982	61	39
June 1981	52	48

*The "undecided" and "no opinion" responses have been allocated proportionally.

Do you approve or disapprove of the way the representative from your own congressional district is handling his or her job?

Approve 66%
Disapprove 19
No opinion 15

Selected National Trend

	Approve	Dis-approve	No opinion
March 1977	55%	17%	28%

Note: This November, George Bush and the Republicans seem likely to escape the heavy losses that usually characterize the outcome of midterm congressional elections. A new Gallup Poll of voting intentions for the 1990 congressional contests shows GOP candidates running stronger than they have in previous off-year elections over the past twenty years.

In the last ten midterm elections, the party in the White House has lost an average of twenty-five seats in the House of Representatives. (The Republican loss of only six seats in the 1986 election was a notable exception.) Indications at this point, however, are that 1990 may be a repeat of 1986; it is even possible that the party in the White House may gain a few seats, which has not happened since 1934.

President George Bush's high popularity helps boost the Republicans' congressional prospects, but changes in the Middle East situation may have a strong influence on the outcome of the November elections. For the moment, however, the international crisis seems to benefit neither party. Republicans are helped by the public's tendency to rally around the president at a time of international crisis. Democrats, however, with their big advantage in congressional seats, benefit from the public's similar tendency to support incumbents when international tensions are high.

Gallup traditionally has found higher levels of support for Democratic candidates in August or September of midterm election years than in the current measure, when only 51% say that they would like to see the Democratic candidate win in their congressional district, as opposed to an average of 56% in the last ten off-year elections. Forty-nine percent in the most recent survey say that they would vote for the Republican candidate.

Over the years, Gallup has found that people have much more positive feelings about their own congressman than they do about Congress as an institution. This year's early measure may reflect the general anti-Congress mood of the country. On election day, however, people will vote for or against individual candidates, and Gallup's numbers do not indicate a groundswell of anti-incumbent sentiment.

Asked if they approve or disapprove of the way their own representative handles the job, two thirds (66%) say that they approve. This rating has increased from 55% when last asked in 1977, at a time when congressional confidence was at an all-time high of 40%.

SEPTEMBER 19
AMERICA'S LARGE CITIES

Interviewing Date: 9/10–11/90
Survey #GO 922017

Now, thinking about large cities—including both those you have visited and those you have never visited—from what you know and have read, do you consider each of the following cities to be safe to live in or visit, or not?

	Safe	Not safe	No opinion
New York	11%	85%	4%
Miami	17	76	7
Washington, DC	22	71	7
Detroit	18	68	14
Chicago	26	65	9
Los Angeles	26	64	10
San Francisco	44	43	14
Philadelphia	40	40	20
Atlanta	45	39	16
Boston	53	29	18
San Diego	56	28	16
Dallas	55	26	19
Houston	55	25	20
Seattle	68	16	16
Minneapolis	66	11	22

Note: Americans have an overwhelmingly negative perception of the safety of many of the nation's large cities. A new Gallup Poll shows that a surprisingly high number think that several of the largest and most popular tourist sites are unsafe places in which to live or work. Among those that share a reputation for being dangerous, New York leads the list, seen as not safe by almost nine in ten Americans (85%). It is followed by Miami (76%), Washington, DC (71%), Detroit (68%), Chicago (65%), and Los Angeles (64%).

The picture is not entirely dismal, however. Several large cities are seen as generally safe: Minneapolis, viewed as unsafe by only 11%; Seattle (16%), Houston (25%), Dallas (26%), San Diego (28%), and Boston (29%).

Interestingly, some cities suffer a worse reputation for safety among those living in the immediate vicinity than among people living elsewhere. Los Angeles, Philadelphia, Atlanta, Boston, Houston, and Dallas, for instance, are all seen as less safe by people living nearby than by residents of other regions. On the other hand, for certain cities the situation is just the opposite. San Francisco and Chicago are perceived as safer by people who live in that city's region than by those who do not.

SEPTEMBER 21
MISS AMERICA PAGEANT

Interviewing Date: 9/14–16/90
Survey #GO 922018

Did you happen to watch the recent Miss America pageant last Saturday, or not?

	Yes
National	25%

If you had a daughter, would you be proud and encourage her if she wanted to enter the Miss America pageant, or not?

Yes	65%
No	30
No opinion	5

There are four areas used in judging the Miss America pageant: swimsuit, evening gown, talent, and the interview questions. Just your opinion, what percentage out of 100 do you think each should be given as a criterion in judging the contestants:

Swimsuit?

None	12%
1 to 10%	21
11 to 20%	17
21 to 30%	33
31 to 40%	2
41 to 50%	2
Over 50%	1
No opinion	12

Evening gown?

None	6%
1 to 10%	14
11 to 20%	19
21 to 30%	39
31 to 40%	3
41 to 50%	4
Over 50%	3
No opinion	12

Talent?

None	7%
1 to 10%	4
11 to 20%	9
21 to 30%	43
31 to 40%	13
41 to 50%	9
Over 50%	4
No opinion	11

Interview?

None	9%
1 to 10%	7
11 to 20%	10
21 to 30%	38
31 to 40%	12
41 to 50%	8
Over 50%	4
No opinion	12

Some people say that the Miss America pageant is degrading and insulting to women. Do you agree with this, or not?

Yes	18%
No	77
No opinion	5

Some people think that the Miss America pageant should be a contest that judges contestants primarily on their looks. Others think that the Miss America pageant should judge contestants primarily on their talent and intelligence. Which comes closer to your opinion?

Looks 11%
Talent and intelligence 70
Both (volunteered) 16
No opinion 3

Do you think the Miss America pageant should stay in Atlantic City, or do you think it should be held somewhere else?

Stay in Atlantic City 38%
Held somewhere else 30
No opinion 32

Note: The Miss America pageant began seventy years ago as a beauty contest and as a way to publicize Atlantic City, New Jersey, after the summer season. Due in part to protests from feminists and others, much more attention now is given to contestants' nonphysical attributes.

A Gallup Poll conducted immediately after the most recent pageant shows that the public agrees that the pageant should reward women for talent and intelligence, not just looks. When given a choice, 70% say that talent and intelligence should be primary, with only 11% opting for looks.

Asked to allocate 100 points among four areas as criteria for judging contestants, respondents give talent the most importance and the swimsuit competition the least. However, very few (12%) want the swimsuit competition dropped altogether, and, feminist protests to the contrary, only 18% agree that the Miss America pageant is degrading and insulting to women. About two thirds (65%) say that they would be proud and encouraging if a daughter wanted to enter the pageant, but almost one third (30%) reply that they would not.

SEPTEMBER 21
U.S.-SOVIET RELATIONS

Interviewing Date: 9/10–11/90
Survey #GO 922017

I'd like your overall opinion of Mikhail Gorbachev. Is your overall opinion of him very favorable, mostly favorable, mostly unfavorable, or very unfavorable?

Very favorable 16%
Mostly favorable 54
Mostly unfavorable 13
Very unfavorable 8
No opinion 9

Selected National Trend

	Very, mostly favorable	Mostly, very unfavorable	No opinion
May 1990	68%	21%	11%
Aug. 1989	77	15	8
Dec. 1988	72	21	7

How about the Soviet Union? Is your overall opinion of it very favorable, mostly favorable, mostly unfavorable, or very unfavorable?

Very favorable 7%
Mostly favorable 51
Mostly unfavorable 23
Very unfavorable 9
No opinion 10

Selected National Trend

	Very, mostly favorable	Mostly, very unfavorable	No opinion
May 1990	64%	26%	10%
Aug. 1989	51	40	9
Dec. 1988	44	46	10

As far as you know, is there still a "cold war" between the United States and the Soviet Union, or is the "cold war" over?

Still exists 40%
Over 50
No opinion 10

Selected National Trend

	Still exists	Over	No opinion
May 1990	52%	40%	8%

Do you trust what Soviet President Gorbachev says, or not?

Yes 49%
No 42
No opinion 9

Selected National Trend

	Yes	No	No opinion
May 1990	43%	49%	8%

Did you happen to hear, read, or see anything about the summit this weekend in Helsinki, Finland, between President Bush and Soviet President Gorbachev?

Yes 52%
No 48
No opinion .... *

*Less than 1%

Do you think that the fact that the United States and the Soviet Union have agreed to work together to solve the current crisis in the Mideast will improve the chances for a peaceful settlement of the situation, decrease the chances of a peaceful settlement, or don't you think it will make a difference either way?

Improve chances 65%
Decrease chances 2
No difference 30
No opinion 3

Do you think the Soviet Union should send troops and ships to support our efforts in the Middle East, or do you think it is better that they do not get directly involved in the peacekeeping force?

Send troops 60%
Not get involved 32
No opinion 8

As you may know, some countries have offered to help the United States with the cost of keeping troops in Saudi Arabia. Do you think the Soviet Union should help share these costs, or not?

Yes 78%
No 16
No opinion 6

Note: About two thirds of the public think that chances for peace in the Middle East are improved because the Soviet Union and United States are working together to resolve the situation there. There is a strong feeling among respondents, however, that the Soviets should participate more actively in the situation in the Middle East. Six out of ten (60%) think that the Soviet Union should send troops and ships to aid U.S. efforts, but about one third (32%), apparently uneasy about the USSR's active participation, do not think that they should be involved. Almost eight out of ten (78%) say that the USSR should help share the costs of the efforts with the United States and other nations who are footing the bill.

The recent summit did not significantly change basic opinions of either Mikhail Gorbachev or the Soviet Union. Gorbachev is viewed favorably by 70%, a number that has not changed markedly since 1988. Six out of ten (58%) now have a favorable opinion of the Soviet Union—essentially unchanged from earlier this year but substantially up from much more unfavorable perceptions measured in 1988 and in the years following World War II.

The summit may have helped accelerate Americans' perceptions that the Cold War is over. One half (50%) now say that it is, up from the 40% who thought that way in May of this year.

SEPTEMBER 26
CRIME/GUN CONTROL

Interviewing Date: 9/10–11/90
Survey #GO 922017

Is there more crime in your area than there was a year ago, or less?

More 51%
Less 17
Same (volunteered) 24
No opinion 8

Selected National Trend

	More	Less	Same	No opinion
1989				
June	53%	18%	22%	7%
January	47	21	27	5
1983	37	17	36	10
1981	54	8	29	9
1977	43	17	32	8
1975	50	12	29	9
1972	51	10	27	12

Is there more crime in the United States than there was a year ago, or less?

More 84%
Less 3
Same (volunteered) 7
No opinion 6

Selected National Trend

	More	Less	Same	No opinion
June 1989	84%	5%	5%	6%

Is there any area near where you live—that is, within a mile—where you would be afraid to walk alone at night?

	Yes
National	40%

Selected National Trend

	Yes
1989	43%
1983	45
1981	45
1977	45
1975	45
1972	42

How about at home at night—do you feel safe and secure, or not?

	Yes
National	90%

Selected National Trend

	Yes
1989	90%
1983	84
1981	84
1977	85
1975	80
1972	83

In your opinion, what factors are most responsible for crime in the United States today?

Drugs 60%
Unemployment 4
Breakdown of family, social values 6
Courts too lenient 2
Punishment too lax 2
Television violence 1
Lack of education 2
Guns 2
Poverty 2
Justice system .... *
Other 11
No opinion 8

*Less than 1%

What is the most important thing that can be done to help reduce crime?*

Cut, eliminate drugs 7%
Harsher punishment 15
Teach values and respect for law 7
Reduce unemployment 5
More police 8
Try cases faster .... **
Legalize drugs 1
Education 10
Tighten judicial system 2
Community watch or involvement 1
Gun control 1

Death penalty; kill drug dealers 3
Other 16
No opinion 12

*Multiple responses were given.
**Less than 1%

To lower the crime rate in the United States, some people think additional money and effort should go to attacking the social and economic problems that lead to crime through better education and job training. Others feel more money and effort should go to deterring crime by improving law enforcement with more prisons, police, and judges. Which comes closer to your view?

Spend money on social and economic
  problems 57%
Spend money on improving law
  enforcement 36
No opinion 7

Do you think there should or should not be a law that would ban the possession of handguns except by the police and other authorized persons?

Should 41%
Should not 55
No opinion 4

Selected National Trend

	Should	Should not	No opinion
October 1987	42%	50%	8%
June 1981	41	54	5
December 1980	38	51	11

Would you favor or oppose the registration of all handguns?

	Favor
National	81%

Selected National Trend

	Favor
1985	70%
1982	66

Would you favor or oppose a law requiring that any person who carries a gun outside his home must have a license to do so?

	Favor
National	81%

Selected National Trend

	Favor
1988	84%

Would you favor or oppose a national law requiring a seven-day waiting period before a handgun could be purchased, in order to determine whether the prospective buyer has been convicted of a felony or is mentally ill?

	Favor
National	95%

Selected National Trend

	Favor
1988	91%

In general, do you feel that the laws covering the sale of firearms should be made more strict, less strict, or kept as they are now?

More strict 78%
Less strict 2
Kept the same 17
No opinion 3

Selected National Trend

	More strict	Less strict	Kept the same	No opinion
1986	60%	8%	30%	2%
1983	59	4	31	6
1981	65	3	30	2
1980	59	6	29	6
1975	69	3	24	4

Would you favor or oppose federal legislation banning the manufacture, sale, and possession of the following types of weapons:

Cheap handguns known as "Saturday night specials"?

Favor 68%
Oppose 26
No opinion 6

Selected National Trend

	Favor	Oppose	No opinion
1989	71%	25%	4%

Plastic guns invisible to metal detectors?

Favor 76%
Oppose 18
No opinion 6

Selected National Trend

	Favor	Oppose	No opinion
1989	75%	20%	5%

Semiautomatic assault guns, such as the AK-47?

Favor 72%
Oppose 22
No opinion 6

Selected National Trend

	Favor	Oppose	No opinion
1989	72%	23%	5%

Do you have a gun in the house?

	Yes
National	47%

Selected National Trend

	Yes
1989	47%
1985	44
1983	58
1980	45
1975	44
1972	43

Asked of gun owners: What is the total number of guns kept in your house?

One 27%
Two 22
Three 14
Four or more 31
Not sure 6

Note: Nationwide support for gun control is at the highest levels recorded by the Gallup Poll since the early 1970s. But while Americans now very strongly favor stricter controls on guns, including registration and seven-day waiting periods, a majority of them oppose a total ban on handgun ownership. The most dramatic change is the percentage who want laws covering the sale of firearms to be made more strict, now favored by 78% of the public compared to 60% when Gallup last asked the question in 1986.

Additionally, over eight out of ten (81%) now support registration of handguns, up 11 percentage points since 1985. Eight out of ten (81%) also support the idea that anyone carrying a gun must have a license, and there is near universal support (95%) for a seven-day waiting period before a handgun can be purchased. Moreover, respondents strongly favor a total ban on plastic guns that are invisible to metal detectors (76%) and on semiautomatic assault weapons (72%).

However, less than one half (41%) want a total ban on handguns; this has not changed essentially since 1980. One seemingly conflicting note: When handguns are described as "cheap handguns known as Saturday night specials," the figure favoring a total ban jumps to 68%. Interestingly, there is at least one gun in about one half (47%) of all households—essentially the same as in most measurements for the last two decades.

Despite the increased interest in gun control, the recent Gallup Poll suggests that the real impact of crime on people's daily lives is no more severe now than in the past. Americans continue to think that crime is increasing rather than decreasing, with about 51% saying that crime is increasing in their area and 84% saying that crime is increasing across the United States. However, respondents have been saying the same thing since

1972. Fifty-one percent said that crime was on the increase in their area as long ago as 1972 (53% said that crime was on the increase last year).

More significant, perhaps, is the fact that there have been slight decreases in two of Gallup's measures. Forty percent now say that there is an area near where they live where they would be afraid to walk alone at night, compared to 43% last year and down even more from the 45% measured as far back as 1975. Only 10% now say that they do not feel safe and secure at home at night, a considerably smaller number than the 20% registered in 1975 and the 16% measured in 1981 and 1983 (the number is unchanged from last year).

Americans strongly believe that the central cause of crime is drugs (60%). Asked what can be done to curb crime, they talk about eliminating drugs and imposing harsher and surer punishment. However, the majority also favors (although less strongly than before) spending more money on social and economic problems as well.

OCTOBER 3
PRESIDENT BUSH/SATISFACTION INDEX/ PERSONAL FINANCES

Interviewing Date: 9/27–30/90
Survey #GO 122005

Do you approve or disapprove of the way George Bush is handling his job as president?

Approve	67%
Disapprove	20
No opinion	13

Selected National Trend

	Approve	Dis- approve	No opinion
Sept. 14–16	73%	17%	10%
Sept. 10–11	76	16	8
August 30– Sept. 2	74	17	9
August 23–26	76	16	8
August 16–19	75	16	9

August 9–12	74	16	10
July 19–22	60	25	15

How likely do you think it is that there will be a recession in the country during the next twelve months—very likely, fairly likely, not too likely, or not at all likely?

Very likely	41%
Fairly likely	36
Not too likely	13
Not at all likely	5
No opinion	5

Selected National Trend

1990	Very, fairly likely	Not too, not at all likely	No opinion
Aug. 23–26	69%	23%	8%
Aug. 9–12	65	28	7
Jan. 1979	62	31	7

In general, are you satisfied or dissatisfied with the way things are going in the United States at this time?

Satisfied	37%
Dissatisfied	58
No opinion	5

Selected National Trend

	Satisfied	Dis- satisfied	No opinion
September	51%	44%	5%
August	43	51	6
July	45	51	4
February	55	39	6

Looking ahead, do you expect that at this time next year you will be financially better off than now, or worse off than now?

Better	51%
Worse	20
Same (volunteered)	17
No opinion	12

Selected National Trend

	Better	Worse	Same	No opinion
August	57%	20%	16%	7%
July	58	18	17	7
February	65	16	13	6

Note: A new Gallup Poll shows increasing evidence of concern over the U.S. economy, which in turn may be beginning to have a negative effect on President George Bush and the Republican party. Most telling is the substantial drop in the number of Americans who are satisfied with the way things are going domestically. That measure is now at 37%, the lowest since the recession years of 1983 and a remarkable drop of 14 percentage points from the 51% level of early September.

This "satisfied" measure is very sensitive to current events. The 51% in early September was a sharp upswing from the earlier, pre-Iraq months of the summer, during which time the figure was down to 45%.

Bush's overall approval level also has dropped from the stratospheric levels attained immediately after the American involvement in the Persian Gulf, while respondents' concerns over the economy are sharply up. Seventy-seven percent now say that it is very or fairly likely that there will be a recession within the next twelve months, up from the 69% and 65% found by Gallup in August of this year.

Additionally, President Bush's job approval, which registered a sharp jump immediately after the Kuwaiti invasion, is now at 67%—still a high number but below the ratings in the 70s that Bush enjoyed after the invasion of Panama and as the Kuwaiti situation developed. In short, it appears that two key measures of America's psychological well-being—satisfaction with the way things are going in the country and approval of the president—are beginning to slip, in spite of the fact that approval for our Iraq involvement is constant.

There has been a downward turn in the percentage who think that they will be better off financially at this time next year. Fifty-one percent now say that they will be better off, down from

57% in August and 65% in February of this year and, in fact, the lowest measured by Gallup since 1983. Thus, it may be that President Bush's continuing support from the public and the fate of Republican candidates in this fall's elections may be more dependent on economic considerations than on events in the Middle East.

OCTOBER 3
GERMAN REUNIFICATION

Interviewing Date: 9/27–30/90
Survey #GO 122005

Do you think the reunification of East and West Germany would be a good thing for the United States and its Western allies, or a bad thing?

Good	73%
Bad	10
Neither good nor bad (volunteered)	3
No opinion	14

Selected National Trend

	Good	Bad	Neither	No opinion
July 1990	72%	12%	4%	12%
February 1990	72	12	4	12
December 1989	63	21	5	11

How concerned are you that if East and West Germany are reunited into one country that it might become an aggressor nation like it was in World War II?

Very concerned	10%
Fairly concerned	18
Not too concerned	36
Not at all concerned	30
No opinion	6

Selected National Trend

	Very, fairly concerned	Not too, not at all concerned	No opinion
July 1990	35%	60%	5%
February 1990	38	59	3
December 1989	35	60	5

Note: A significant majority of Americans continues to see the impending reunification of East and West Germany as good for the United States and its Western allies. According to the latest Gallup Poll, nearly three quarters (73%) think that a reunified Germany would be good.

Even more respondents are in favor of reunification now than they were ten months ago when this question was first asked. Only one in ten (10%) currently thinks that it would be bad for the United States, down from 21% in December 1989. And most (66%) are not concerned that Germany will become a military aggressor as it did in the 1930s; only 28% think it very or fairly likely that a reunified Germany will be militarily aggressive.

OCTOBER 5
FEDERAL BUDGET

Interviewing Date: 10/3–4/90
Survey #GO 922019

As you may know, President Bush and leaders in Congress have agreed on a new federal budget plan. In general, do you favor or oppose this proposed budget plan?

Favor 33%
Oppose 41
Have not heard enough to make a
    decision (volunteered) 20
No opinion 6

If the federal budget plan is not passed, the Gramm-Rudman-Hollings deficit-reduction law will take effect which will force the federal government to cut its budget 30 to 40 percent. Which would you prefer—passing the proposed federal budget plan or letting the Gramm-Rudman-Hollings deficit-reduction law take effect?

Budget plan 52%
Gramm-Rudman-Hollings law 25
Neither (volunteered) 5
No opinion 18

Here are some of the proposals that are currently included in the proposed federal budget plan. Please tell me if you favor or oppose each as I read them:

Putting an additional 10% tax on luxury items, such as automobiles over $30,000, yachts over $100,000, and jewelry and furs over $5,000?

Favor 85%
Oppose 14
No opinion 1

Raising the effective income tax rate for those with adjusted incomes of over $100,000?

Favor 82%
Oppose 16
No opinion 2

Raising taxes on cigarettes by eight cents per pack?

Favor 78%
Oppose 21
No opinion 1

Raising taxes on beer, wine, and liquor?

Favor 76%
Oppose 23
No opinion 1

Holding spending on domestic programs to the rate of inflation?

Favor 64%
Oppose 29
No opinion 7

Cutting defense spending?

Favor 54%
Oppose 42
No opinion 4

Applying the current payroll Medicare tax to wages up to $73,000, up from the current $51,300 ceiling?

Favor 49%
Oppose 37
No opinion 14

Raising taxes on airline tickets?

Favor 47%
Oppose 48
No opinion 5

Cutting farm subsidies?

Favor 30%
Oppose 64
No opinion 6

Raising the federal gasoline tax by twelve cents per gallon?

Favor 19%
Oppose 81
No opinion .... *

Cutting Medicare benefits for older Americans?

Favor 6%
Oppose 93
No opinion 1

*Less than 1%

Here are several proposals not currently included in the proposed federal budget plan. Please tell me if you favor or oppose each as I read them:

Raising taxes on those with adjusted incomes of $200,000 and over?

Favor 84%
Oppose 14
No opinion 2

Reducing spending on defense further?

Favor 46%
Oppose 50
No opinion 4

Reducing the tax on capital gains?

Favor 41%
Oppose 49
No opinion 10

Reducing spending on domestic programs such as Social Security, financial aid to the needy, and veterans' benefits?

Favor 12%
Oppose 87
No opinion 1

Note: The recently defeated federal budget plan, backed by President George Bush and key leaders in Congress, lacked strong support from the American public. According to a recent Gallup Poll, only 33% said that they favored the plan, while 41% opposed it and one quarter (26%) did not have an opinion. Reasons behind this lack of support are evident: respondents thought that the plan mainly raised taxes, hit the middle class hardest, and would not necessarily lower the federal budget deficit.

Despite the lack of support for the proposed plan, there was also little support for the alternative: letting the Gramm-Rudman-Hollings deficit-reduction law take effect. Given a choice, most respondents (52%) opted for the plan; only one quarter (25%) favored letting Gramm-Rudman take effect. Even among the 41% who opposed the plan, 39% would support it over Gramm-Rudman, compared to 38% who favor Gramm-Rudman.

Three provisions of the plan engendered the strongest opposition: cutting Medicare benefits for older Americans (93% opposed), raising the federal gasoline tax by 12 cents per gallon (81%), and cutting farm subsidies (64%). Taxing the wealthy and nonessential items, as well as holding domestic spending to the rate of inflation and cutting defense spending, are more palatable. Most respondents favor an additional 10% tax on luxury items (85%), raising the effective income tax on those with adjusted incomes of $100,000 or more (82%), and raising taxes on cigarettes (78%) or alcohol (76%). Two thirds (64%) support holding domestic spending to the rate of inflation and a slight majority (54%) favors cutting defense spending.

What other options could be included in a new budget reduction effort? Most Americans (84%) say that they would support raising taxes on persons with adjusted incomes of $200,000 or more. In contrast, nine in ten (87%) would oppose reducing spending on domestic programs such as Social Security, financial aid to the needy, and veterans' benefits. There is mixed reaction to reducing the capital gains tax (41% favor, 49% oppose) and reducing defense spending further (46% favor, 50% oppose).

OCTOBER 5
DISCOVERY OF AMERICA

Interviewing Date: 10/3–4/90
Survey #GO 922019

> Here's a different question that people find interesting to answer. Can you please tell me who first discovered America?

Christopher Columbus	55%
Leif Eriksson, the Vikings	14
Indians	7
Other	13
No opinion	11

Note: Nearly five hundred years after Christopher Columbus's epic voyage to the New World, only one half (55%) of the public credits him with the initial discovery of America. Fourteen percent cite Leif Ericksson or the Vikings, and 7% say that the native Indian population of America were the first discoverers. Thirteen percent name someone else, and 11% do not have an opinion.

While Columbus is named by the majority in all population groups, college graduates are far less likely than those with less than a high-school education to credit the Italian explorer with the discovery of America (46% versus 64%). And while college graduates are more likely to name Leif Ericksson and the Vikings, younger Americans favor the Columbus theory of discovery.

OCTOBER 8
TELEVISION PROGRAMS

Interviewing Date: 8/16–19/90
Survey #GO 922016

> What is your favorite way to spend an evening?

Watching television	24%
Reading	15
Home with family	14
Resting, relaxing	9
Visiting with friends	5
Dining out	4
Movies, theater	4
House, yard work	2
Drinking, going to bars	2
Cards, games	1
Dancing	1
Listening to music, radio	1
Sewing, needlework	1
Other	16
No opinion	1

> On an average weekday—Monday through Friday—about how many hours do you personally watch television?

None	3%
Less than one	5
One to three	35
Four to six	39
Six or more	17
No opinion	1

> On an average weekend day—that is, Saturday or Sunday—about how many hours do you personally watch television?

None	8%
Less than one	4
One to three	33

Four to six 38
Six or more 17
No opinion .... *

*Less than 1%

Asked of television set owners: How many televisions do you own?

One 29%
Two 37
Three 20
Four 10
Five or more 4

*All in all, what would you say is the best thing about television—that is, the thing that you think is most positive about television as far as you are concerned?**

News; news reports or programs 34%
Educational programs or channels 7
Entertainment value 7
Information in general 6
Up-to-date; current events; keeps
  you informed 6
PBS; public television 4
Sports 4
Immediate, instant source of
  information 3
Keeping in touch with rest of world 3
Children's programs 2
CNN 2
Choice; variety of programs 2
Movies 2
Other 17
None 3
No opinion 3

*Multiple responses were given.

*And, all and all, what would you say is the worst thing about television—that is, the thing that you think is most negative about television?**

Not enough educational programs 34%
Foul language, profanity 7
Unrealistic portrait of real life 7

MTV 6
Negative influence on children 6
Pornography, sex 4
Reruns 4
Movies—general 3
It's addictive 3
Bad programs, shows (nonspecific) 2
Biased news, opinions 2
Comedy channels 2
News 2
Violence 1
Other 16
None 3
No opinion 3

*Multiple responses were given.

Thinking about your nonworking time each day, do you think that you spend too much time or too little time watching television?

Too much 42%
Too little 23
Just right (volunteered) 33
No opinion 2

As far as you are concerned, is watching television a good use of your time or not a good use of your time?

Good use 58%
Not a good use 38
No opinion 4

*If someone came along and took all your television sets away, what would you be most likely to find yourself doing to fill in the time you usually spend watching television?**

Reading, reading books 39%
Listen to radio, stereo, music 16
Spend time with family 4
Outdoor activities 3
Work 3
Gardening, yard work 3
Cleaning, clean house, housework 3
Crafts 2
Exercising 2
Go out with friends 2

Read newspaper 2
Sewing 2
Shopping 2
Working around house, house projects 2
Other 13
None 1
No opinion 2

*Multiple responses were given.

*As far as you are concerned, what's the best
television show of all time—that is, the one
that you enjoyed watching most over the
years?**

Bill Cosby/Cosby show 7%
60 Minutes 4
Evening news/news 4
M*A*S*H 4
Cheers 3
I Love Lucy/Lucille Ball 3
Dallas 2
Star Trek 2
Other 69
None 5
No opinion 9

*Multiple responses were given.

*The following four questions were asked of
those with a child/children under age 18 living at home:*

*How many hours a day would you say that
your oldest child spends watching television?*

None 5%
Less than one hour 3
One hour 5
Two hours 14
Three hours 13
Four to five hours 8
Six or more 5
No opinion 47

*As far as you're concerned, does this child
watch television too much, not enough, or is*

*the amount of television he or she watches
about right?*

Too much 16%
Not enough 1
About right 35
No opinion 48

*Do you put any restrictions on the number of
hours your children watch television?*

Yes 24%
No 29
No opinion 47

*Do you put any restrictions on the types of
programs your children can watch?*

Yes 42%
No 11
No opinion 47

*Thinking more generally, would you say that
television has been good for our society, been
bad for American society, or hasn't made
much difference either way?*

Good for society 40%
Bad for society 35
No difference 15
Both good and bad (volunteered) 9
No opinion 1

*Do you consider yourself addicted to televi-
sion, or not?*

	Yes
National	13%

*What is your feeling about advertisements or
commercials on television—do you love
them, like them, not have any strong feelings
about them, dislike them, or hate them?*

Love commercials 1%
Like commercials 15
No strong feelings 41
Dislike commercials 30
Hate commercials 12
No opinion 1

Do you find advertisements on television useful—that is, do you use the information in commercials to make purchase and buying decisions, or not?

	Yes
National	39%

What if commercials and advertisements would be eliminated from television if you would agree to pay an extra $50 a month to help support the price of programming? Would you pay this $50 per month in order to have commercial-free television, or not?

	Yes
National	14%

As far as you're concerned, what are the one or two types of programs or shows that you would like to see more of on television which would most interest you?*

Comedies, sitcoms	11%
Family-oriented shows, programs	9
Educational programs, shows	8
Documentaries	6
News shows, programs	5
Sports	4
Good movies (nonspecific)	3
Westerns	3
Nature programs	3
Children's programs	2
Drama	2
Information shows, programs	2
Musicals	2
Old movies	2
PBS programs, public broadcasting	2
Religious programs	2
Other	30
None	3
No opinion	6

*Multiple responses were given.

Trying to be as honest as you can, what would be the impact on your life if television was taken out of your home altogether? Would it make life much worse, make life somewhat worse, not make much difference either way, make life somewhat better for you, or make life a lot better for you?

Much worse	6%
Somewhat worse	29
Not much difference	46
Somewhat better	14
A lot better	5
No opinion	*

*Less than 1%

Does your household have a VCR, or video cassette recorder, or not?

	Yes
National	77%

Do you have a remote control on at least one television set such that you can change channels from a distance, or not?

	Yes
National	80%

Note: Television. The average American watches four hours per day and appreciates television's ability to bring him in touch with the world around him. Yet, at the same time, many viewers feel increasingly guilty about spending so much time with television and are less likely than ever before to claim it as their favorite way to spend an evening. In fact, according to a recent Gallup Mirror of America survey, a good number think that their lives would be no worse off if television disappeared, and they list a wide variety of activities—most prominently, reading—that they would pursue if they could not watch television.

The best thing about television, in the minds of respondents, is that it brings them news and news reports from around the world (34%), followed by educational programs (7%), information of all sorts (6%) and current events (6%), and public television broadcasts (4%). Smaller percentages list entertainment, sports, or other types of noninformational programming. What social psychologists call presentation-of-self biases are evident in these types of replies. To some degree, viewers are talking about what they think they should be valuing rather than what they really watch.

It may not be surprising, then, to find that the number one complaint about television is that there are not enough informative and educational programs (34%). Other complaints vary widely and include: too much foul language (7%), unrealistic portrayal of life (7%), MTV (6%), negative influence on children (6%), and too much sex (4%). Surprisingly, only 1% mention violence.

Commercials are the life blood of local, network, and a good deal of cable television, but that does not mean that they have endeared themselves to the public. About four out of ten (42%) either dislike or hate them, but just as many profess no strong feelings either way, and 16% of us like or love them. Less than a majority (39%) says that the information in commercials is useful in making buying and purchasing decisions. However, these advertisements are apparently better than the alternative: paying for commercial-free television. Only 14% say that they would be willing to pay $50 per month to watch television without commercials.

OCTOBER 16
MIDDLE EAST SITUATION

Interviewing Date: 10/11–14/90
Survey #GO 922020

I'd like your overall opinion of a foreign country. Is your opinion of Israel very favorable, mostly favorable, mostly unfavorable, or very unfavorable?

Very favorable 10%
Mostly favorable 38
Mostly unfavorable 26
Very unfavorable 13
No opinion 13

Selected National Trend

	Those saying "very," "mostly favorable"
February 1990	44%
August 1989	45
February–March 1989	49

In the Middle East situation, are your sympathies more with the Israelis or more with the Palestinian Arabs?*

Israelis 48%
Palestinian Arabs 23
Both; neither (volunteered) 19
No opinion 10

Selected National Trend

	Israelis	Palestinian Arabs	Both; neither	No opinion
Aug. 1989	50%	14%	15%	21%
Dec. 1988*	46	24	16	14
May 1986*	43	20	20	17
1982				
July	41	12	31	16
June	52	10	29	9
May	51	12	26	11
Jan.	49	14	23	14
1981				
Aug.	44	11	34	11
1979				
March	34	11	31	14
Jan.	40	14	31	15
1978				
Nov.	39	13	30	18
Sept.	42	12	29	17
Aug.	42	11	30	17
May	44	10	33	13
March	38	11	33	18
Feb.	33	14	28	25
1977				
Dec.	44	10	27	19
Oct.	46	11	21	22
June	44	8	28	20
1975				
Jan.	44	8	22	26

1973				
Dec.	50	7	25	18
1970				
Oct.	47	6	22	25
March	44	3	32	21
1969				
Jan.	50	5	28	17
1967				
June	56	4	25	15

*Based on the informed group; that is, those who have read or heard about the situation in the Middle East.

*Do you favor or oppose the establishment of an independent Palestinian nation within the territories occupied by Israel in the 1967 war?**

Favor 41%
Oppose 32
No opinion 27

Selected National Trend

	Favor	Oppose	No opinion
May 1988*	38%	30%	32%

*Based on the informed group

Some people feel that the Israelis rely too much on military force in dealing with the Palestinian Arabs and others in the region who oppose them. Other people feel that the Israelis have used only as much force as they need to protect themselves. Which comes closer to your view?

Israelis rely too much on military force 34%
Israelis only protecting themselves 52
No opinion 14

Selected National Trend

	Rely on force	Protecting themselves	No opinion
August 1989	34%	49%	17%
August 1982	47	41	12

*Do you think there will or will not come a time when Israel and the Arab nations will be able to settle their differences and live in peace?**

Yes 46%
No 49
No opinion 5

Selected National Trend

	Yes	No	No opinion
May 1988*	55%	37%	8%

*Based on the informed group

Asked of those who responded in the affirmative (46%): Do you think this will happen during the next five years, or not?

Yes 18%
No 24
No opinion 4
                                      ——
                                      46%

Note: Recent violence in Jerusalem and the UN resolution condemning Israel's actions have not significantly changed the way that Americans view Israel or the Israeli-Palestinian conflict. The latest Gallup Poll does indicate, however, increasing pessimism that the two sides will be able to settle their differences and live in peace.

About one half of Americans (48%) have a favorable opinion of Israel, not significantly different from earlier this year or in 1989. Also, one half (48%) of informed respondents—those who are following the recent developments very or somewhat closely—side with the Israelis in the conflict, while one quarter (23%) side with the Palestinian Arabs and 19% choose both or neither side in the conflict. This pattern has not changed substantially since Gallup began asking the question in 1986.

Slightly more than one half of informed Americans (52%) think that Israel uses only as much force as it needs for self defense and 34% say that Israel relies too much on military force in dealing with the Palestinians. These attitudes have not changed since August 1989, when the question was last asked, despite the death of about twenty Palestinians in the recent riots and the condemnation by the United Nations of Israel's actions.

Support for an independent Palestinian state has increased only slightly since 1988. Forty-one percent currently favor this solution versus 38% in May 1988.

The recent events have taken their most significant toll on optimism that there will ever be a peaceful solution to the differences that exist between Palestinians and Israelis. Nearly one half (49%) now think that there never will be a time when the two parties will settle their differences and live in peace. This is a sharp increase from the 37% who thought that way in May 1988.

OCTOBER 17

PERSIAN GULF SITUATION/ SATISFACTION INDEX/PERSONAL FINANCES

Interviewing Date: 10/11–14/90
Survey #GO 922020

Do you approve or disapprove of the way George Bush is handling his job as president?

Approve 56%
Disapprove 33
No opinion 11

Do you approve or disapprove of the way George Bush is handling this current situation in the Middle East involving Iraq and Kuwait?

Approve 65%
Disapprove 29
No opinion 7

Selected National Trend

	Approve	Dis-approve	No opinion
October 3–4	69%	25%	6%
September 27–30	71	22	7
September 14–16	74	16	10
September 10–11	76	17	7
August 30– September 2	74	18	8
August 23–26	76	17	7
August 16–19	79	14	7
August 9–12	80	12	8
August 3–4	52	16	32

Do you approve or disapprove of the U.S. decision to send U.S. troops to Saudi Arabia as a defense against Iraq?

Approve 70%
Disapprove 27
No opinion 3

Selected National Trend

	Approve	Dis-approve	No opinion
October 3–4	72%	23%	5%
September 27–30	72	21	7
September 14–16	73	18	9
September 10–11	72	22	6
August 30- September 2	74	20	6
August 23–26	80	16	4
August 16–19	76	19	5
August 9–12	78	17	5

In view of the developments since we first sent our troops to Saudi Arabia, do you think the United States made a mistake in sending troops to Saudi Arabia, or not?

Yes 27%
No 68
No opinion 5

Selected National Trend

	Yes	No	No opinion
October 3–4	21%	71%	8%
September 27–30	20	73	7
September 14–16	18	73	9
September 10–11	19	76	5

August 30–
September 2	16	76	8
August 23–26	18	76	6
August 16–19	17	75	8

In general, are you satisfied or dissatisfied with the way things are going in the United States at this time?

Satisfied 29%
Dissatisfied 67
No opinion 4

Selected National Trend

1990	Satisfied	Dis- satisfied	No opinion
September	37%	58%	5%
August	43	51	6
July	45	51	4
February	55	39	6

In general, are you satisfied or dissatisfied with the way things are going in your own personal life?

Satisfied 82%
Dissatisfied 16
No opinion 2

Selected National Trend

1990	Satisfied	Dis- satisfied	No opinion
September	85%	13%	2%
August	85	13	2
July	81	17	2
February	83	16	1

We are interested in how people's financial situation may have changed. Would you say that you are financially better off now than you were a year ago, or are you financially worse off now?

Better 32%
Worse 41
Same (volunteered) 26
No opinion 1

Selected National Trend

1990	Better	Worse	Same	No opinion
September	40%	27%	32%	1%
August	43	27	29	1
July	44	28	27	1
February	49	24	26	1

Looking ahead, do you expect that at this time next year you will be financially better off than now or worse off than now?

Better 48%
Worse 30
Same (volunteered) 13
No opinion 9

Selected National Trend

1990	Better	Worse	Same	No opinion
September	51%	17%	20%	12%
August	57	16	20	7
July	58	17	18	7
February	65	13	16	6

Note: Three weeks before a midterm election, Americans are not in a very positive mood this month—confronted with protracted efforts by their elected representatives to ratify a federal budget and with the country's most massive involvement of its military power on foreign territory since Vietnam. The percentage who are satisfied with the way things are going in the United States is now at the lowest level measured by Gallup since the early recession years of the Reagan administration: only 29% are satisfied, with two thirds (67%) saying that they are dissatisfied.

These responses have a history of quick change. As recently as last February, 55% professed to be satisfied with the way things were going in the United States; satisfaction dropped this past summer to 43% but rebounded to 51% immediately after the deployment of U.S. troops to Saudi Arabia. Now, it is back down to the lowest levels of the Bush administration.

Behind this dissatisfaction are two overriding reasons: the economy and an increasing concern over the situation in the Persian Gulf. Gallup's personal financial measures show how economic concerns really may be hitting home. In the course of only two weeks, the percentage who believe themselves worse off financially now than last year has jumped from 27% to 41%. And in the past two weeks the number who say that they will be worse off financially one year from now has jumped from 17% to 30%. While it is important to note that 48% continue to think positively about next year, the 30% "worse" projection is as high as Gallup has recorded since the last months of the Carter administration and the early years of Ronald Reagan's.

Gradual erosion of the public's support for our actions in the Persian Gulf continues. Gallup first noticed this erosion in the middle of September, and it has continued on a gradual but steady decline. Disapproval of the way that President George Bush is handling the situation first rose above 20% in late September and is now at 29%. However, two thirds (65%) still say that they approve of Bush's handling of the situation. Other measures of support for our Persian Gulf intervention are slipping as well: 27% now say that it was a mistake to get involved, somewhat higher than the 17% to 21% levels measured in seven previous polls. Overall disapproval of the decision to get involved is also now at 27%.

OCTOBER 24
UNITED NATIONS

Interviewing Date: 10/18–21/90
Survey #GO 122006

In general, do you think the United Nations is doing a good job or a poor job in trying to solve the problems it has had to face?

Good job 54%
Poor job 34
No opinion 12

Selected National Trend

	Good job
August 1985	28%
February 1985	38
October 1983	36
June 1982	36
September 1980	31
February 1978	40
November 1975	33
November 1971	35
September 1970	44

Do you think the United States should give up its membership in the United Nations, or not?

Yes 8%
No 88
No opinion 4

Selected National Trend

	Yes
August 1985	11%
October 1983	12
June 1982	12
November 1975	16
July 1967	10
November 1963	8
January 1962	5
November 1951	11

A proposal has been made to build up the United Nations' emergency force to a size great enough to deal with "brush fires" or small wars throughout the world. Does this sound like a good idea or a poor idea to you?

Good idea 61%
Poor idea 27
No opinion 12

Selected National Trend

	Good idea	Poor idea	No opinion
April 1964	62%	19%	19%
January 1961	66	17	17
July 1960	72	12	16
February 1958	66	15	19

The United Nations is now forty-five years old. Do you think it will be more important or less important, say, five years from now?

More important 67%
Less important 19
About the same (volunteered) 7
No opinion 7

Selected National Trend

	More impor- tant	Less impor- tant	About the same	No opinion
May 1950*	45%	28%	12%	15%

*The question was worded: "The United Nations is now five years old."

Is your respect for the United Nations increasing or decreasing as the years go by?

Increasing 50%
Decreasing 28
No change (volunteered) 16
No opinion 6

Selected National Trend

	In- creasing	De- creasing	No opinion
Feb. 1972	18%	50%	32%
May 1951	25	40	35
Dec. 1950	32	19	49

Do you think the amount of money the United States currently contributes to the United Nations' budget is too much, too little, or about the right amount?

Too much 40%
Too little 5
About right 31
No opinion 24

How effective has the United Nations been in helping deal with the current crisis involving Iraq's invasion of Kuwait? Would you say it has been very effective, fairly effective, not too effective, or not at all effective?

Very effective 14%
Fairly effective 45
Not too effective 26
Not at all effective 8
No opinion 7

Do you happen to know where the United Nations Headquarters is located? (If yes) Where is that?

Yes, New York (correct) 49%
Yes, incorrect answer 48
No opinion 3

Note: On United Nations Day 1990, a new Gallup Poll indicates that American support for the United Nations—some forty-five years after the adoption of its charter in October 1945—is higher than it has been in over twenty years. Fifty-four percent now think that the United Nations has done a good job of solving the problems it has had to face, while 34% say that it has done a poor job. This is a significantly more positive attitude than Gallup's measurements throughout the 1970s and 1980s, when no more than 44% thought that the United Nations was doing a good job.

This positive attitude no doubt is due in part to the general decrease in East-West hostility evidenced over the past two years, including rapprochement between the USSR and the United States and the dissolution of the Iron Curtain in Eastern Europe. The UN role in the current crisis in the Persian Gulf also may be a part of its improved image: almost six out of ten (59%) think that it has been effective in helping deal with the current crisis, with only 8% saying that it has not been at all effective.

Americans' respect for the United Nations is increasing, and two thirds (67%) think that the organization will become more important rather than less important in the coming years. Both of these measurements are up significantly from previous Gallup surveys of the same issues.

OCTOBER 24
PRESIDENT BUSH/CONGRESS

Interviewing Date: 10/18–21/90
Survey #GO 122006

Do you approve or disapprove of the way George Bush is handling his job as president?

Approve 53%
Disapprove 37
No opinion 10

Selected National Trend

	Approve	Dis-approve	No opinion
1990			
October 11–14	56%	33%	11%
October 3–4	66	25	9
September 27–30	67	20	13
September 14–16	73	17	10
September 10–11	76	16	8

Do you approve or disapprove of the way Congress is handling its job?

Approve 23%
Disapprove 64
No opinion 13

Selected National Trend

	Approve	Dis-approve	No opinion
September 1987	42%	49%	9%
April 1983	33	43	24
June 1982	29	54	17
June 1981	38	40	22
June 1979	19	61	20
September 1978	29	49	22
March 1977	36	42	22
November 1975	28	54	18
April 1974	30	47	23

Do you approve or disapprove of the way the representative from your own congressional district is handling his or her job?

Approve 49%
Disapprove 30
No opinion 21

Selected National Trend

	Approve	Dis-approve	No opinion
August 1990	66%	19%	15%
June 1982	69	15	16
March 1977	55	17	28

Note: Two weeks before the 1990 midterm elections, the job approvals given by Americans to both President George Bush and the U.S. Congress continue to deteriorate, and both are now at record lows. President Bush's job approval is 53%, the lowest rating of his administration (except for the very first taken immediately after his inauguration in January 1989, when many Americans had yet to form an opinion). Bush's current job approval is 23 points lower than on September 10–11 of this year, when it was at 76%, and it is down 3 percentage points from last week. The 37% disapproval Bush now gets is also the highest of his administration.

Job approval for Congress is now at one of its lowest points since 1974, when Gallup began measuring it, with only 23% saying that they approve of the way Congress is handling its job, and a full 64% disapproving. Respondents tend to rate the job being done by their own representative higher than that of Congress in general. Still, job approval by this measure is at 49%, with 30% disapproving, and also represents the lowest point measured by Gallup since 1977. This also reflects a drop of 17 points since August.

OCTOBER 31
SATISFACTION INDEX/
CONGRESSIONAL ELECTIONS

Interviewing Date: 10/25–28/90
Survey #GO 122007

Do you approve or disapprove of the way George Bush is handling his job as president?

Approve 54%
Disapprove 36
No opinion 10

Selected National Trend

	Approve	Dis-approve	No opinion
1990			
October 18–21	53%	37%	10%
October 11–14	56	33	11
October 3–4	66	25	9
September 27–30	67	20	13
September 14–16	73	17	10
September 10–11	76	16	8

In general, are you satisfied or dissatisfied with the way things are going in the United States at this time?

Satisfied 31%
Dissatisfied 66
No opinion 3

Selected National Trend

	Satisfied	Dis-satisfied	No opinion
1990			
October 11–14	29%	67%	4%
September	37	58	5
August–September	51	44	5

Asked of those who expressed dissatisfaction: Why are you dissatisfied with the way things are going in the United States?

Economy; unemployment 20%
Federal budget; budget deficit 12
Taxes 9
Middle East; Iraq 9
Washington not doing their job; no
   leadership 6
Congress 4
Politicians in general 3
President; administration 3
Spending too much overseas 3
Drugs; crime 3
Gas prices 2

Medicare; health care 1
Cut spending 1
Savings and Loan scandal 1
Other 19
None 1
No opinion 3

Do you approve or disapprove of the way Congress is handling its job?

Approve 24%
Disapprove 68
No opinion 8

Selected National Trend

	Approve	Dis-approve	No opinion
1990			
October 18–21	23%	64%	13%
October 11–14	28	65	7

Asked of those who disapprove: Why do you disapprove of the way Congress is handling its job?

Budget; won't cut spending 23%
Too worried about staying in office;
   too much politics 6
Not getting anything done 20
Not working together; can't agree on
   anything 11
Too concerned about themselves and
   not whom they represent 6
Voted themselves a pay raise 3
Raising taxes 2
Other 23
None 1
No opinion 5

Do you approve or disapprove of the way the representative from your own congressional district is handling his or her job?

Approve 61%
Disapprove 19
No opinion 20

Selected National Trend

	Approve	Dis-approve	No opinion
1990			
October 18–21	49%	30%	21%
October 11–14	55	33	12
August	66	19	15

Would you like to see your representative in Congress be reelected in November, or not?

Yes	62%
No	22
Not running (volunteered)	2
No opinion	14

Asked of registered voters: If the elections for Congress were being held today, which party's candidate would you like to see win in your congressional district—the Democratic party's candidate or the Republican party's candidate?

Democratic candidate	55%*
Republican candidate	45

*The "undecided" and "no opinion" responses have been allocated proportionally.

Asked of registered voters: Which political party—the Republican or the Democratic—will do a better job of keeping the country prosperous?

Republican	37%
Democratic	35
No difference; no opinion	28

Selected National Trend

	Republican	Democratic	No difference; no opinion
Aug. 1990	46%	30%	24%
Sept. 1988	52	34	14
Aug. 1984	48	36	24
Oct. 1982	34	43	23
Sept. 1980	35	36	29

Looking ahead for the next few years, which political party do you think would be more likely to keep the United States out of World War III—the Republican or the Democratic party?

Republican	34%
Democratic	36
No difference; no opinion	30

Selected National Trend

	Republican	Democratic	No difference; no opinion
Aug. 1990	37%	34%	29%
Sept. 1988	43	33	24
Aug. 1984	36	40	24
Oct. 1982	29	38	33
Sept. 1980	25	42	33

How likely do you think it is that there will be a recession in the country during the next twelve months—very likely, fairly likely, not too likely, or not at all likely?

Very likely	42%
Fairly likely	37
Not too likely	12
Not at all likely	4
No opinion	5

Selected National Trend

	Very, fairly likely	Not too, not at all likely	No opinion
1990			
October 11–14	76%	19%	5%
October 3–4	77	18	5
September 27–30	77	18	5
August 23–26	69	23	8
August 9–12	65	28	7

We are interested in how people's financial situation may have changed. Would you say that you are financially better off now than you were a year ago, or are you financially worse off now?

Better	.... 38%
Worse	 35
Same (volunteered)	 26
No opinion	 1

Selected National Trend

1990	Better	Worse	Same	No opinion
Oct. 18–21	27%	41%	30%	2%
Oct. 11–14	32	41	26	1
September	40	27	32	1
August	43	27	29	1
July	44	28	27	1
February	49	24	26	1

Looking ahead, do you expect that at this time next year you will be financially better off than now or worse off than now?

Better	.... 50%
Worse	 27
Same (volunteered)	 15
No opinion	 8

Selected National Trend

1990	Better	Worse	Same	No opinion
Oct. 18–21	41%	34%	16%	9%
Oct. 11–14	48	30	13	9
September	51	17	20	12
August	57	16	20	7
July	58	17	18	7
February	65	13	16	6

Note: While there is deep dissatisfaction among Americans with the way things are going in this country and a fairly widely held opinion that Congress is inept, data from the latest Gallup Poll do not necessarily suggest that there will be a massive vote against incumbents in the upcoming midterm election. In fact, a majority approve of the job being done by their own congressional representative and say that they plan to vote for his or her reelection. In short, the mood of America one week before the 1990 midterm election is muddled.

Two trains of thought among respondents are clearly apparent. First, the largest number since the early 1980s are dissatisfied with the way things are going in the country today. And second, approval of the job being done by Congress is at the lowest level since Gallup began asking the question in 1974.

There are two root causes for these negative measures: one economic, the other a more general complaint. Forty-four percent who are dissatisfied explain that it is because of the country's economic problems; 16% explain their dissatisfaction in terms of the inability of Washington, Congress, politicians, or the president to get things done.

Forty-six percent of those who disapprove of Congress express their frustrations with such comments as "they're not getting anything done in Washington," and "they're too worried about staying in office." Only 23% mention the budget problems directly.

Will this general dissatisfaction and low job approval of Congress translate into a massive rejection of incumbents? Not necessarily. Only 24% approve of the job being done by Congress in general, but 61% approve of the way that the representative from their own congressional district is handling his or her job. Two thirds (62%) say that they will vote to reelect their congressman, while only 22% say that they will not.

There is some indication that Democrats have gained standing in recent weeks. They are now just as likely as Republicans to be perceived as the party that can keep the country prosperous (37% say Republicans, 35% Democrats, a dramatic change from August, when it was 46% to 30% in the Republicans' favor). However, respondents' overall preference in voting for the Republican or Democrat from their district has not changed substantially this year: 55% now say that they will vote for the Democrat from their district, while 45% say the Republican.

Finally, there is the Bush factor. The historical record indicates that the midterm performance of the party in the White House is affected by the incumbent's job approval. George Bush's presidential job approval is now 54%, down dramatically from the highs it attained after the U.S. entry into the Persian Gulf in August and September.

NOVEMBER 2
CONGRESSIONAL ELECTIONS

Interviewing Date: 10/25–28/90
Survey #GO 122007

Asked of registered voters: If the elections for Congress were being held today, which party's candidate would you like to see win in your congressional district—the Democratic party's candidate or the Republican party's candidate?

Democratic candidate 54%*
Republican candidate 46

*The "undecided" and "no opinion" responses have been allocated proportionally.

As you may know, there has been a lot of attention paid to the current situation involving the federal budget in Washington. Has the way the federal budget been handled in Washington made you more likely or less likely to:

Vote for the reelection of the congressman from your district?

More likely 45%
Less likely 31
No difference (volunteered) 11
No opinion 13

Vote for a Republican candidate for Congress from your district?

More likely 35%
Less likely 42
No difference (volunteered) 13
No opinion 10

Vote for a Democratic candidate for Congress from your district?

More likely 42%
Less likely 34
No difference (volunteered) 12
No opinion 12

Want to vote at all in the November election?

More likely 58%
Less likely 22
No difference (volunteered) 16
No opinion 4

As you feel today, which political party—the Republican or the Democratic—do you think serves the interests of the following groups best:

People like yourself?

Republican 38%
Democratic 44
No difference (volunteered) 10
No opinion 8

Selected National Trend

	Republican	Democratic	No difference; no opinion
1985	43%	38%	19%

Poor people?

Republican 18%
Democratic 64
No difference (volunteered) 9
No opinion 9

Wealthy people?

Republican 70%
Democratic 16
No difference (volunteered) 5
No opinion 9

Women?

Republican 26%
Democratic 45
No difference (volunteered) 13
No opinion 16

Selected National Trend

	Republican	Democratic	No difference; no opinion
1985	25%	48%	27%

Blacks?

Republican	17%
Democratic	59
No difference (volunteered)	10
No opinion	14

Selected National Trend

	Republican	Democratic	No difference; no opinion
1985	19%	60%	21%

Retired people?

Republican	28%
Democratic	51
No difference (volunteered)	10
No opinion	11

Selected National Trend

	Republican	Democratic	No difference; no opinion
1985	28%	48%	24%

Farmers?

Republican	27%
Democratic	49
No difference (volunteered)	9
No opinion	15

Selected National Trend

	Republican	Democratic	No difference; no opinion
1985	31%	45%	24%

Business and professional people?

Republican	65%
Democratic	19
No difference (volunteered)	5
No opinion	11

Selected National Trend

	Republican	Democratic	No difference; no opinion
1985	69%	16%	15%

Small-business people?

Republican	36%
Democratic	45
No difference (volunteered)	7
No opinion	12

Selected National Trend

	Republican	Democratic	No difference; no opinion
1985	35%	45%	20%

White-collar workers?

Republican	56%
Democratic	25
No difference (volunteered)	7
No opinion	12

Selected National Trend

	Republican	Democratic	No difference; no opinion
1985	59%	23%	18%

Skilled workers?

Republican	38%
Democratic	40
No difference (volunteered)	8
No opinion	14

Selected National Trend

	Republican	Democratic	No difference; no opinion
1985	41%	39%	20%

Unskilled workers?

Republican 20%
Democratic 60
No difference (volunteered) 7
No opinion 13

Selected National Trend

	Republican	Democratic	No difference; no opinion
1985	22%	58%	20%

Labor union members?

Republican 22%
Democratic 55
No difference (volunteered) 6
No opinion 17

Selected National Trend

	Republican	Democratic	No difference; no opinion
1985	24%	58%	18%

Unemployed people?

Republican 20%
Democratic 59
No difference (volunteered) 10
No opinion 11

Selected National Trend

	Republican	Democratic	No difference; no opinion
1985	26%	52%	22%

Note: Prospects for Republican congressional candidates in the November 6 election seem less promising than they did one month ago. In the aftermath of the Washington budget battle and with fear of a recession on the rise, political momentum has shifted toward the Democrats.

Gallup's latest measure of intentions among likely voters shows 54% supporting the Democratic candidate for Congress in their district and 46% supporting the Republican. Similar vote distributions have been measured throughout the summer and fall despite the Iraqi invasion of Kuwait, the budget crisis, and recent talk of a recession. These figures do not translate directly into numbers of seats that each party will hold in the next Congress, but it would appear that the GOP's prospects for avoiding any losses in the House, and perhaps even making gains, have been sharply reduced.

The edge that the Republicans used to hold over the Democrats on the issues of competency and compassion has evaporated. Coupled with a slowing economy, these changes in voter perceptions on economic and class issues raise Democrats' hopes for larger gains in Tuesday's elections than they might have expected before the budget drama unfolded in Washington.

The Republicans also have lost ground as the party that voters say best represents their interests. Thirty-eight percent think that the GOP cares about "people like yourself" compared to 44% for the Democratic party. Five years ago these percentages were reversed. In this instance it is not just a single group of the population that has abandoned the Republicans—it shows up among all groups.

The federal budget battle in Washington has helped the Democratic congressional members more than their Republican counterparts, who cannot count on similar levels of support. When asked whether they would vote for a Republican candidate in their congressional district, 42% of respondents reply that they are less likely to do so, while only 35% are more likely.

NOVEMBER 5
QUALITY OF GOODS

Interviewing Date: 10/11–14/90
Survey #GO 922020

In general, do you think that the quality of goods manufactured in the United States is a lot better now than it was a few years ago, a

*little better, a little worse, or is the quality
of goods a lot worse now?*

Lot better 21%
Little better 46
Same (volunteered) 8
Little worse 16
Lot worse 7
No opinion 2

*Thinking now about the quality of goods
manufactured in the United States compared
with the quality of goods manufactured in
Asian countries like Japan, South Korea, Taiwan, and Hong Kong—in comparison to
these other countries, do you think the United
States has gained ground or lost ground in
the last few years in the quality of the goods
it manufactures?*

Has gained ground 51%
Has lost ground 43
Neither (volunteered) 3
Depends on which country
      (volunteered) 2
No opinion 1

*Now looking ahead to the next few years—
in comparison to these other countries, do
you think the United States will gain ground
or lose ground in the quality of goods pro-
duced during the next few years?*

Will gain ground 68%
Will lose ground 24
Neither (volunteered) 2
Depends on which country
      (volunteered) 5
No opinion 1

*We would like your opinion about who is to
blame for the quality of goods not being
higher than it is in the United States. Some
people blame employees. Other people blame
management. Still others blame the government. Now, let's assume you have ten chips
and you can use them to assign blame among
these three—employees, management, and*

*government. How many chips would you give
to:*

	Total chips assigned
Management	38%
Government	34
Employees	28

Note: Most Americans remain optimistic about
being able to improve the quality of goods manufactured in this country during the next few
years. Despite growing recession fears, fully two
thirds (68%) of respondents to a new Gallup Business Poll expect the United States to gain ground
in comparison to Asian competitors such as Japan, South Korea, Taiwan, and Hong Kong. Only
24% expect the United States to fall behind.

If these optimistic expectations are realized,
many people will see it as an improvement over
what they believe has happened in the past few
years. Only one half (51%) now say that U.S.
quality has gained compared to these competitors.
Nearly as many (43%) say that we have not kept
pace during the past few years.

Many respondents believe that the overall quality of goods manufactured in the United States is
only a little better now (46%) than it was a few
years ago. Fewer say either that quality is a lot
better now (21%) or that it has become worse
(23%).

When asked who is to blame for U.S. quality
not being better than it is, respondents allocate
the blame fairly evenly among management
(38%), government (34%), and employees (28%).
The great majority says that the blame is shared
by more than one of these three. Interestingly,
those who assign most blame to management are
more likely than other respondents to have favorable attitudes toward the quality of U.S. goods.
They less often believe either that our country
has fallen behind Asia in the past few years or
will do so in the next few years. In contrast, those
who blame employees tend to have relatively less
favorable attitudes.

NOVEMBER 6

ELECTION DAY 1990: THE MOOD OF THE NATION

Interviewing Date: 11/1–4/90
Survey #GO 922021

Do you approve or disapprove of the way George Bush is handling his job as president?

Approve 58%
Disapprove 32
No opinion 10

Selected National Trend

	Approve	Dis-approve	No opinion
1990			
October 25–28	54%	36%	10%
October 18–21	53	37	10
October 11–14	56	33	11
October 3–4	66	25	9
September 27–30	67	20	13
September 14–16	73	17	10
September 10–11	76	16	8

In general, are you satisfied or dissatisfied with the way things are going in the United States at this time?

Satisfied 31%
Dissatisfied 64
No opinion 5

Selected National Trend

	Satisfied	Dis-satisfied	No opinion
1990			
October 25–28	31%	66%	3%
October 11–14	29	67	4

In general, are you satisfied or dissatisfied with the way things are going in your own personal life?

Satisfied 85%
Dissatisfied 13
No opinion 2

Selected National Trend

	Satisfied	Dis-satisfied	No opinion
1990			
October 25–28	87%	11%	2%
October 11–14	82	16	2

Asked of registered voters: If the elections for Congress were being held today, which party's candidate would you like to see win in your congressional district—the Democratic party's candidate or the Republican party's candidate?

Democratic candidate 54%*
Republican candidate 46

*The "undecided" and "no opinion" responses have been allocated proportionally.

Asked of registered voters supporting the Democratic candidate: Why would you like to see the Democratic candidate win in your congressional district?

Always vote Democratic 22%
Like the candidate 10
For the people, people like me 9
Don't like the incumbent 8
Like stand on issues 7
Don't like the Republicans 7
Like the incumbent 5
More in tune with values 5
Represents the poor 4
Just the way I vote 2
Believe in the party 2
Other 13
No reason 1
No opinion 7

*Multiple responses were given.

Asked of registered voters supporting the Republican candidate: Why would you like to see the Republican candidate win in your congressional district?

Always vote Republican 9%
More in tune with values 11
Like the candidate 10
Like stand on issues 9
Don't like the Democrats 7
Like the incumbent 6
Fiscal responsibility 4
Believe in the party 3
Don't like the incumbent 2
Because of taxes 2
For the people, people like me 2
Other 18
No reason 1
No opinion 8

*Multiple responses were given.

What do you think is the most important problem facing this country today?

Economic
Economy in general 11%
Cost of living; inflation 2
Federal budget deficit; failure to
    balance budget 11
Trade deficit 1
Unemployment 3
Taxes 3
Recession 1
Other 1

Noneconomic
Drugs; drug abuse 8
Crime 2
Poverty; homelessness 6
Environment 2
Education 2
Ethics, morals 6
Fear of war 3
Kuwait, Iraq 17
Dissatisfaction with government 3
Oil crisis; fuel 2
Medicare 1
International 1
Health care 1
Other 7

No opinion 5

*Multiple responses were given.

How closely have you followed news about the situation involving the invasion of Kuwait by Iraq and the sending of U.S. troops to Saudi Arabia? Would you say you have followed it very closely, fairly closely, not too closely, or not at all closely?

Very closely 37%
Fairly closely 49
Not too closely 12
Not at all closely 2
No opinion .... *

*Less than 1%

Do you approve or disapprove of the way George Bush is handling this current situation in the Middle East involving Iraq and Kuwait?

Approve 61%
Disapprove 29
No opinion 10

Do you approve or disapprove of the U.S. decision to send U.S. troops to Saudi Arabia as a defense against Iraq?

Approve 67%
Disapprove 27
No opinion 6

In view of the developments since we first sent our troops to Saudi Arabia, do you think the United States made a mistake in sending troops to Saudi Arabia, or not?

Yes 25%
No 67
No opinion 8

How likely do you think it is that the U.S. forces in and around Saudi Arabia will become engaged in combat?

Very likely 40%
Somewhat likely 36
Not too likely 13
Not at all likely 5
No opinion 6

Just from what you have heard, read, or seen, which of these statements comes closer to how you, yourself, feel about the U.S. presence in the Mideast?

United States should begin to withdraw its troops 20%
United States should continue its present level of troop presence 41
United States should increase the level of its troops to force Iraq to leave Kuwait 32
No opinion 7

Do you approve or disapprove of the way Congress is handling its job?

Approve 26%
Disapprove 63
No opinion 11

Do you approve or disapprove of the way the representative from your own congressional district is handling his or her job?

Approve 55%
Disapprove 28
No opinion 17

Interviewing Date: 10/25–28/90
Survey #GO 122007

Do you think the United States currently has enough federal laws and regulations aimed at reducing race, religion, and sex discrimination, or does the Congress need to pass additional laws and regulations aimed at reducing this type of discrimination?

Has enough laws 61%
Needs additional laws 33
No opinion 6

Have you heard or read anything about the new Civil Rights Act of 1990 which is now being discussed in Congress?

                                      Yes
National 38%

Asked of those who responded in the affirmative: Do you have an opinion about the Civil Rights Act of 1990, or not?

                                      Yes
National 56%

Asked of those who have an opinion: Do you approve or disapprove of the Civil Rights Act of 1990?

Approve 32%
Disapprove 62
No opinion 5

Looking back over the last ten years, do you think the quality of life of blacks has gotten better, stayed about the same, or gotten worse?

Better 61%
About the same 21
Worse 13
No opinion 5

By Ethnic Background
White
Better 64%
About the same 21
Worse 10
No opinion 5

Black
Better 44%
About the same 24
Worse 31
No opinion 1

Note: On the eve of Election Day 1990, here is a brief run-down on the mood of the nation according to the Gallup Poll.

- Americans are dissatisfied with the way things are going in the United States. In fact, the satisfaction level (31%) is the lowest recorded since 1982. Dissatisfaction is based primarily on economic concerns.
- The most important problem facing our country is the economy and related economic issues, cited by one third. There has been an increase in concern over the Persian Gulf and other international tensions, with 20% currently naming these as the most important problem. Drugs, which had led the list as recently as July, are now seen as the number one problem by only 8%.
- President George Bush's job approval is now at 58%, down from post-Iraqi invasion highs.
- Approval of the job being done by Congress remains very low at 26%, continuing a trend evident throughout October. However, approval of the job being done by respondents' own congressman is much higher than that of Congress in general. Fifty-five percent approve of their own representative.
- Congressional vote intentions have remained constant all year; 54% now say that they will vote for the Democrat, 46% for the Republican. There has been no essential change throughout the turmoil of the Middle East situation and the federal budget debates.
- Voters are unable to articulate any one issue driving the way they plan to vote for congressional candidates this year. When pressed, they are more likely to say that they are simply voting for their party rather than give any other explanation; others talk about particular candidates involved, while some discuss the values of the two parties and how well they represent "people like me."
- Anticipation of U.S. involvement in a war in the Persian Gulf is up. Almost three quarters (76%) say that it is very or somewhat likely, up from two measurements in August. Support for the U.S. position there remains strong, although approval of Bush's handling of the situation (61%) is down somewhat from August and September measurements. About one quarter (25%) say that U.S. involvement is a mistake, but only 20% of the public favors an immediate withdrawal. Forty-one percent say that we should stand pat for the time being, and 32% think that we should accelerate

U.S. involvement in order to force Iraq out of Kuwait.
- A majority (62%) opposes the recent civil rights bill (vetoed by President Bush), thinking that legislation already on the books is adequate. On a related issue, 61% overall say that the quality of life for blacks has gotten better over the last ten years. However, whites see blacks' lives as 64% better and 10% worse, while blacks see themselves as only 44% better and 31% worse.

NOVEMBER 14
PRESIDENT BUSH/VICE PRESIDENT QUAYLE

Interviewing Date: 11/8–11/90
Survey #GO 922022

Do you approve or disapprove of the way George Bush is handling his job as president?

Approve	58%
Disapprove	34
No opinion	8

Would you like to see George Bush run for president in 1992, or not?

Yes	53%
No	39
No opinion	8

Thinking ahead to the 1992 presidential election, do you think President Bush should be reelected, or not?

Yes	45%
No	43
No opinion	12

Based on what you know about Vice President Dan Quayle, do you think he is qualified to serve as president if it becomes necessary, or not?

Yes	33%
No	59
No opinion	8

Selected National Trend

	Yes	No	No opinion
1990			
March	31%	54%	15%
1989			
May	34	52	14
1988			
October	46	42	12
September	34	47	19
August	41	40	19

Do you approve or disapprove of the way Dan Quayle is handling his job as vice president?

Approve 47%
Disapprove 33
No opinion 20

Selected National Trend

	Approve	Dis-approve	No opinion
1990			
August	47%	23%	30%
July	44	30	26
May	48	27	25
February	46	27	27
1989			
November	43	29	28

If President Bush runs for reelection in 1992, do you think he should keep Dan Quayle as his vice presidential running mate or choose someone else?

Keep Quayle 36%
Choose someone else 55
No opinion 9

Selected National Trend

	Keep Quayle	Choose someone else	No opinion
March 1990	35%	49%	16%

I'd like you to rate Vice President Quayle using a scale that goes from the highest possible rating of +5 for someone you have a very favorable opinion of, all the way down to the lowest position of −5 for someone you have a very unfavorable opinion of. How far up or down the scale would you rate Vice President Dan Quayle?

Highly favorable (+5, +4) 14%
Mildly favorable (+3, +2, +1) 36
Mildly unfavorable (−1, −2, −3) 15
Highly unfavorable (−4, −5) 13
No opinion 22

Selected National Trend

	Highly, mildly favorable	Mildly, highly unfavor-able	No opinion
March 1990	46%	27%	27%

What do you think is President Bush's greatest achievement to date this year?

	Feb.	July	Nov.
Sending troops to Saudi Arabia; standing up to Hussein	–	–	17%
Nothing	6	13	15
Foreign policy; foreign affairs; peace in world	7	9	9
Changes in USSR; getting along with Gorbachev	7	24	5
Leadership qualities ...	2	1	4
Drug war	9	4	3
Panama invasion, Noriega capture	18	3	2
Economy; budget	1	1	2
Getting elected	3	1	1
Changes in Eastern Europe; Berlin Wall	2	4	1
Taxes	1	*	1
Education	–	–	1
Keeping things together; status quo	–	–	1
Abortion stand	1	1	*

Supreme Court
  nominations ....   –   –   *
Other   9   12   9
No opinion; can't say   36   27   29

*Less than 1%

How would you rate President George Bush on the following questions, after nearly two years in office? Would you say his performance has been excellent, good, only fair, or poor on:

Making good appointments to cabinet and other positions?

Excellent 8%
Good 37
Fair 37
Poor 11
No opinion 7

Selected National Trend

	Excellent	Good	Fair	Poor	No opinion
1990					
July	5%	40%	36%	7%	12%
Feb.	7	42	32	6	13

Being an efficient manager of government?

Excellent 7%
Good 40
Fair 37
Poor 13
No opinion 3

Selected National Trend

	Excellent	Good	Fair	Poor	No opinion
1990					
July	7%	45%	33%	11%	4%
Feb.	10	52	28	5	5

Developing programs to address the pressing problems America faces?

Excellent 5%
Good 29
Fair 40
Poor 23
No opinion 3

Selected National Trend

	Excellent	Good	Fair	Poor	No opinion
1990					
July	4%	31%	42%	19%	4%
Feb.	8	39	35	13	5

Communicating his ideas to the American public?

Excellent ....,........ 12%
Good 41
Fair 33
Poor 13
No opinion 1

Selected National Trend

	Excellent	Good	Fair	Poor	No opinion
1990					
July	9%	46%	30%	13%	2%
Feb.	16	49	26	7	2

Following through on his ideas and initiatives?

Excellent 5%
Good 34
Fair 38
Poor 20
No opinion 3

Selected National Trend

	Excellent	Good	Fair	Poor	No opinion
1990					
July	4%	36%	38%	18%	4%
Feb.	10	45	32	7	6

Working effectively with Congress?

Excellent 5%
Good 31
Fair 39
Poor 22
No opinion 3

Selected National Trend

1990	Excellent	Good	Fair	Poor	No opinion
July	5%	46%	35%	7%	7%
Feb.	7	46	34	6	7

Being a good representative or symbol of the United States?

Excellent 19%
Good 44
Fair 27
Poor 9
No opinion 1

Selected National Trend

1990	Excellent	Good	Fair	Poor	No opinion
July	22%	49%	22%	6%	1%
Feb.	24	52	18	4	2

Being an inspirational leader to the American people?

Excellent 10%
Good 37
Fair 32
Poor 20
No opinion 1

Selected National Trend

1990	Excellent	Good	Fair	Poor	No opinion
July	10%	45%	30%	13%	2%
Feb.	17	47	27	8	1

Please tell me which word or phrase better describes your impression of George Bush.

If you feel neither phrase describes Bush, please say so.

Sincere 74%
Insincere 19
Neither; no opinion 7

Selected National Trend

1990	Sincere	Insincere	No opinion
July	75%	18%	7%
February	85	9	6

Steady, reliable 67%
Undependable 23
Neither; no opinion 10

Selected National Trend

1990	Steady, reliable	Undependable	No opinion
July	72%	19%	9%
February	83	8	9

Intelligent 65%
Only average 33
Neither; no opinion 2

Selected National Trend

1990	Intelligent	Only average	No opinion
July	66%	31%	3%
February	72	25	3

Confident 72%
Insecure 22
Neither; no opinion 6

Selected National Trend

1990	Confident	Insecure	No opinion
July	76%	18%	6%
February	82	12	6

Warm, friendly 80%
Cold, unfriendly 11
Neither; no opinion 9

Selected National Trend

	Warm, friendly	Cold, unfriendly	No opinion
1990			
July	84%	7%	9%
February	86	5	9

Strong 62%
Weak 22
Neither; no opinion 16

Selected National Trend

	Strong	Weak	No opinion
1990			
July	63%	21%	16%
February	73	14	13

A leader 68%
A follower 20
Neither; no opinion 12

Selected National Trend

	A leader	A follower	No opinion
1990			
July	67%	24%	9%
February	75	18	7

An active president 71%
A passive president 21
Neither; no opinion 8

Selected National Trend

	An active president	A passive president	No opinion
1990			
July	70%	22%	8%

Here is a list of some problems and respon-sibilities facing the president and his ad-ministration. After nearly two years in office,

do you think George Bush is making progress or is not making progress on handling each of these different problems:

Keeping the nation out of war?

Making progress 37%
Not making progress 55
No opinion 8

Selected National Trend

	Making progress	Not making progress	No opinion
1990			
February	77%	17%	6%

Keeping America prosperous?

Making progress 41%
Not making progress 54
No opinion 5

Selected National Trend

	Making progress	Not making progress	No opinion
1990			
February	59%	33%	8%

Increasing respect for the United States abroad?

Making progress 62%
Not making progress 32
No opinion 6

Selected National Trend

	Making progress	Not making progress	No opinion
1990			
February	73%	21%	6%

Improving educational standards?

Making progress 42%
Not making progress 48
No opinion 10

Selected National Trend

	Making progress	Not making progress	No opinion
1990			
February	48%	44%	8%

Improving the quality of the environment?

Making progress 50%
Not making progress 43
No opinion 7

Selected National Trend

	Making progress	Not making progress	No opinion
1990			
February	46%	45%	9%

Improving the lot of minorities and the poor?

Making progress 28%
Not making progress 62
No opinion 10

Selected National Trend

	Making progress	Not making progress	No opinion
1990			
February	35%	54%	11%

Reducing the crime rate in the United States?

Making progress 27%
Not making progress 65
No opinion 8

Selected National Trend

	Making progress	Not making progress	No opinion
1990			
February	37%	54%	9%

Reducing the federal budget deficit?

Making progress 24%
Not making progress 70
No opinion 6

Selected National Trend

	Making progress	Not making progress	No opinion
1990			
February	30%	58%	12%

Getting the drug crisis under control?

Making progress 47%
Not making progress 49
No opinion 4

Selected National Trend

	Making progress	Not making progress	No opinion
1990			
February	57%	39%	4%

Avoiding raising taxes?

Making progress 21%
Not making progress 74
No opinion 5

Selected National Trend

	Making progress	Not making progress	No opinion
1990			
February	54%	36%	10%

At this point, would you say George Bush is doing a better job as president than you expected or not as good a job as you expected?

Better 36%
Not as good 38
As well as expected (volunteered) 24
No opinion 2

Selected National Trend

	Better	Not as good	As well as ex- pected	No opinion
1990				
July	50%	30%	17%	3%
1989				
Nov.	44	21	28	7
March*	32	26	30	12

Newsweek survey conducted by the Gallup Organization

Note: Midway through his first term in office, President George Bush seems more vulnerable to an election challenge in 1992 than he did just a few months ago. His job approval rating (58%) is significantly below the average rating for his term to date (66%). The percentage of the public who see him making progress on specific issues has decreased, in some cases dramatically, and respondents divide equally on whether he should be reelected (45% versus 43%).

For the first time, Americans are as likely to say that Bush has been a worse president (38%) than they expected as they are to say he has exceeded their expectations (36%). In July, 50% thought that he was doing better, and only 30% thought that he was doing worse. Before Bush faces the voters again, however, public attitudes toward him are likely to evolve further. His viability as a candidate in 1992 will depend not only on how he handles the current situation but also on his performance in handling new situations that may arise.

As a candidate, Bush's pledge not to raise taxes contributed to his victory; as president, the Persian Gulf situation has boosted his approval ratings. Today, neither is a clear Bush asset. In fact, the percentages who give him credit for keeping the country out of war (37%) and avoiding a tax increase (21%) have fallen by over 30 percentage points since February.

Respondents also have become less willing to credit Bush with making progress in other areas, particularly in keeping America prosperous (41%) and increasing respect for the United States abroad (62%). He also gets less credit for helping solve the drug crisis (47%) and for keeping the crime rate under control (27%). However, Bush now does get slightly more credit for his handling of the environment (50%).

Perhaps as a result of the recent protracted budget negotiations between Capitol Hill and the White House, ratings of Bush on working effectively with Congress (36%) have fallen 15 percentage points since July. His images as an inspirational leader (47%) and a good representative or symbol of the United States (63%) have also declined.

There has been no change in his ratings on other presidential qualities, however, including making good appointments to cabinet and other positions (45%), developing programs to address the pressing problems America faces (34%), and communicating his ideas to the public (53%). His ratings are off only slightly in terms of being an efficient manager of government (47%).

There also has been very little change in the public's perception of his character. The Gallup Poll shows no major change in opinions on eight character traits, measured for the third time this year—thus suggesting that Bush's drop in job approval has not yet begun to materially affect views of his basic persona.

Bush's greatest achievements in office, according to the public, have always centered on foreign policy. In February, it was the invasion of Panama; in July, the changes with the Soviet Union; now, it is the movement of troops to Saudi Arabia, cited by 17%.

All in all, despite Bush's tarnished image, 53% would like to see him run again for the presidency in 1992. This is considerably higher than the 36% in 1983 who thought that Ronald Reagan should run again in 1984, at a time when Reagan was enduring his lowest job approval ratings.

There has been some discussion that Vice President Dan Quayle may have improved his standing by virtue of his actions in the recent budget situation. If so, there is no sign of it from the American public: the percentage who think that Quayle is not qualified to be president (59%) has actually gone up slightly, not down; and the percentage of those who think that Bush should dump him in 1992 (55%) is up 6 points. Quayle's overall job approval rating (47%) is unchanged; however, disapproval is up as "no opinion" replies have gone down.

NOVEMBER 15
THE BIBLE

Interviewing Date: 11/1–4/90
Survey #GO 922021

How often do you read the Bible?

Daily or more often	17%
Weekly or more often	23
Monthly or more often	13
Less than monthly	25
Rarely or never	20
No opinion	2

Asked of those who had ever read the Bible: Just your best guess, about how much of the Old Testament of the Bible would you say you have ever read? And how about the New Testament, about how much of it would you say you have ever read?

	Old Testament	New Testament
All	26%	35%
Most	18	20
About half	24	19
Less than half	20	13
Little or none	11	12
No opinion	1	1

Will you tell me the names of the first four books of the New Testament of the Bible—that is, the first Four Gospels?

Matthew	44%
Mark	40
Luke	41
John	45
Named at least one	50
Named all four	37

Which, if any, of the following are you involved in or do you practice?

Bible study groups	21%
Prayer, meditation groups	21
Religious education classes	20
All three of the above	7

Do you happen to know whether or not the public schools of your community do the following:

Teach about the major religions of the world?

Yes	21%
No	39
No opinion	40

Use the Bible in literature, history, and social studies classes?

Yes	9%
No	52
No opinion	39

Make facilities available after school hours for use by student religious groups or organizations?

Yes	21%
No	40
No opinion	39

Offer elective courses in Bible studies?

Yes	8%
No	60
No opinion	32

Note: On the fiftieth anniversary of National Bible Week, celebrated this year on November 18–25, the Bible is still widely read and studied, but ignorance about its contents may be increasing.

The Bible undoubtedly is the most widely read book in America. A new Gallup Poll indicates that 17% of adults read it daily, and an additional 23% read it weekly. The Bible is read at least monthly by an additional 13% of all adults, while one in four (25%) read it less often than that and 20% say that they never read it.

Among adult Bible readers, the New Testament is slightly more widely read than the Old Testament: almost one half say that they have read all (26%) or most (18%) of the Old Testament, while a majority has read all (35%) or most (20%) of the New Testament. Moreover, about one adult in five (21%) belongs to a Bible study group.

Despite the impressive statistics concerning reading and study of the Bible, it is apparent that ignorance of its contents is widespread. In 1990 only one half (50%) of the adults interviewed nationwide could name any one of the four Gospels of the New Testament. Just 37% could name all four, compared to 42% who were able to cite the four titles correctly in 1982.

At the same time there is widespread lack of awareness of whether or not religious and Bible studies are offered in the public schools of the respondents' communities; between three and four in ten say that they do not know. Unlike school prayer, which the Supreme Court has prohibited on constitutional grounds, the activities covered in the latest Gallup Poll are permissible under the First Amendment.

NOVEMBER 21
PERSIAN GULF SITUATION

Interviewing Date: 11/15–18/90
Survey #GO 122008

Do you approve or disapprove of the way George Bush is handling his job as president?

Approve 54%
Disapprove 33
No opinion 13

Do you approve or disapprove of the way George Bush is handling this current situation in the Middle East involving Iraq and Kuwait?

Approve 54%
Disapprove 35
No opinion 11

Selected National Trend

	Approve	Disapprove	No opinion
Nov. 8–11	61%	34%	5%
Nov. 1–4	61	29	10
Oct. 25–28	61	31	8
Oct. 11–14	64	29	7

As you may know, President Bush has recently decided to send up to 150,000 additional troops to the Middle East. Do you approve or disapprove of this decision to send more troops at this time?

Approve 47%
Disapprove 46
No opinion 7

If the current situation in the Middle East involving Iraq and Kuwait does not change by January, would you favor or oppose the United States going to war with Iraq in order to drive the Iraqis out of Kuwait?

Favor 37%
Oppose 51
No opinion 12

Which of the following comes closest to your own view? The president should be able to go to war against Iraq without getting approval from Congress, or the president should be able to go to war against Iraq only if Congress approves of the decision?

President alone 22%
President and Congress 74
No opinion 4

Do you feel you have a clear idea of what the U.S. military involvement in the Iraqi situation is all about—that is, why our troops are in Saudi Arabia?

Yes 69%
No 29
No opinion 2

Selected National Trend

	Yes	No	No opinion
Sept. 27–30	75%	23%	2%
Aug. 30–			
Sept. 2	76	23	1
Aug. 23–26	70	28	2
Aug. 16–19	74	24	2

Why do you think we are involved in the Iraqi situation and why are our troops in Saudi Arabia?

	Aug. 16–19	Nov. 15–18
Defend oil interests	49%	38%
We should be; have to		
defend other countries ...	17	9
Stop Iraqi aggression	11	23
Defend Saudi Arabia	6	5
Protect U.S. citizens	4	4
Get Iraq out of Kuwait	1	5
Other	6	10
None	1	1
No opinion	5	5

All in all, which of these courses of action do you agree with:

United States should keep troops, planes, and ships in and around Saudi Arabia as long as is necessary to prevent Iraq from invading Saudi Arabia but without initiating a war? 65%

United States should initiate a war against Iraq in order to drive Iraq out of Kuwait and bring the situation to a close? 28

No opinion 7

Note: Although a majority of Americans still supports the White House's original decision to send troops to the Persian Gulf to halt a possible Iraqi attack on Saudi Arabia, only 47% approve of President George Bush's recent decision to send at least another 150,000 men and women to the region. And, according to a recent Gallup Poll, only 37% say that we should initiate a war to drive the Iraqis out of Kuwait if the current situation in the Middle East does not change by January.

Sixty-five percent say that the United States should keep its forces in and near Saudi Arabia as long as needed to prevent an Iraqi invasion. Only 28% say that we should make war on Iraq to drive it out of Kuwait.

The ambivalence over recent escalation of U.S. involvement is reflected in a continuing deterioration in approval of President Bush's handling of the situation. Only 54% now approve of his handling of the Persian Gulf crisis, down from 80% approval in early August and 61% approval one week ago—the same percentage as his current overall job approval.

Most Americans still profess to know why we are in the Persian Gulf. When asked to explain their views of U.S. involvement in their own words, they continue to cite national self-interest: defending U.S. oil and national interests (38%), followed by stopping Iraqi aggression (23%). Others reply: to defend and come to the aid of other countries (9%), to defend Saudi Arabia (5%), to get Iraq out of Kuwait (5%), and to protect U.S. citizens (4%).

Respondents firmly believe that Congress should be involved if war does occur. Seventy-four percent say that the president should be able to go to war against Iraq only if Congress approves of the decision, while only 22% say that Bush should be able to act without congressional approval.

NOVEMBER 22
THANKSGIVING

Interviewing Date: 11/15–18/90
Survey #GO 122008

With Thanksgiving only a short time away, what do the people of this country have the most to be thankful for this year?*

Not in war 31%

Freedom 17

Health 12

Employment; prosperity 6

Living in America 6

Family 3

Food			3
The president			1
Everything			2
Other			6
Nothing			4
No opinion			13

*Multiple responses were given.

And what about yourself—this year? *

Health	47%
Family	30
Good jobs	15
Spiritual, God	3
Material things; roof over head	6
Living in America	3
Everything	3
Peace; end of war	**
Other	12
Nothing	1
No opinion	4

*Multiple responses were given.
**Less than 1%

Note: On Thanksgiving Day 1990, Americans say that people in this country should be most thankful for peace, freedom, health, and prosperity. They personally are most thankful for their health, family, job, and material things such as a roof over their heads.

NOVEMBER 28
PAST PRESIDENTS

Interviewing Date: 11/8–11/90
Survey #GO 922922

From what you have heard, read, or remember about some of our past presidents, please tell me if you approve or disapprove of the way they handled their job as president:

	Approve	Dis- approve	No opinion
Roosevelt	75%	17%	8%
Truman	68	8	24
Eisenhower	70	10	20
Kennedy	84	9	7
Johnson	40	43	17
Nixon	32	62	6
Ford	55	34	11
Carter	45	52	3
Reagan	54	44	2

Retrospective versus Actual Approval Ratings during Presidency

	1990 approval	*Average approval*	*Final approval*
Roosevelt	75%	75%*	66%
Truman	68	41	31
Eisenhower	70	65	59
Kennedy	84	71	58
Johnson	40	56	49
Nixon	32	48	24
Ford	55	47	53
Carter	45	47	34
Reagan	54	52	63

*Only measures Roosevelt's third and fourth terms, from September 1941 onward

Now, let's think about the four living past presidents. Would you say you approve or disapprove of their performance since they left office?

	Approve	Dis- approve	No opinion
Nixon	54%	33%	13%
Ford	67	15	18
Carter	74	17	9
Reagan	58	32	10

Note: How do the passing years affect Americans' evaluation of their presidents? In a new Gallup Poll conducted in mid-November, retrospective opinions about the job done in office by the last several presidents were compared to the actual job evaluations given them while they were in office.

Harry Truman has fared the best; his retrospective approval rating of 68% is 27 points higher than his average while in office (41%). His historical improvement is all the more remarkable given that he left office with a dismal approval rating of 31%.

John F. Kennedy, whose 71% average approval ratings while in office were the highest recorded since Franklin Roosevelt, has continued to improve over time, gaining another 13 points. Kennedy has achieved almost mythic stature twenty-seven years after his assassination, with a phenomenal 84% now approving of his 1,000-day administration.

Both Dwight Eisenhower (plus 5 points, to 70%) and Gerald Ford (plus 8, to 55%) also are more positively remembered than during their tenures. The two most recent presidents, Ronald Reagan and Jimmy Carter, show the least change, perhaps because their terms in office are still fresh in the public's mind. Reagan, at 54% approval, is 2 points higher than his average while in office; Carter, at 45%, is 2 points lower.

The biggest losses over time have been sustained by Lyndon Johnson and Richard Nixon, both of whom now receive approval ratings 16 points below their averages while actually in office. Nixon's presidency is now approved by only 32%—dead last among the presidents rated—a strong indicator that revisionist thinking about his foreign policy achievements overcoming the stigma of Watergate has not taken hold among the public. There also has been no overhauling of Johnson, whose presidency now is approved by only 40%, 9 percentage points lower than when he left office at the end of 1968.

What about the four living ex-presidents (Nixon, Ford, Carter, and Reagan) since they left office? What do Americans think about how well they have comported themselves as "former" presidents?

The big winner is Jimmy Carter. The public, perhaps mindful of his peacemaking efforts in Africa, his work with Habitat for Humanity, and his avoidance of postpresidential perquisites, give him a 74% approval rating. Ford's postpresidential performance rates 67%, while Ronald Reagan, just two years out of office, receives a 58% rating. Nixon's recent efforts to rehabilitate his image do not seem to have been very effective; at 54%, his is the lowest postpresidential rating.

DECEMBER 2
WEIGHT AND WEIGHT REDUCTION

Interviewing Date: 10/11–14/90
Survey #GO 122006

How would you describe your own personal weight situation right now?

	Total	Women	Men
Very overweight	7%	10%	3%
Somewhat overweight	41	41	40
About right	46	43	49
Somewhat underweight	5	4	7
Very underweight	1	2	1
No opinion	*	*	*

*Less than 1%

Has your weight situation ever caused you any of the following:

To be depressed or deeply worried?

	Total	Women	Men
Yes	12%	19%	4%
No	87	80	96
No opinion	1	1	*

*Less than 1%

To lose out on job opportunities or promotions?

	Total	Women	Men
Yes	2%	2%	2%
No	97	97	97
No opinion	1	1	1

Trouble with relationships, making friends, or difficulty in social situations?

	Total	Women	Men
Yes	4%	6%	3%
No	96	94	97
No opinion	*	*	*

*Less than 1%

Health problems?

	Total	Women	Men
Yes	10%	13%	7%
No	89	86	93
No opinion	1	1	*

*Less than 1%

How often do you worry about your weight? Would you say you worry all of the time, some of the time, not too often, or never?

	Total	Women	Men
All of the time	7%	13%	2%
Some of the time	27	33	19
Not too often	33	32	33
Never	33	22	46
No opinion	*	*	*

*Less than 1%

Would you like to lose weight, put on weight, or stay at your present weight?

	Total	Women	Men
Lose weight	52%	62%	42%
Put on weight	7	3	10
Stay at present weight	40	34	47
No opinion	1	1	1

Selected National Trend
Total Personal Weight Situation

	1990	1955	1953	1951
Lose weight	52%	37%	35%	31%
Put on weight	7	13	14	17
Stay at present weight	40	48	48	50
No opinion	1	2	3	2

At this time, are you seriously trying to lose weight?

	Total	Women	Men
Yes	18%	24%	11%
No	82	76	88
No opinion	*	*	1

*Less than 1%

Selected National Trend
Total

	1990	1955	1953	1951
Yes	18%	17%	25%	19%
No	82	83	75	81
No opinion	*	*	*	*

*Less than 1%

Asked of those who are seriously trying to lose weight: Are you trying to lose weight more to improve your appearance or more to improve your health?

	Total	Women	Men
Improve appearance ...	21%	25%	11%
Improve health	51	44	68
Both (volunteered)	27	31	18
No opinion	1	*	3

*Less than 1%

Also asked of those who are seriously trying to lose weight: What are you doing to try and lose weight?

	Total	Women	Men
Dieting; changing eating habits	69%	75%	59%
Exercising	31	26	42
Other	2	1	6
Nothing	2	3	**
No opinion	1	1	**

*Multiple responses were given.
**Less than 1%

Also asked of those who are seriously trying to lose weight: Is this weight loss program working for you, or not?

	Total	Women	Men
Yes	84%	83%	86%
No	10	9	11
No opinion	6	8	3

How many different times, if any, have you seriously tried to lose weight in your life?

	Total	Women	Men
Once or twice	30%	32%	28%
Three to ten times	18	25	10
More than ten times ..	5	8	1
Never	44	31	59
No opinion	3	4	2
Average number of times	6	9	1

Also asked of those who have ever seriously tried to lose weight: At about what age did you first try to lose weight?

	Total	Women	Men
17 years or younger ...	23%	28%	14%
18 to 24 years	26	28	22
25 to 34 years	21	20	22
35 to 44 years	15	13	18
45 years and older	14	10	23
No opinion	1	1	1
Average age	28	26	33

All in all, from your experience, what do you think is the most effective way to lose weight?

Watch what you eat; eat sensibly	17%
Eat less food, smaller portions	16
Exercise	13
Stop eating, fasting	7
Diet	5
Walking	5
Aerobics; bicycling; jogging	5
Willpower, self-control	4
Eat foods low in fat	3
Cut calories	2
Weight Watchers	2
Other	11
Nothing	2
No opinion	8

I am going to read you some ways people try to lose weight. Please tell me, from what you know, if you think each can really be an effective way to lose weight, or not:

Eating healthier and low-calorie foods?

Yes	97%
No	2
No opinion	1

Exercising?

Yes	95%
No	4
No opinion	1

Eating less food or smaller portions?

Yes	93%
No	6
No opinion	1

Avoiding or drinking less alcohol?

Yes	76%
No	15
No opinion	9

Attending a commercial weight-loss program such as Weight Watchers or Nutri-System?

Yes	61%
No	33
No opinion	6

Attending a hospital or doctor-based program like Optifast?

Yes	50%
No	34
No opinion	6

Using a liquid diet such as Slim Fast?

Yes	32%
No	61
No opinion	7

Skipping meals or fasting?

Yes	21%
No	78
No opinion	1

Psychotherapy or hypnosis?

Yes 19%
No 64
No opinion 17

Taking over-the-counter diet medication or appetite suppressants?

Yes 9%
No 87
No opinion 4

If you had to take a physical fitness test involving such things as running, push-ups, and sit-ups, what kind of physical shape would it show you to be in—excellent, good, only fair, or poor?

	Total	Women	Men
Excellent	11%	7%	15%
Good	42	37	49
Fair	32	37	27
Poor	13	18	8
No opinion	2	1	1

Note: The average American woman today is 5 feet, 4 inches tall and weighs 142 pounds. The average American man is 5 feet 10 inches and weighs 180. This state of affairs is not ideal: women would like to be 5 feet 6 and weigh 129, while men would like to be 5 feet 11 and weigh 171.

A significant percentage of respondents of both sexes consider themselves to be overweight and think that they should be on a diet. This weight consciousness is much higher now than it was forty years ago. At the same time, less than one out of five is dieting today, a number that has stayed remarkably constant over the last forty years.

In other words, Americans are dieting as before but worrying more. They think that society's emphasis on "thinness" is too extreme. They are generally satisfied with how attractive they are, although very few think that they are either beautiful or ugly. These are among the findings of the latest Gallup Mirror of America survey, which shows that nearly one half of all adults perceive themselves as overweight.

DECEMBER 12
PERSIAN GULF SITUATION

Interviewing Date: 11/29–12/2; 12/6–12/9/90
Survey #GO 12209; GO 922023

Do you approve or disapprove of the way George Bush is handling his job as president?

Approve 58%
Disapprove 33
No opinion 9

How closely have you followed news about the situation involving the invasion of Kuwait by Iraq [and the sending of U.S. troops to Saudi Arabia]? Would you say you have followed it very closely, fairly closely, not too closely, or not at all closely?*

	Nov. 29–Dec. 2	Dec. 6–9
Very closely	40%	43%
Fairly closely	49	46
Not too closely	9	9
Not at all closely	2	2
No opinion	**	**

*All questions asked after August 16–19 included the phrase in brackets.
**Less than 1%

Selected National Trend

	Very, fairly closely	Not too, not at all closely	No opinion
Nov. 15–18	78%	22%	*%
Nov. 8–11	87	13	*
Nov. 1–4	86	14	*
Oct. 25–28	88	12	*
Oct. 18–21	84	16	*
Oct. 3–4	85	15	*
Sept. 27–30	85	15	*
Sept. 14–16	86	14	*
Sept. 10–11	84	16	*

Aug. 30–Sept. 2	......	86	13	1
Aug. 23–26	....	86	14	*
Aug. 16–19	....	87	13	*
Aug. 9–12	....	83	17	*
Aug. 3–4	....	57	43	*

*Less than 1%

Do you approve or disapprove of the way George Bush is handling this current situation in the Middle East involving Iraq and Kuwait?

	Nov. 29–Dec. 2	Dec. 6–9
Approve	....	58%	57%
Disapprove	....	33	36
No opinion	....	9	7

Selected National Trend

	Approve	Dis-approve	No opinion
Nov. 15–18	....	54%	35%	11%
Nov. 8–11	....	60	34	6
Nov. 1–4	....	61	29	10
Oct. 25–28	....	61	31	8
Oct. 18–21	....	61	29	10
Oct. 11–14	....	64	29	7
Oct. 3–4	....	69	25	6
Sept. 27–30	....	71	22	7
Sept. 14–16	....	74	16	10
Sept. 10–11	....	76	17	7
Aug. 30–Sept. 2	......	74	18	8
Aug. 23–26	....	76	17	7
Aug. 16–19	....	79	14	7
Aug. 9–12	....	80	12	8
Aug. 3–4	....	52	16	32

Do you approve or disapprove of the U.S. decision to send U.S. troops to Saudi Arabia as a defense against Iraq?

	Nov. 29–Dec. 2	Dec. 6–9
Approve	....	65%	63%
Disapprove	....	30	33
No opinion	....	5	4

Selected National Trend

	Approve	Dis-approve	No opinion
Nov. 8–11	....	67%	28%	5%
Nov. 1–4	....	67	27	6
Oct. 25–28	....	70	23	7
Oct. 18–21	....	66	27	7
Oct. 11–14	....	70	27	3
Oct. 3–4	....	72	23	5
Sept. 27–30	....	72	21	7
Sept. 14–16	....	73	18	9
Sept. 10–11	....	72	22	6
Aug. 30–Sept. 2	......	74	20	5
Aug. 23–26	....	80	16	4
Aug. 16–19	....	76	19	5
Aug. 9–12	....	78	17	5

In view of the developments since we first sent our troops to Saudi Arabia, do you think the United States made a mistake in sending troops to Saudi Arabia, or not?

	Nov. 29–Dec. 2	Dec. 6–9
Yes	....	29%	28%
No	....	66	66
No opinion	....	5	6

Selected National Trend

	Yes	No	No opinion
Nov. 15–18	....	27%	65%	8%
Nov. 8–11	....	27	68	5
Nov. 1–4	....	25	67	8
Oct. 25–28	....	24	71	5
Oct. 18–21	....	26	67	7
Oct. 11–14	....	26	68	6
Oct. 3–4	....	21	71	8
Sept. 27–30	....	20	73	7
Sept. 14–16	....	18	73	9
Sept. 10–11	....	19	76	5
Aug. 30–Sept. 2	......	16	76	8
Aug. 23–26	....	18	76	6
Aug. 16–19	....	17	75	8

All in all, is the current situation in the Mideast worth going to war over, or not?

	Nov. 29–	
	Dec. 2	Dec. 6–9
Yes	51%	47%
No	41	45
No opinion	8	8

Selected National Trend

	Yes	No	No opinion
Nov. 15–18	46%	45%	9%
Sept. 27–30	49	41	10
Aug. 30–Sept. 2	45	44	11
Aug. 23–26	49	41	10

Asked of those who say it is worth going to war: If it were necessary for thousands of American troops to be killed in order to win such a war, would you still think the situation worth going to war over, or not?

	Nov. 29–Dec. 2
Yes	72%
No	19
No opinion	9

If the current situation in the Middle East involving Iraq and Kuwait does not change by January, would you favor or oppose the United States going to war with Iraq in order to drive the Iraqis out of Kuwait?

	Nov. 29–	
	Dec. 2	Dec. 6–9
Favor	53%	53%
Oppose	40	40
No opinion	7	7

Selected National Trend

	Favor	Oppose	No opinion
Nov. 15–18	37%	51%	12%

Which of the following three statements comes closest to your opinion:

A) The United States should withdraw its troops from Saudi Arabia.

B) The United States should continue to enforce sanctions and seek some form of peaceful solution to the crisis, no matter how long it takes, without initiating a war to drive Iraq out of Kuwait.

C) The United States should initiate a war to drive Iraq out of Kuwait if Iraq does not change its position within the next several months, in order to draw matters to a close.

	Nov. 29–	
	Dec. 2	Dec. 6–9
Statement A	9%	10%
Statement B	46	41
Statement C	42	46
No opinion	3	3

Some people feel the sanctions imposed by the international community against Iraq should be given more time to work. Other people feel that it is time to take stronger action against Saddam Hussein, including the use of armed force. Which one of these views comes closer to how you feel?

	Nov. 29–	
	Dec. 2	Dec. 6–9
Give sanctions time	46%	47%
Take stronger action against Hussein	48	46
No opinion	6	7

Asked of those who think sanctions should be given more time: About how much longer do you think the sanctions against Iraq should be given before taking military actions to get Saddam Hussein out of Kuwait?

	Nov. 29–	
	Dec. 2	Dec. 6–9
Forever, as long as it takes	10%	10%
One to two more months, until January	29	33
Three to less than six months	21	18

Six months to less than one year	16	16
One to less than two years	6	5
Two to less than three years	*	*
Three to less than five years	*	*
Five years or longer	1	*
Other	2	3
None	1	2
No opinion	14	13

*Less than 1%

Recently, the United Nations Security Council passed a resolution that allows Iraq one final opportunity to pull out of Kuwait by January 15 or else face possible military action. If Iraq lets this deadline pass, would you favor the United States and its allies going to war with Iraq in order to drive the Iraqis out of Kuwait, or not?

	Nov. 29–Dec. 2	Dec. 6–9
Yes	64%	61%
No	31	33
No opinion	5	6

Some people say that if Iraq simply stays in Kuwait with no further aggression, the United States should maintain its troops in Saudi Arabia as a defensive measure almost indefinitely, as we have in Korea, without initiating a war. Others say that the United States should go ahead and initiate a war to drive Iraq out of Kuwait and not allow Iraq to stay in Kuwait indefinitely. Which comes closer to your opinion?

	Nov. 29–Dec. 2	Dec. 6–9
Maintain troops indefinitely	42%	42%
Initiate war	49	48
No opinion	9	10

Do you feel you have a clear idea of what the U.S. military involvement in the Iraqi situation is all about—that is, why our troops are in Saudi Arabia?

	Nov. 29–Dec. 2
Yes	73%
No	26
No opinion	1

Selected National Trend

	Yes	No	No opinion
Nov. 15–18	69%	29%	2%
Sept. 27–30	75	23	2
Aug. 30–Sept. 2	76	23	1
Aug. 23–26	70	28	2
Aug. 16–19	74	24	2

Why do you think we are involved in the Iraqi situation and why are our troops in Saudi Arabia?

	Nov. 29–Dec. 2	Nov. 15–18	Aug. 16–19
Defend oil interests ...	43%	39%	49%
We should be; have to defend other countries	7	9	17
Stop Iraqi aggression	19	23	11
Defend Saudi Arabia	5	5	6
Protect U.S. citizens	5	4	4
Get Iraq out of Kuwait	6	5	1
Other	10	10	6
None	*	*	1
No opinion	5	5	5

*Less than 1%

Would you happen to know the name of the leader of Iraq? Asked of those who responded in the affirmative: What is his name?

	Nov. 29– Dec. 2
Correct response [Saddam Hussein]	75%
Incorrect response	23
No opinion	2

And, just your best guess, about how many troops will the United States have in and around Saudi Arabia after the latest deployment of troops is completed?

	Nov. 29– Dec. 2
Less than 100,000	8%
100,000 to less than 200,000	7
200,000 to less than 300,000	14
300,000 to less than 400,000	11
400,000 to less than 500,000	18
500,000 to less than 600,000	8
600,000 to less than 700,000	1
700,000 to less than 800,000	1
800,000 to less than 900,000	1
900,000 to less than 1 million	1
More than 1 million	1
No opinion	29

Is that more or fewer troops than Iraq has in the region?

	Nov. 29– Dec. 2
More troops	29%
Fewer troops	52
No opinion	19

Here is a list of countries. As I read each one, please tell me if that country has sent troops to the Persian Gulf to support the U.S. stand against Iraq, or not:

England?

	Nov. 29– Dec. 2
Yes	72%
No	16
No opinion	12

France?

	Nov. 29– Dec. 2
Yes	55%
No	27
No opinion	18

Syria?

	Nov. 29– Dec. 2
Yes	34%
No	34
No opinion	32

Egypt?

	Nov. 29– Dec. 2
Yes	49%
No	27
No opinion	24

Japan?

	Nov. 29– Dec. 2
Yes	16%
No	72
No opinion	12

Soviet Union?

	Nov. 29– Dec. 2
Yes	27%
No	61
No opinion	12

Canada?

	Nov. 29– Dec. 2
Yes	32%
No	45
No opinion	23

Jordan?

	Nov. 29– Dec. 2
Yes	25%
No	48
No opinion	27

If you could talk with President Bush for fifteen minutes about the Iraqi situation in the Persian Gulf, what would you tell him to do?

	Nov. 29– Dec. 2
Continue on; wait for sanctions	20%
Take action now; bomb Iraqis	12
Get out; withdraw troops	11
Do something or get out	5
Take it slow; be cautious; wait more	5
Get it over with	5
Avoid war or fighting at all costs	4
Use diplomacy, allies to talk to Iraq	4
Should have taken military action by now	2
Pray	1
Other	12
None	3
No opinion	16

If you knew that Iraq and Saddam Hussein would have nuclear weapons within two years, would you favor or oppose going to war against Iraq within the next several months to destroy Iraq's nuclear capability?

	Nov. 29– Dec. 2
Favor	70%
Oppose	25
No opinion	5

Asked of those who oppose military action: Regardless of how you feel now, if the United States does go to war against Iraq after the deadline passes, would you actively oppose U.S. involvement by participating in demonstrations, writing letters, and so forth, or not?

	Nov. 29– Dec. 2
Would actively oppose U.S. involvement	37%
Would not take such actions	58
No opinion	5

If you knew that the price of gas at the pump would go up by $1.00 a gallon if Iraq stays in Kuwait indefinitely, would you favor or oppose going to war against Iraq to drive it out of Kuwait within the next several months?

	Nov. 29– Dec. 2
Favor	43%
Oppose	51
No opinion	6

I am going to read you a list of several possible concessions the United States could make to Iraq. For each, please tell me whether or not you would favor it as a possible way to resolve the crisis, short of war:

Allow Iraq to redraw the border between Iraq and Kuwait to give Iraq some of Kuwait's territory and oil fields?

	Nov. 29– Dec. 2
Favor	30%
Oppose	64
No opinion	6

Agree to host an international summit combining discussion of the Iraq-Kuwait situation with discussion of the Palestinian problem in Israel?

Favor 68%
Oppose 26
No opinion 6

Agree to allow Iraq to stay in Kuwait but with a treaty agreement that it would not invade any other country?

Nov. 29–
Dec. 2

Favor 22%
Oppose 75
No opinion 3

Agree that an American envoy would meet directly with Saddam Hussein and try to negotiate terms under which Iraq would leave Kuwait?

Nov. 29–
Dec. 2

Favor 81%
Oppose 16
No opinion 3

Agree that President Bush should meet directly with Saddam Hussein to negotiate terms under which Iraq would leave Kuwait?

Nov. 29–
Dec. 2

Favor 74%
Oppose 24
No opinion 2

Here is a different question on the Persian Gulf situation. Do you think President Bush should stick closely to American public opinion when deciding what steps to take next— including the results of polls like this one— or should President Bush do what he thinks is best regardless of what the American public thinks?

Nov. 29–
Dec. 2

Bush should stick closely to public opinion when deciding 56%
Bush should do what he thinks is best regardless of what public thinks 41
No opinion 3

More generally, do you think the results of public opinion polls on the Persian Gulf crisis like this one should be widely published and discussed, or not?

Nov. 29–
Dec. 2

Yes 83%
No 14
No opinion 3

Are you aware that President Saddam Hussein has agreed to release all foreign hostages from Iraq by Christmas, or not?

Nov. 29–
Dec. 2

Yes 87%
No 13
No opinion .... *

*Less than 1%

How likely do you think it is that Hussein will actually follow through and release the hostages by Christmas? Is it very likely, only a 50-50 chance, or not very likely?

Nov. 29–
Dec. 2

Very likely 29%
Only 50-50 46
Not very likely 23
No opinion 2

If Hussein does follow through and release the hostages, what, if anything, do you think that the United States and its allies should do differently regarding Hussein and the Iraq-Kuwait situation?

	Nov. 29– Dec. 2

Do nothing different; keep things as
  they are 21%

Talk to Hussein; negotiate; peace talks;
  diplomacy 9

Get out; pull out troops; withdraw
  from there 8

Bomb; take action; initiate war 7

Wait a little longer; give Hussein,
  sanctions more time 6

Get Hussein out of Kuwait 4

Make sanctions even tougher 1

Other 5

Nothing 15

No opinion 24

Note: More than four months after President George Bush's initial decision to send troops to Saudi Arabia, the American public is deeply split over the implications and future of U.S. involvement in the Persian Gulf. The latest Gallup Poll finds that a majority still approves of the initial deployment, but there is no emerging consensus about what should be done next.

This could mean that if the United States initiates a war against Iraq in January, President Bush inevitably will face a sizable opposition. As many Americans think the situation is not worth going to war over as think it is. Depending on how the scenario plays out, anywhere from 40% to 55% will not approve of initiating military action.

Moreover, approval for the way President Bush is handling the crisis is down more than 20 percentage points from August, to 57%, and is now in the range maintained by President Lyndon Johnson in the early years of Vietnam and by President Richard Nixon at various points in his prosecution of that war. In short, respondents give Bush only an average—not exceptional—level of support for his handling of the Persian Gulf crisis.

They also, perhaps predictably, are souring somewhat on U.S. involvement in the Iraq-Kuwait situation. Approval of the decision to send troops to Saudi Arabia is down to 63% from an initial 80% in August, with 33% now disapproving.

Paradoxically, the proportion who supports U.S. initiation of war to drive Iraq out of Kuwait is up from earlier measures—although, as is often the case with public opinion, this measure varies widely depending on the context in which the situation is put to Americans, the alternatives they are given, and other factors. This volatility may be another indication of the unstable nature of U.S. attitudes toward war. The strongest support comes when the war is linked to several hypothetical situations: for example, that Iraq has a definite nuclear capability (70%).

The crucial point here is that large numbers of Americans remain unconvinced that war is necessary. If they could talk to President Bush for fifteen minutes, they most often would tell him to continue the current efforts and wait for the sanctions to have an effect (20%). There is also strong support for diplomatic efforts to avert a war, including the types of face-to-face talks being proposed between U.S. and Iraqi leaders (81%). Respondents strongly endorse the idea of Bush's talking directly with Saddam Hussein (74%), if necessary, and do not object to bringing in the Palestinian issue if that would help (68%).

A consistent 80% to 90% say that they have followed news reports of the Persian Gulf situation over the past four months. In the most recent Gallup Poll, 43% reply that they are following the story very closely, with another 46% saying fairly closely. Only 11% admit that they are not following it closely at all.

Public opinion polls routinely reveal that Americans have a low level of factual knowledge about stories in the news. However, public awareness of the specifics of the current Persian Gulf situation is remarkably high. Seventy-five percent can name the leader of Iraq (Saddam Hussein) without prompting—a surprisingly high number compared to factual questions asked of the public about other events.

A good number also can come close to correctly estimating how many U.S. troops are involved in the Persian Gulf area. Forty-three percent guess between 200,000 and 500,000—numbers that are or will be fairly accurate. Only 15% say less than 200,000, and only 13% guess more than one-half million (about three out of ten do not hazard a guess). Further, slightly over one half (52%) correctly say that the United States has fewer troops than Iraq (29% say that we have more).

Respondents also were asked, in a poll conducted near the end of November, to indicate which of eight countries do or do not have troops committed to the Persian Gulf area in support of U.S. efforts. Although there were a good many "no opinion" responses, the overall pattern conforms to the actual situation. For example, 72% correctly say that England has troops, while only 16% incorrectly cite Japan.

Despite various reports that President Bush has failed to articulate the reasons for U.S. involvement in the Persian Gulf, Americans continue to claim that they do have a clear idea of why we are there. In the most recent Gallup Poll, 73% say that they have a clear idea of why we are involved, not significantly different from the 74% who so claimed in mid-August.

A significant majority further say, in the most recent poll, that they are aware of Hussein's pledge to release all foreign hostages held in Kuwait and Iraq before Christmas. But there is no strong evidence that his move has had an impact on American public opinion. Basic attitudes toward U.S. actions in the Persian Gulf did not change substantially from the weekend of November 29–December 2, before Hussein had made his surprise announcement. Asked what the United States and its allies should do differently regarding Hussein and the Iraq-Kuwait situation as a result of the hostage release, only 6% respond that we should wait a little longer or give him more time, while 21% propose that nothing different be done.

There is no consensus among Americans about what moves should be made next in the Persian Gulf. A majority favors U.S. initiation of war in some circumstances, but not in others. In general, ongoing Gallup measurements in mid-November showed a jump in support for initiating a war to drive Iraq out of Kuwait, coinciding with the UN resolution, and for setting a firm last-chance date of January 15. The percentage who agreed that the United States should initiate a war after mid-January if Iraq did not leave Kuwait rose from 37% to 53% during the period from immediately

before Thanksgiving to one week afterward. The stronger support level has been maintained to date.

Additionally, when Americans are reminded of the UN resolution, the fact that allies would be supporting the United States, and the January 15 deadline, 61% say that they would approve our going to war with Iraq in order to drive the Iraqis out of Kuwait.

On the other hand, questions that do not specifically stress the January deadline or UN involvement generate lower levels of support for U.S.-initiated action. Given a choice between allowing the sanctions imposed by the international community against Iraq more time to work and taking stronger action against Hussein, including the use of armed force, the public splits down the middle: 47% to 46%.

The impact of polls on the current situation is interesting. A majority of respondents (56%) believes that President Bush should stick closely to American public opinion when deciding what steps to take next—"including the results of polls like this one," while 41% answer that he should do what he thinks best, regardless of what the public thinks. More generally, 83% say that the results of public opinion polls relating to the Persian Gulf crisis should be widely published and discussed.

DECEMBER 12
CHRISTMAS GIFTS

Interviewing Date: 11/29–12/2/90
Survey #GO 122009

Asked of those who celebrate Christmas or Christmas and Hanukkah: Roughly how much money do you think you personally will spend on Christmas gifts this year?

Less than $50	3%
$50 to $99	4
$100 to $249	19
$250 to $499	23
$500 to $749	20
$750 to $999	5
$1,000 to $1,499	10

$1,500 to $1,999 3
$2,000 or more 4
No opinion 9

> *Is that more, less, or about the same amount as you spent last Christmas?*

More 15%
Less 26
Same amount 57
No opinion 2

Note: 'Tis the season to be jolly—but once again Americans are grumbling about the mercenary side of Christmas. They appear to be spending slightly less this year than last on gifts, with an increase of about 6% in the group who say that they will be spending under $250 on their Christmas presents; there has been no change in the number who claim that they will be spending $1,000 or more. All in all, 26% say that the amount they are spending is less than last year, while 15% say it is more.

Compare your spending to the average American: The median amount being spent this year on Christmas gifts is $458. If you are spending under $250, you are a Scrooge compared to most people—about 65% will be spending more than that. On the other hand, if you are spending over $1,000, only 17% will be spending that amount or more.

What are the popular gifts for kids this year? More girls are asking for dolls than anything else, followed by clothes, Nintendo, bikes, and toys related to New Kids on the Block. For boys, the two gifts leading their wish list did not exist five years ago: Nintendo and Teenage Mutant Ninja Turtles.

DECEMBER 12
SUPER BOWL SITE

Interviewing Date: 11/29–12/2/90
Survey #GO 122009

> *As you may know, the commissioner of the National Football League has recommended that the NFL move the 1992 Super Bowl out of Arizona because the state's voters did not pass a proposal to make Martin Luther King, Jr., Day a state holiday. Do you favor or oppose the NFL moving the Super Bowl out of Arizona for this reason?*

Favor 25%
Oppose 63
No opinion 12

Note: Almost two thirds of respondents (63%) are opposed to moving the 1992 Super Bowl out of Arizona. The move has been recommended by the commissioner of the National Football League because Arizona voters have rejected a bill that would make Martin Luther King, Jr., Day a state holiday.

There is a difference by race in these attitudes, but perhaps not as much as might be expected. Sixty-six percent of whites and 40% of blacks oppose the move (58% of blacks support the idea).

DECEMBER 12
ALCOHOLIC BEVERAGES

Interviewing Date: 12/6–9/90
Survey #GO 122009

> *Do you have occasion to use alcoholic beverages such as liquor, wine, or beer, or are you a total abstainer?*

	Those who drink
National	57%

Selected National Trend

	Those who drink
1989	56%
1988	63
1987	65
1984	64
1981	70
1978	71
1976	71
1966	65
1958	55
1947	63
1939	58

Asked of those who drink (57% of the sample): When did you last take a drink of any kind of alcoholic beverage?

	1990	1987	1984
Within last 24 hours ..	29%	38%	39%
Over 1 day to 1 week ago	23	29	29
Over 1 week ago	47	32	31
No opinion	1	1	1

Asked of those who had a drink in the last seven days: Approximately how many drinks of any kind of alcoholic beverage did you drink in the past seven days?

1 to 7 drinks	78%
8 to 19	13
20 or more	5
No opinion	4

Also asked of those who had a drink in the last seven days: Do you most often drink liquor, wine, or beer?

Liquor	23%
Wine	22
Beer	51
All about equally (volunteered)	4
Cordials	*
No opinion	*

*Less than 1%

Asked of those who drink: Do you sometimes drink more than you think you should?

	Yes
National	23%

Selected National Trend

	Yes
1989	35%
1987	29
1985	32
1978	23

Also asked of those who drink: Do you plan to cut down or quit drinking within the next year?

Yes, cut down	12%
Yes, quit	8
Neither	78
No opinion	2

Selected National Trend

	Yes, cut down	Yes, quit	Neither	No opinion
1989	18%	7%	74%	1%
1987	12	3	82	3
1984	14	2	83	1

Asked of the entire sample: Has drinking ever been a cause of trouble in your family?

	Yes
National	23%

Selected National Trend

	Yes
1989	19%
1987	24
1985	21
1984	17
1981	22
1978	22
1976	17
1974	12
1966	12
1950	14

Note: Fifty-seven percent of Americans drink alcoholic beverages such as liquor, wine, or beer. The rest (43%) are total abstainers. These percentages are essentially unchanged from 1989.

The frequency of drinking has dropped significantly this year, however, perhaps as a result of continuing emphasis on the dangers of drinking while driving or while pregnant. Only 52% of those who define themselves as drinkers (that is, not total abstainers) recall having had a drink within the week before the survey. In 1989, 67% said that they had had their most recent drink within the week before the survey, as was also the case in two earlier surveys in the 1980s.

Only a small percentage admits to averaging more than one drink per day. And a significant majority of drinkers claim that they can handle their alcohol with no problem: only 23% admit that they sometimes drink more than they should, and only 20% say that they have any plans to cut back or quit drinking.

Still, 23% of all Americans, regardless of whether or not they themselves drink, say that alcohol has been a cause of trouble in their family. This number is roughly in line with Gallup's findings for the past twelve years, but higher than the numbers polled in the 1950s and 1960s.

DECEMBER 26
MOST ADMIRED MAN

Interviewing Date: 12/6–9/90
Survey #GO 922023

What man whom you have heard or read about, living today in any part of the world, do you admire the most? And who is your second choice?

The following are listed in order of frequency of mention, with first and second choices combined.

George Bush
Mikhail Gorbachev
Ronald Reagan
Pope John Paul II
Billy Graham
Nelson Mandela
Jesse Jackson
Donald Trump
Jimmy Carter
Lech Walesa

By way of comparison, the following are the results of the 1989 audit:

George Bush
Mikhail Gorbachev
Ronald Reagan
Pope John Paul II

Billy Graham
Lech Walesa
Donald Trump
Lee Iacocca
Jesse Jackson
Jimmy Carter ⎫
Bill Cosby ⎭ tied

Note: The man whom Americans admire the most in 1990 is the president of the United States, George Bush. For the third consecutive year Soviet Premier Mikhail Gorbachev is in second place. Others rounding out the top ten are former President Ronald Reagan, Pope John Paul II, evangelist Billy Graham, South Africa's Nelson Mandela, the Reverend Jesse Jackson, businessman Donald Trump, former President Jimmy Carter, and Polish leader Lech Walesa.

This is the first time ever for Nelson Mandela on the list. Lee Iacocca and Bill Cosby were among the top ten last year, but not in 1990.

There are a wide number of others mentioned this year. Sports heroes include Michael Jordan, Larry Bird, Bo Jackson, Muhammad Ali, Richard Petty, Clyde Drexler, Tom Landry, David Robinson, Joe Montana, Magic Johnson, Joe Paterno, Dan Marino, and A. J. Foyt. In entertainment, Bill Cosby, Marlon Brando, Kenny Rogers, Billy Dee Williams, Sylvester Stallone, David Bowie, radio talk-show host Rush Limbaugh, Bob Hope, Robert Redford, Johnny Carson, Clint Eastwood, Mel Gibson, Neil Diamond, Tom Cruise, Chevy Chase, Arsenio Hall, Martin Scorsese, Sean Connery, Phil Collins, Michael Landon, Bruce Willis, Frank Sinatra, Stephen Spielberg, and Arnold Schwarzenegger are named. And in politics and public life, Dan Quayle, Henry Kissinger, "the commander in the Persian Gulf," Jack Kemp, Louis Farrakhan, James Baker, Ted Kennedy, Bishop Desmond Tutu, Doug Wilder, Oliver North, Harvey Gant, Dick Cheney, Sam Nunn, "the new prime minister from England," Helmut Kohl, Strom Thurmond, Daniel Moynihan, and Bob Kerrey are among those cited.

DECEMBER 26
MOST ADMIRED WOMAN

Interviewing Date: 12/6–9/90
Survey #GO 922023

Which woman whom you have heard or read about, living today in any part of the world, do you admire the most? And who is your second choice?

The following are listed in order of frequency of mention, with first and second choices combined.

Margaret Thatcher
Barbara Bush
Mother Teresa of Calcutta
Nancy Reagan
Oprah Winfrey
Elizabeth Taylor
Cher
Elizabeth Dole
Jacqueline Kennedy Onassis
Corazon Aquino ⎫
Betty Ford   ⎬ tied
Jeane Kirkpatrick ⎭

By way of comparison, the following are the results of the 1989 audit:

Margaret Thatcher
Mother Teresa of Calcutta
Barbara Bush
Nancy Reagan
Corazon Aquino
Oprah Winfrey
Betty Ford
Diana, Princess of Wales
Sandra Day O'Connor
Jacqueline Kennedy Onassis

Note: First Lady Barbara Bush has moved from third place on last year's most admired list to second this year. Mother Teresa, second last year, is now third, while first is still British Prime Minister Margaret Thatcher. Other women in the top ten include former First Lady Nancy Reagan,

talk show hostess Oprah Winfrey, actress Elizabeth Taylor, actress and singer Cher, former Secretary of Labor Elizabeth Dole, former First Lady Jacqueline Kennedy Onassis, President Corazon Aquino of the Philippines, former First Lady Betty Ford, and former UN ambassador Jeane Kirkpatrick.

Diana, Princess of Wales, and Supreme Court Justice Sandra Day O'Connor are no longer on the top ten. A perennial favorite, however, is former First Lady Jacqueline Kennedy, who has appeared twenty-six times since her first listing in 1960.

The other mentions tend to come from the entertainment and news fields and include such women as Jane Fonda, Katharine Hepburn, Heather Locklear, Jessica Lange, Jane Pauley, Maria Shriver, Dolly Parton, Bernadette Peters, Madonna, Diana Ross, Eartha Kitt, Joan Collins, Lena Horne, Racquel Welch, Connie Chung, Bette Midler, Emmylou Harris, Julia Roberts, Carol Burnett, Whitney Houston, Whoopi Goldberg, Barbara Walters, Meryl Streep, Tina Turner, Barbra Streisand, Michelle Pfeiffer, and Joan Rivers. Also named are women in politics and public life, including Benazir Bhutto, Sandra Day O'Connor, Queen Elizabeth, Princess Diana, "the new lieutenant governor in Iowa," Diane Feinstein, Ann Richards, Barbara Jordan, Winnie Mandela, Pat Schroeder, Raisa Gorbachev, Rose Kennedy, Houston Mayor Kathy Whitmire, "the woman who started MADD," Pat Nixon, Rosalyn Carter, Coretta Scott King, and Kitty Dukakis.

DECEMBER 28
SALARIES OF OFFICIALS AND EXECUTIVES

Interviewing Date: 11/15–18/90
Survey #GO 122008

For each of the following groups, please tell me whether you think the pay they receive is more than they are worth or less than they are worth: The top executives of the one hundred largest U.S. corporations? Top elected officials; for example, U.S. senators, congressmen, and governors? The one hundred top administration officials in the U.S. government; for example, department heads and the like? In general, would you say they are paid too much or too little for what they do?

Asked of those who replied "too much" or "too little": Are they paid a lot (too much/too little), or only a little (too much/too little)?

	Business executives	Elected officials	Appointed officials
A lot too much	58%	47%	41%
A little too much	13	22	18
About right	10	12	11
A little too little	2	7	7
A lot too little	1	2	3
Some too much, some too little (volunteered)	15	10	19
No opinion	1	*	1

*Less than 1%

Percent Saying Paid a Lot Too Much

	Business executives	Elected officials	Appointed officials
National	58%	47%	41%

By Income

Under $30,000	59%	56%	47%
$30,000–$49,999	63	45	46
$50,000 and over	55	33	27

By Education

College graduate	60%	34%	29%
Some college	55	45	43
No college	58	54	46

By Politics

Conservative Democrats	56%	54%	51%
Moderate, liberal Democrats	69	44	39
Republicans	56	46	38
Independents	59	47	39

Note: Despite the fact that many U.S. congressmen and senators claim that they are paid too little, Americans have little sympathy for their financial plight. Over two thirds (69%) think that the top one hundred elected officials in the federal government are paid too much, while only 9% think that they are paid too little. Additionally, 59% say that appointed government officials make too much money.

Not just congressmen and senators are perceived as making too much, however. There is even less approval of the pay levels of top corporate executives in this country. Seventy-one percent of respondents think that top business leaders are paid too much.

INDEX

A

Aaron, Hank
    as greatest baseball player, 46
Abortion
    favor Idaho law to make illegal, 45
    favor New Hampshire law to legalize, 45
    as issue handled by Bush, 74
        national trend, 74
    legal under any circumstances, 45
        national trend, 45
    stand on, as Bush's greatest achievement, 18, 75, 152
Advertising practitioners
    honesty rating, 23
        national trend, 24
Aerobics
    as most effective way to lose weight, 164
    your participation in, 43
        by women, 44
        frequency of participation, 44
AIDS
    cure will be found, by year 2000, 1
    as most important problem, 38, 84
Alcoholic beverages
    avoiding, as effective way to lose weight, 164
    drinking as cause of trouble in your family, 175
        national trend, 175
    how many did you drink in past seven days, 175
    increase taxes on, to reduce federal budget deficit, 56
    in federal budget plan, favor raising taxes on beer, wine, and liquor, 128
    most often drink liquor, wine, or beer, 175
    plan to cut down or quit within next year, 175
        national trend, 175
    problems with will increase by year 2000, 3
    sometimes drink more than you should, 175
        national trend, 175
    when did you last take a drink, 175
    your use of, 174
        national trend, 174

America
    who first discovered (listed), 130
Aquino, Corazon
    as most admired woman, 177
Arabs
    peace between Israelis and, by year 2000, 2
    See also Palestinian Arabs; Saudi Arabia
Archery
    your participation in, 43
Atlanta
    safe to live in or visit, 119
Atomic bomb
    approve of using, on Japanese cities in 1945, 91-92
        national trend, 92
    ever been used on an enemy in wartime, 91
    good or bad that it was developed, 92
        national trend, 92
    in another world war, should we use it, 92
        national trend, 92
    where was it used, 91
Auto racing
    your favorite sport to watch, 33

B

Babbitt, Bruce
    have heard of, 51
    as nominee for Democratic presidential candidate, 50
Badminton
    your participation in, 43
Bankers
    honesty rating, 23
        national trend, 24
Banks
    your confidence in, 102
        national trend, 102
Baseball
    are professional players overpaid, 36
    heard about possible strike, 20
    how interested are you in following, 34
    how many hours do you spend watching, 36
    if a strike, do you favor owners or players, 20
    major league, and adding two to four more teams to, 37
    major league, and allowing players to use aluminum bats, 37
    major league, and designated-hitter rule, 37
    major league, and elimination of designated hitter in both leagues, 37
    major league, greatest player of all time, 46
        national trend, 46
    major league, and increase in number of teams, 37
    major league, and increases in salary paid to players, 37
    major league, and increasing use of artificial turf, 37

Baseball (*continued*)

    major league, and interleague play during regular
        season, 37

    major league, more fun to watch today than years
        ago, 36

    major league, and playoffs to determine World
        Series, 37

    major league, and use of designated hitter in both
        leagues, 37

    major league, and use of domed stadiums, 37

    players care more about the game today than
        years ago, 36

    requires its players to be the best athletes, 36

    will there be a strike this season, 20

    your favorite major league team (listed), 35

    your favorite sport to watch, 33

        national trend, 33

    your participation in, 43

Basketball

    are professional players overpaid, 36

    how interested are you in following, 34

    how many hours do you spend watching, 36

    requires its players to be the best athletes, 36

    you and your friends participate in, 27

    your favorite NBA team (listed), 35–36

    your favorite sport to watch, 33

        national trend, 33

    your participation in, 43

        by men, 44

Bentsen, Lloyd

    have heard of, 51

    as nominee for Democratic presidential candidate,
        50

Berlin Wall

    as Bush's greatest achievement, 18, 75, 152

Bible

    how much of the Old Testament and New Testa-
        ment have you ever read, 158

    how often do you read, 158

    involved in study groups or classes, 158

    know whether public schools make facilities
        available after hours for student religious
        groups, 158

    know whether public schools offer elective
        courses in, 158

    know whether public schools teach about major
        religions, 158

    know whether public schools use in classes, 158

    tell me the names of the first Four Gospels, 158

Bicycle touring and racing

    your participation in, 43

        by women, 44

Bicycling

    as most effective way to lose weight, 164

    your participation in, 43

        by men, 43

        by women, 44

        frequency of participation, 44

        participation changes by decade, 44

Biden, Joseph

    have heard of, 51

    as nominee for Democratic presidential candidate,
        50

Big business

    your confidence in, 103

        national trend, 103

Billiards

    your participation in, 43

        by men, 44

        by women, 44

        participation changes by decade, 44

Blacks

    quality of life has gotten better for, 150

    Republican or Democratic party best serves, 145

        national trend, 145

    what percent of population, 31

    See also Racial tolerance; South Africa

Bodybuilding

    your participation in, 43

Boston

    safe to live in or visit, 119

Bowling

    your favorite sport to watch, 33

    your participation in, 43

        by men, 44

        by women, 44

        frequency of participation, 44

        participation changes by decade, 44

Boxing

    your favorite sport to watch, 33

Bradley, Bill

    have heard of, 51

    as nominee for Democratic presidential candidate,
        50

Budget, federal

    favor additional tax on luxury items, 128

    favor applying payroll Medicare tax to wages up
        to $73,000, 129

    favor cutting defense spending, 128

    favor cutting farm subsidies, 129

    favor cutting Medicare benefits, 129

    favor holding spending on domestic programs to
        rate of inflation, 128

    favor proposed plan, 128

    favor raising federal gasoline tax, 129

    favor raising income tax rate, 128

    favor raising taxes on airline tickets, 129

    favor raising taxes on beer, wine, and liquor,
        128

    favor raising taxes on cigarettes, 128

    pass proposed plan or let Gramm-Rudman-
        Hollings law take effect, 128

    raise taxes on those with adjusted incomes of
        $200,000 and over, 129

    as reason for dissatisfaction, 141

    reduce spending on defense further, 129

    reduce spending on domestic programs, 129

    reduce tax on capital gains, 129

Budget deficit, federal
approve of Bush's announcement that he would
increase taxes to reduce, 78
Bush making progress on reducing, 19, 156
national trend, 156
as Bush's greatest achievement, 18, 75, 152
Bush should consider new taxes to help reduce,
57
expense of Vietnam War led to growing, 49
handled by Bush, 73
national trend, 73
how important is reducing, 56
if taxes were raised to reduce, which one would
be your first choice (listed), 56
as most important problem, 38, 84, 149
national trend, 84
as reason for dissatisfaction, 141
reduce, if defense budget is cut, 6
reduce by reducing spending or raising taxes, 56
Building contractors
honesty rating, 23
national trend, 24
Bumpers, Dale
have heard of, 51
as nominee for Democratic presidential candidate,
51
Bush, Barbara
as most admired woman, 177
Bush, George
and abortion issue, 74
national trend, 74
and agenda at Washington summit, 54
approval rating, 6, 17–18, 55, 73, 84, 96, 99,
126, 136, 140, 140–41, 148, 151, 159,
165
national trend, 7, 55, 73, 84, 96, 99, 126,
140, 141, 148
approval rating compared to predecessors, 7
approve of his announcement that he would increase taxes to reduce deficit, 78
approve of his decision to send 150,000 additional troops to Middle East, 159
approve of his invitation to De Klerk, 22
and budget deficit, 73
national trend, 73
and Central America situation, 7, 75
national trend, 7, 75
described as an active or passive president, 78,
155
national trend, 155
described as confident or insecure, 77, 154
national trend, 77, 154
described as intelligent or only average, 77,
154
national trend, 77, 154
described as a leader or follower, 77, 155
national trend, 78, 155
described as sincere or insincere, 77, 154
national trend, 77, 154

described as steady or undependable, 77, 154
national trend, 77, 154
described as strong or weak, 77, 155
national trend, 77, 155
described as warm or cold, 77, 155
national trend, 77, 155
doing better job as president than you expected,
75, 156
national trend, 75, 157
do you think he should be reelected, 151
and drug problem, 8, 74
national trend, 8, 74
and Eastern Europe situation, 7, 74
national trend, 7, 74
and economic conditions, 73
national trend, 73
and education policy, 74
national trend, 74
and environmental issues, 74
national trend, 74
favor proposed federal budget plan of, 128
and foreign policy, 74
national trend, 74
greatest achievement (listed) to date, 18, 75,
152–53
have heard of, 51
happen to hear about summit in Helsinki between
Bush and Gorbachev, 122
and homelessness, 74
national trend, 74
if he does choose someone new, appoint Quayle
to cabinet post, 29
if you could talk with him about the situation in
the Persian Gulf, what would you tell him
to do (listed), 170
making progress on avoiding raising taxes, 19,
156
national trend, 156
making progress on getting drug crisis under
control, 19, 156
national trend, 156
making progress on improving educational standards, 19, 155
national trend, 156
making progress on improving the lot of minorities and the poor, 19, 156
national trend, 156
making progress on improving quality of the environment, 19, 156
national trend, 156
making progress on increasing respect for the
United States abroad, 19, 155
national trend, 155
making progress on keeping America prosperous,
19, 155
national trend, 155
making progress on keeping nation out of war,
19, 155
national trend, 155

Bush, George (*continued*)
  making progress on reducing the crime rate, 19,
      156
    national trend, 156
  making progress on reducing federal budget defi-
      cit, 19, 156
    national trend, 156
  as most admired man, 176
  most to blame for Savings and Loan crisis, 86
  as nominee for Republican presidential candidate,
      51
  performance rating on his being an efficient man-
      ager, 75, 153
    national trend, 75, 153
  performance rating on his being a good represen-
      tative of the United States, 76, 154
    national trend, 76, 154
  performance rating on his being an inspirational
      leader, 76, 154
    national trend, 76, 154
  performance rating on his communicating his
      ideas to the public, 76, 153
    national trend, 76, 153
  performance rating on his developing programs to
      address pressing problems, 76, 153
    national trend, 76, 153
  performance rating on his following through on
      his ideas, 76, 153
    national trend, 76, 153
  performance rating on his making good appoint-
      ments, 75, 153
    national trend, 75, 153
  performance rating on his working effectively
      with Congress, 76, 154
    national trend, 76, 154
  and Persian Gulf situation, 93, 95, 97, 104, 114,
      136, 149, 159, 166
    national trend, 95, 97, 104, 114, 136, 159,
        166
  and poverty, 74
    national trend, 74
  as reason for dissatisfaction, 141
  and relations with Soviet Union, 74
    national trend, 74
  and Savings and Loan crisis, 75
  should be able to go to war against Iraq without
      approval from Congress, 159
  should keep pledge not to raise taxes, 57
  should keep Quayle as running mate, 29
  should stick closely to public opinion when de-
      ciding what steps to take next on Persian
      Gulf situation, 171
  as U.S. concession, agree that he should meet
      with Hussein to negotiate terms, 171
  whether he keeps Quayle, as important in your
      vote, 29
  will be able to keep his pledge of no new taxes,
      57

  would like to see him run for president in 1992,
      151
Bush administration
  and progress in combating drugs, 8
  as reason for dissatisfaction, 141
Business and professional people
  Republican or Democratic party best serves, 145
Business executives
  honesty rating, 23
    national trend, 24
  paid too much or too little, 177-78

C

Calisthenics
  your participation in, 43
Camping
  your participation in, 43
    by men, 44
    by women, 44
    frequency of participation, 44
Canada
  has sent troops to the Persian Gulf, 170
Cancer
  cure will be found, by year 2000, 1
Canoeing
  your participation in, 43
Cars
  important to own expensive car, 70
  in federal budget plan, favor additional tax on lux-
      ury automobiles, 128
  kept car running clean, to improve quality of the en-
      vironment, 42
  types people will drive, by year 2000, 2
Car salesmen
  honesty rating, 23
    national trend, 24
Carter, Jimmy
  approval rating, 161
    retrospective versus actual ratings, 161
  approval rating compared to Bush, 7
  approval rating since he left office, 161
  as most admired man, 176
Cats. *See* Pets
Census, U.S.
  confident that Census Bureau will not release infor-
      mation, 30
  government should estimate to count minorities and
      the poor, 30
  has your household received 1990 form, 44
  have you filled out form, 44
  how complicated was it, 45
  how many people currently live in the United
      States, 31
  taken every year, 30
  what percent of population is black, 31
  what percent of population is Hispanic, 31
  what percent of population is Jewish, 31

D

Dallas
  safe to live in or visit, 119
Darts
  your participation in, 43
Defense, national
  amount of money Washington should spend for, 99
    national trend, 99
  in federal budget plan, favor cutting defense spend-
    ing, 128
  reduce spending further, 129
  See also Military spending
De Klerk, F. W.
  approve of Bush's invitation to, 22
Democratic party
  best serves blacks, 145
    national trend, 145
  best serves business and professional people, 145
    national trend, 145
  best serves farmers, 145
    national trend, 145
  best serves labor union members, 146
    national trend, 146
  best serves people like yourself, 144
    national trend, 144
  best serves poor people, 144
  best serves retired people, 145
    national trend, 145
  best serves skilled workers, 145
    national trend, 145
  best serves small-business people, 145
    national trend, 145
  best serves unemployed people, 146
    national trend, 146
  best serves unskilled workers, 146
    national trend, 146
  best serves wealthy people, 144
  best serves women, 144
    national trend, 144
  better at keeping country prosperous, 118, 142
    national trend, 118, 142
  for Congress, which party's candidate would you
    like to see win, 118, 142, 144, 148
    national trend, 118, 142
  likely to vote for candidate for Congress from your
    district, 144
  more likely to keep United States out of war, 117,
    142
    national trend, 118, 142
  nominees for presidential candidate, 50-51
  why (listed) would you like to see the Democratic
    candidate win in your congressional district,
    148
  your affiliation with, 51
    national trend, 52
Dentists
  honest rating, 23
    national trend, 24

Depression
  as most important problem, 38
  will happen by year 2000, 1
Detroit
  safe to live in or visit, 119
Diana, Princess of Wales
  as most admired woman, 177
DiMaggio, Joe
  as greatest baseball player, 46
Discrimination
  enough federal laws aimed at reducing, 150
Distance and marathon running
  your participation in, 43
Divorce rate
  will increase or decrease, by year 2000, 3
Doctors, medical
  honesty rating, 23
    national trend, 23
Dogs. *See* Pets
Dole, Elizabeth
  have heard of, 51
  as nominee for Republican presidential candidate,
    51
  as most admired woman, 177
Dole, Robert
  have heard of, 51
  as nominee for Republican presidential candidate,
    51
Druggists and pharmacists
  honesty rating, 23
    national trend, 23
Drugs and drug problem
  activities (listed) in government's fight against, 8-9
    national trend, 8, 9
  Bush making progress on getting crisis under con-
    trol, 19, 156
    national trend, 156
  confidence in border patrol to fight against, 9
  confidence in courts in fight against, 9
  confidence in drug treatment centers in fight
    against, 9
  confidence in federal drug agents in fight against, 9
  confidence in police in fight against, 9
  confidence in public schools in fight against, 9
  eliminate, to help reduce crime, 123
  as factor most responsible for crime, 123
  increase spending on, if defense budget is cut, 6
  legalization, and government's efforts to educate
    people about dangers of, 10-11
    national trend, 11
  legalization a good or bad idea, 9-10
  legalize, to help reduce crime, 123
  legalized drugs, and getting addicts to participate in
    treatment programs, 10
  legalized drugs would increase amount of drug-
    related crime, 10
    national trend, 10
  legalized drugs would increase drug overdoses, 10
    national trend, 10

Drugs and drug problem (*continued*)
    legalized drugs would increase drug use in public
        schools, 10
        national trend, 10
    legalized drugs would increase number of addicts,
        10
        national trend, 10
    as most important problem, 38, 84, 149
        national trend, 84
    problem handled by Bush, 8, 74
        national trend, 8, 74
    problems with drug abuse will increase, by year
        2000, 3
    progress made by Bush administration in combating,
        8
    as reason for dissatisfaction, 141
    war on, as Bush's greatest achievement, 18, 75,
        152
Dukakis, Michael
    have heard of, 51
    as nominee for Democratic presidential candidate,
        51
Du Pont, Pierre
    have heard of, 51
    as nominee for Republican presidential candidate,
        51

E

Eastern Europe
    changes in, as Bush's greatest achievement, 18, 75,
        152
    defense spending affected by changes in, 5
    defense spending reduced, as result of changes in, 5
    situation in, handled by Bush, 7, 74
        national trend, 7, 74
Economic conditions
    handled by Bush, 73
        national trend, 73
Economy
    as Bush's greatest achievement, 18, 75, 152
    local, and reduced defense spending, 6
    as most important problem, 38, 84, 149
    as reason for dissatisfaction, 141
    U.S., and reduced defense spending, 5-6
Education
    Bush making progress on improving standards, 19,
        155
    as Bush's greatest achievement, 152
    developing best system of, 4
    easier or harder for parents to afford college, by
        year 2000, 3
    increase spending on, if defense budget is cut, 6
    know whether public schools make facilities availa-
        ble after hours for student religious groups,
        158

    know whether public schools offer elective courses
        in Bible studies, 158
    know whether public schools teach about major
        religions, 158
    know whether public schools use Bible in classes,
        158
    lack of, as factor most responsible for crime, 123
    legalized drugs would increase drug use in public
        schools, 10
        national trend, 10
    policy handled by Bush, 74
        national trend, 74
    quality of, as most important problem, 38, 84, 149
    to help reduce crime, 123
    way children are taught, by year 2000, 2
    your confidence in public schools, 101
        national trend, 101
    your confidence in public schools in fight against
        drugs, 9
    See also Racial tolerance
Egypt
    has sent troops to the Persian Gulf, 169
Eisenhower, Dwight
    approval rating, 161
        retrospective versus actual ratings, 161
    approval rating compared to Bush, 7
    as president most responsible for getting country
        into Vietnam War, 47
Elderly people
    having pets would provide them with a more satis-
        fying life, 108
    in federal budget plan, favor cutting Medicare bene-
        fits for, 129
    way they are cared for, by year 2000, 2
Energy
    clean source will be developed, by year 2000, 1
    crisis will occur, by year 2000, 1
    doing anything to reduce your use of, 96; and what
        is that (listed), 96
        national trend, 96
    how serious is the energy situation, 96
Engineers
    honesty rating, 23
        national trend, 24
England
    has sent troops to the Persian Gulf, 169
Environment
    are you a strong environmentalist, 38
    better or worse, by year 2000, 1
    Bush making progress on improving quality of, 19,
        156
        national trend, 156
    business and industry is too worried about, 41
    consider yourself to be an environmentalist, 38
        national trend, 38
    does your community require sorting so that materi-
        als can be recycled, 42

favor a new clean air law, 41

government is too worried about, 41

have avoided buying a product because it was not recyclable, 42

have avoided using aerosol sprays, 41

have boycotted a company's products, 42

have contributed money to group, 42

have done other things (listed) to improve quality of, 42

have done volunteer work, 42

have used cloth rather than disposable diapers, 42

have voluntarily recycled, 41

how much progress have we made in dealing with environmental problems, 41

issues handled by Bush, 74
    national trend, 74

life will continue without major disruptions only if (actions listed), 40

as most important problem, 38, 84, 149

protection of the environment, or economic growth, should be given priority, 42
    national trend, 42

public today is too worried about, 41

United States does more than other countries, 41

we will have our environmental problems well under control in twenty years, 41

worry about acid rain, 40
    national trend, 40

worry about air pollution, 39
    national trend, 39

worry about contamination by radioactivity, 40
    national trend, 40

worry about contamination by toxic waste, 39
    national trend, 39

worry about damage to ozone layer, 40
    national trend, 40

worry about the "greenhouse effect," 40
    national trend, 40

worry about loss of natural habitats for wildlife, 39
    national trend, 39

worry about loss of tropical rain forests, 40
    national trend, 40

worry about ocean and beach pollution, 39
    national trend, 39

worry about pollution of drinking water, 38

worry about pollution of rivers, lakes, and reservoirs, 39
    national trend, 39

Eriksson, Leif
    first discovered America, 130

Ethnic group tensions
    better or worse, by year 2000, 1

Europe
    on Washington summit agenda, reduce U.S. and Soviet forces in, 54

reduce defense spending, by reducing number of U.S. troops based in, 5
See also Eastern Europe

F

Families
    breakdown of family, as factor most responsible for crime, 123
    family life better or worse, by year 2000, 1
    more or less time will be spent on, by year 2000, 2
    and women's movement, easier or harder to earn comfortable living, 13
    See also Children; Men; Women

Farmers
    Republican or Democratic party best serves, 145
    national trend, 145

Farm subsidies
    in federal budget plan, favor cutting, 129

Feinstein, Dianne
    have heard of, 51
    as nominee for Democratic presidential candidate, 51

Figure skating
    your favorite sport to watch, 33

Financial situation
    better or worse, by year 2000, 1
    chance to become rich today, 70
    consider yourself to be rich or poor, 68-69
    distribution of wealth is fair, 69
        national trend, 69
    does America benefit from having class of rich people, 72
    easier to get rich today than it used to be, 70
    envy rich people, 70
    important not to worry about unexpected expenses, 70
    important to contribute to charities, 71
    important to do anything you want to, 71
    important to entertain lavishly, 71
    important to gain recognition, 71
    important to have servants, 70
    important to own big house, 70
    important to own expensive car, 70
    important to own expensive clothes, 70
    important to pass money on to your children, 71
    important to quit worrying about losing your job, 71
    important to send your children through college without financial strain, 71
    important to travel around world, 70
    job the rich do in contributing back to society, 172
    likely that you ever will be rich, 69
    more difficult for rich than poor person to love God and one's neighbors, 72
    more often the case if person is rich, effort or luck, 69

energy crisis will occur, 1
environmental pollution, better or worse, 1
family life, better or worse, 1
financial situation, better or worse, 1
health, better or worse, 1
homelessness, better or worse, 1
inflation rate will increase or decrease, 3
international terrorism, better or worse, 1
job, better or worse, 1
kinds of food will be different, 2
kinds of jobs will be different, 2
kinds of music will be different, 2
kinds of programs on television will be different, 2
life expectancy will have risen, 1
life will be very different, 2
life will get easier or harder, 2
more or less time will be spent on families, 2
more or less time will be spent on household chores, 2
more or less time will be spent on jobs, 2
more or less time will be spent on leisure and recreational activities, 2
nuclear war between Soviet Union and United States will happen, 2
nuclear war will be started, 2
number of couples choosing not to have children will increase or decrease, 3
number of working mothers will increase or decrease, 3
optimistic or pessimistic about future of United States, 1
optimistic or pessimistic about future of world, 1
optimistic or pessimistic about your future, 1
peace between countries, better or worse, 1
peace between Israelis and Arabs will happen, 2
poverty, better or worse, 1
problems with alcohol and drug abuse will increase or decrease, 3
quality of life, better or worse, 1
Soviet communism will have vanished, 2
Soviet Union and West will live peacefully together, 1
tensions between racial and ethnic groups, better or worse, 1
types of cars will be different, 2
types of homes will be different, 2
types of medical care will be different, 2
unemployment rate will increase or decrease, 3
U.S. forces will be drawn into Central America, 1
way children are raised will be different, 2
way children are taught will be different, 2
way elderly are cared for will be different, 2
way people dress will be different, 2
way people shop will be different, 2
way people spend free time will be different, 2
way people worship will be different, 2
workers will be replaced by robots, 1
world hunger will be eliminated, 2
worldwide economic depression will happen, 1

G

Gasoline
increase taxes on, to reduce federal budget deficit, 56
in federal budget plan, favor raising federal tax on, 129
Gasoline crisis
by how many cents have prices gone up, 96
doing anything to reduce your use of gasoline, 96; and what is that (listed), 96
national trend, 96
has the price gone up, 96
how serious is the energy situation, 96
if the price of gas goes up by $1.00 a gallon if Iraq stays in Kuwait, would you favor going to war, 170
if there is another gas crisis, would you favor direct U.S. military action against Iraq, 93
price increase was necessary because of Iraqi situation, 96
prices, as reason for dissatisfaction, 141
Gehrig, Lou
as greatest baseball player, 46
national trend, 46
Gephardt, Richard
have heard of, 51
as nominee for Democratic presidential candidate, 51
German reunification
good or bad for United States and its allies, 22, 127
national trend, 22, 127
if reunited, country might become aggressor nation, 22-23, 127
national trend, 23, 127
Golf
requires its players to be the best athletes, 36
your favorite sport to watch, 33
your participation in, 43
frequency of participation, 44
participation changes by decade, 44
Gorbachev, Mikhail
and agenda at Washington summit, 54
do you trust what he says, 54, 122
national trend, 122
getting along with, as Bush's greatest achievement, 18, 75, 152
hear about summit in Helsinki between Bush and, 122
as most admired man, 176
your overall opinion of, 53, 121
national trend, 53, 121
Government
dissatisfaction with, as most important problem, 38, 84, 149
Government officials, top
paid too much or too little, 178
Government spending
cut, as reason for dissatisfaction, 141
likely to be reduced next year, 56

Government spending (*continued*)
    overseas, as reason for dissatisfaction, 141
    reduce to reduce budget deficit, 56
Governors
    paid too much or too little, 178
Graham, Billy
    as most admired man, 176
Gun control
    ban possession of handguns except by police, 124
        national trend, 124
    favor law requiring person who carries gun to have
        a license, 124
        national trend, 124
    favor law requiring seven-day waiting period before
        purchase, 124
        national trend, 124
    favor legislation banning possession of plastic guns
        invisible to metal detectors, 125
        national trend, 125
    favor legislation banning possession of "Saturday
        night specials," 124-25
        national trend, 125
    favor legislation banning possession of semiauto-
        matic assault guns, 125
        national trend, 125
    favor registration of all handguns, 124
        national trend, 124
    guns as factor most responsible for crime, 123
    have a gun in the house, 125
        national trend, 125
    laws covering sale of firearms should be more strict,
        124
        national trend, 124
    number of guns kept in your house, 125

H

Haig, Alexander
    have heard of, 51
    as nominee for Republican presidential candidate,
        51
Handball
    your participation in, 43
Handicapped people
    having pets would provide them with a more satis-
        fying life, 108
Hanukkah gifts
    how much money will you spend on, this year, 173-
        74
Hart, Gary
    have heard of, 51
    as nominee for Democratic presidential candidate,
        51
Health
    better or worse, by year 2000, 1
    has your weight ever caused you health problems,
        163

    trying to lose weight more to improve your appear-
        ance or your, 163
Health care
    as most important problem, 149
    as reason for dissatisfaction, 141
Hiking
    your participation in, 43
        by men, 44
        by women, 44
Hispanic people
    what percent of population, 31
Homelessness
    better or worse, by year 2000, 1
    handled by Bush, 74
        national trend, 74
    increase spending on, if defense budget is cut, 6
    as most important problem, 38, 84, 149
        national trend, 84
Home ownership
    in the next ten years, if you bought a house, would
        it be worth a lot more money ten years from
        now, 104
    ten years ago, if you had bought a house, would it
        now be worth a lot more than you paid for
        it, 103-4
Honesty and ethical standards
    rating by profession (listed), 23
        national trend, 23-24
Horseback riding
    your participation in, 43
        frequency of participation, 44
        participation changes by decade, 44
Horse racing
    your favorite sport to watch, 33
Household chores
    how much of each job (listed) do you usually do
        yourself, 13-14
    more or less time will be spent on, by year 2000, 2
    your household has domestic help to help with, 14
    your husband/wife share work equally, 16
Housing
    blacks have as good a chance as whites to get,
        63
    easier or harder to buy a house, by year 2000, 3
    types of homes people will live in, by year 2000,
        2
    See also Home ownership
Houston
    safe to live in or visit, 119
Hunger
    as most important problem, 38
    will be eliminated, by year 2000, 2
Hunting
    your participation in, 43
        frequency of participation, 44
        participation changes by decade, 44
Hussein, Saddam. *See* Persian Gulf situation

I

Iacocca, Lee
  as most admired man, 176
Ice hockey
  are professional players overpaid, 36
  how interested are you in following, 34
  how many hours do you spend watching, 36
  requires its players to be the best athletes, 36
  your favorite sport to watch, 33
Ice skating
  your favorite sport to watch, 33
  your participation in, 43
Independents
  your affiliation with, 51
    national trend, 52
Inflation
  as most important problem, 38, 84, 149
Inflation rate
  in federal budget plan, favor holding spending on
    domestic programs to, 128
  will increase or decrease, by year 2000, 3
Insurance salesmen
  honesty rating, 23
    national trend, 24
Interest rates
  as most important problem, 38
International problems
  as most important problem, 38, 149
Iraq
  as most important problem, 149
  See also Persian Gulf situation
Israel
  peace between Israelis and Arabs, by year 2000, 2
  as U.S. concession, agree to summit combining dis-
    cussion of Iraq-Kuwait situation with Pales-
    tinian problem in, 170-71
  See also Middle East situation

J

Jackson, Jesse
  have heard of, 51
  as most admired man, 176
  as nominee for Democratic presidential candidate,
    51
Japan
  has sent troops to the Persian Gulf, 169
  United States has lost ground to, in quality of goods
    it manufactures, 147
Jews
  what percent of population, 31
Jobs
  better or worse, by year 2000, 1
  blacks have as good a chance as whites to get, 62-
    63

describe business conditions in your community, 85-
  86
  national trend, 86
easier or harder for parents to raise children and
  have jobs at same time, by year 2000, 3
easier or harder for young people to find, by year
  2000, 2
has your weight ever caused you to lose out on job
  opportunities or promotions, 162
how many hours per week do you work, 16
important to quit worrying about your job, 71
in ideal family situation, 58
kinds people will have, by year 2000, 2
likely that you will lose your job, 86
  national trend, 86
man and woman earn same amount, 16
more or less time will be spent on, by year 2000, 2
prefer to work for man or woman, 14
women have equal opportunities with men, 14
and women's movement, easier or harder for
  women to combine jobs and family responsibilities, 13
  See also Men; Women
Jogging
  as most effective way to lose weight, 164
  you and your friends participate in, 27
  your participation in, 43
    by men, 44
    by women, 44
John Paul II, Pope
  as most admired man, 176
Johnson, Lyndon
  approval rating, 161
    retrospective versus actual ratings, 161
  approval rating compared to Bush, 7
  as president most responsible for getting country
    into Vietnam War, 47
  as president most responsible for getting country out
    of Vietnam War, 48
  your opinion of his role in Vietnam War, 49
Jordan
  has sent troops to the Persian Gulf, 170
Journalists
  honesty rating, 23
    national trend, 24
Justice system
  as factor most responsible for crime, 123

K

Kemp, Jack
  have heard of, 51
  as nominee for Republican presidential candidate,
    51
Kennedy, John
  approval rating, 161

Kennedy, John (*continued*)
    retrospective versus actual ratings, 161
    approval rating compared to Bush, 7
    as president most responsible for getting country
        into Vietnam War, 47
Kerrey, Bob
  have heard of, 51
  as nominee for Democratic presidential candidate,
    51
Kirkpatrick, Jeane
  have heard of, 51
  as most admired woman, 177
  as nominee for Republican presidential candidate,
    51
Kissinger, Henry
  your opinion of his role in Vietnam War, 49
Kuwait
  as most important problem, 149
  See also Persian Gulf situation

L

Labor, organized
  honesty rating of union leaders, 23
    national trend, 24
  Republican or Democratic party best serves union
    members, 146
    national trend, 146
  your confidence in, 102
    national trend, 102
Lawyers
  honesty rating, 23
    national trend, 24
Leisure and recreational activities
  if someone took your television set away, what
      would you be doing (listed) to fill in time,
      131-32
  more or less time will be spent on, by year 2000, 2
  way people will spend free time, by year 2000, 2
  your favorite way (listed) to spend an evening, 130
Life expectancy
  will have risen, by year 2000, 1
Los Angeles
  safe to live in or visit, 119

M

Mandela, Nelson
  currently in jail or released, 21
  heard or read about, 21
  importance of sanctions in release of, 21
  as most admired man, 176
Mantle, Mickey
  as greatest baseball player, 46
Manufactured goods
  quality of goods is better now than a few years ago,
    146-47

United States has gained ground in the quality of, in
    last few years, 147
United States will gain ground in the quality of,
    during next few years, 147
who is to blame for the quality of goods not being
    higher, 147
Marriage
  what kind is more satisfying, 14
Martial arts
  your participation in, 43
Mays, Willie
  as greatest baseball player, 46
McGovern, George
  your opinion of his role in Vietnam War, 49
Medical care
  easier or harder to afford, by year 2000, 3
  type people will receive, by year 2000, 2
Medicare
  in federal budget plan, favor applying payroll Medi-
    care tax to wages up to $73,000, 129
  in federal budget plan, favor cutting benefits, 129
  as most important problem, 149
  as reason for dissatisfaction, 141
Men
  as capable as women of being good parents, 15
  characteristics of (listed), 15-16
  choice for most admired man, 176
  greater satisfaction from caring for family than from
    job, 15
  have better life than women, 12
    national trend, 12
  household chores (listed) you usually do yourself,
    13-14
  how many hours per week do you work, 16
  main reason men and women are basically different,
    16
  man and woman earn same amount, 16
  man is achiever and woman takes care of home,
    14
  more successful in business world than women, 15
  share household chores equally, 16
  who have successful careers end up sacrificing too
    much, 15
  and women, basically similar or different, 15
  women are more capable of managing household
    than, 15
  women are as successful as, in workplace, 15
  and women's movement, easier or harder to lead
    satisfying lives, 13
Mental health problems, people with
  having pets would provide them with a more satis-
    fying life, 108
Miami
  safe to live in or visit, 119
Middle East situation
  favor establishment of independent Palestinian
    nation within territories occupied by Israel,
    135
    national trend, 135

O

O'Connor, Sandra Day
  as most admired woman, 177
Oil crisis
  as most important problem, 149
  See also Persian Gulf situation
Onassis, Jacqueline Kennedy
  as most admired woman, 177

P

Paddle and platform tennis
  your participation in, 43
Palestinian Arabs
  as U.S. concession, agree to summit combining discussion of Iraq-Kuwait situation with Palestinian problem in Israel, 170-71
  See also Middle East situation
Panama invasion
  as Bush's greatest achievement, 18, 75, 152
Parental leave legislation
  favor Congress passing this type of law, 67
Peace
  better or worse, by year 2000, 1
  between Israelis and Arabs, by year 2000, 2
  Bush making progress on keeping nation out of war, 19, 155
    national trend, 155
  as Bush's greatest achievement, 18, 75, 152
  Republican or Democratic party more likely to keep United States out of war, 117, 142
    national trend, 118, 142
Persian Gulf situation
  America's allies are doing all they should to support U.S. efforts, 95-96, 115
    national trend, 115
  amount of money Washington should spend for defense, 99
    national trend, 99
  approve of Bush's decision to send 150,000 additional troops, 159
  approve of Bush's handling of, 93, 95, 97, 104, 114, 136, 149, 159, 166
    national trend, 95, 97, 104, 114, 136, 159, 166
  approve of calling up reservists to active duty, 106
  approve of U.S. decision to send troops to Saudi Arabia, 95, 97-98, 105, 115, 136, 149, 166
    national trend, 98, 105, 115, 136, 166
  approve of U.S. embargo on all supplies coming into and out of Kuwait and Iraq, 98
  approve of using U.S. troops to force Iraqis to leave Kuwait, 95
  aware that Hussein has agreed to release all foreign hostages by Christmas, 171
  ban all imports from Iraq, including oil, 93
  Bush should stick closely to public opinion when deciding what steps to take next, 171
  by how many cents have gasoline prices gone up, 96
  doing anything to reduce your use of energy, 96; and what is that (listed), 96
    national trend, 96
  encourage U.S. allies to boycott Iraqi oil imports, 93
  favor direct U.S. military action against Iraq, 93
  favor leaving U.S. troops in Saudi Arabia if it becomes a long conflict, 95, 106
  favor reinstating military draft for, 117
  freeze Kuwait's assets, 93
  happen to know the name of the leader of Iraq, 169
  has Canada sent troops, 170
  has Egypt sent troops, 169
  has England sent troops, 169
  has France sent troops, 169
  has Japan sent troops, 169
  has Jordan sent troops, 170
  has the price of gasoline gone up, 96
  has the Soviet Union sent troops, 169
  has Syria sent troops, 169
  have clear idea of what U.S. military involvement is all about, 98, 104, 115, 159, 168
    national trend, 104, 115, 160, 168
  have the media been too critical of President Bush's action in, 116
  how closely have you followed news about, 92-93, 94, 97, 104, 114, 149, 165
    national trend, 95, 97, 105, 114, 165
  how do you, yourself, feel (listed) about the U.S. presence in the Mideast, 98-99, 106, 115, 150
  how effective has the United Nations been in dealing with Iraq's invasion of Kuwait, 139
  how long will U.S. forces remain in the Mideast, 98, 116
  how many troops will the United States have in Saudi Arabia after latest deployment, 169; is that more or fewer than Iraq has, 169
  how much longer should the sanctions be given before taking military actions, 167-68
  how serious is the energy situation, 96
  if Hussein does release hostages, what should the United States do differently (listed), 171-72
  if Iraq and Hussein have nuclear weapons in two years, would you favor going to war to destroy Iraq's nuclear capability, 170
  if Iraq invades Saudi Arabia, would you favor direct U.S. military action against Iraq, 93
  if Iraq invades Saudi Arabia, would you favor sending as many more U.S. troops as necessary, 95
  if Iraq lets January 15 deadline pass, would you favor going to war with Iraq, 168
  if Iraq stays in Kuwait, United States should maintain its troops in Saudi Arabia or initiate war, 168

believe in clairvoyance, 88
  national trend, 89
believe in déjà vu, 88
  national trend, 89
believe in the Devil, 88
  national trend, 89
believe in ESP, 88
  national trend, 89
believe that extraterrestrial beings have visited
    Earth, 88
believe in ghosts, 89
  national trend, 89
believe in psychic or spiritual healing, 88
believe in reincarnation, 89
believe in telekinesis, 89
believe in telepathy, 88
believe in witches, 89
  national trend, 89
believe that houses can be haunted, 88
believe that people are sometimes possessed by the
    Devil, 88
believe that people can communicate with someone
    who has died, 89
believe that pyramids have special healing power,
    89
believe that rock crystals have special healing
    power, 89
ever had each of these experiences (listed), 89-90
ever seen a UFO, 90
  national trend, 90
heard about New Age movement, 90
heard about UFOs, 90
  national trend, 90
how superstitious are you, 87-88
New Age movement is good for traditional relig-
    ions, 91
New Age movement is good for U.S. society, 91
read your horoscope every day, 90
what one or two superstitions (listed) affect you
    most, 88
your opinion of New Age movement, 90
Public schools. *See* Education

Q

Quality of life
  better or worse, by year 2000, 1
  for blacks, has gotten better, 150
Quayle, Dan
  appoint to cabinet post, if Bush does choose some-
    one new, 29
  approval rating, 29, 55, 78, 152
    by degree, 152
    national trend, 29, 56, 78, 152
  Bush should keep, as running mate, 29, 152
    national trend, 152
  have heard of, 51
  as nominee for Republican presidential candidate, 51

qualified to serve as president, 29, 151
  national trend, 29, 152
whether Bush keeps, as important in your vote, 29
your opinion of, 29

R

Racial tolerance
  any objection to sending your children to school
    where a few children are black, 64
  any objection to sending your children to school
    where half of the children are black, 64
  any objection to sending your children to school
    where more than half of the children are
    black, 64
  black children have as good a chance as white chil-
    dren to get good education, 63
  blacks have as good a chance as whites to get hous-
    ing, 63
  blacks have as good a chance as whites to get job,
    62-63
  has society become more tolerant lately, 65
  have number of negative racial comments been in-
    creasing, 64-65
  have you become more tolerant lately, 65
  how much progress made in civil rights, 62
    national trend, 62
  how well are blacks treated in your community,
    62
    national trend, 62
  if black people came to live in your neighborhood,
    would you move, 64
    national trend, 64
  if black people came to live next door, would you
    move, 64
    national trend, 64
  likely to be serious racial trouble in this community,
    62
    national trend, 62
  quality of life of blacks has gotten better, 63-64
    national trend, 64
  racial and ethnic group tensions, better or worse by
    year 2000, 1
Racquetball
  your participation in, 43
Reagan, Nancy
  as most admired woman, 177
Reagan, Ronald
  approval rating, 161
    retrospective versus actual ratings, 161
  approval rating compared to Bush, 7
  approval rating since he left office, 161
  as most admired man, 176
  most to blame for Savings and Loan crisis, 86
Real estate agents
  honesty rating, 23
    national trend, 24

Recession
    likely in the country during the next twelve months,
        106, 126, 142
        national trend, 106, 126, 142
    as most important problem, 38, 149
        national trend, 84
Religion
    any religious training as a child, 68
    aware of presence different from your everyday self,
        68
    believe in life after death, 68
    increasing its influence on American life, 67
        national trend, 67
    it can answer today's problems, 67
        national trend, 67
    its importance in your life, 12, 67
        national trend, 12
    made a commitment to Jesus Christ, 68
    there are clear guidelines about what's good or evil,
        68
    way people will worship, by year 2000, 2
    you and your friends pray together, 27
    your confidence in church or organized, 101
        national trend, 101
    See also Bible; Church; Synagogue
Republican party
    best serves blacks, 145
        national trend, 145
    best serves business and professional people, 145
        national trend, 145
    best serves farmers, 145
        national trend, 145
    best serves labor union members, 146
        national trend, 146
    best serves people like yourself, 144
        national trend, 144
    best serves poor people, 144
    best serves retired people, 145
        national trend, 145
    best serves skilled workers, 145
        national trend, 145
    best serves small-business people, 145
        national trend, 145
    best serves unemployed people, 146
        national trend, 146
    best serves unskilled workers, 146
        national trend, 146
    best serves wealthy people, 144
    best serves women, 144
        national trend, 144
    better at keeping country prosperous, 118, 142
        national trend, 118, 142
    for Congress, which party's candidate would you
        like to see win, 118, 142, 144, 148
        national trend, 118, 142
    likely to vote for candidate for Congress from your
        district, 144
    more likely to keep United States out of war, 117,
        142

    national trend, 118, 142
    nominees for presidential candidate, 51
    why (listed) would you like to see the Republican
        candidate win in your congressional district,
        148-49
    your affiliation with, 51
        national trend, 52
Retarded people
    having pets would provide them with a more satis-
        fying life, 108
Retired people
    Republican or Democratic party best serves, 145
        national trend, 145
Retirement
    easier or harder to afford, by year 2000, 3
Robb, Charles
    have heard of, 51
    as nominee for Democratic presidential candidate,
        51
Robertson, Pat
    have heard of, 51
    as nominee for Republican presidential candidate, 51
Robinson, Jackie
    as greatest baseball player, 46
Rockefeller, Jay
    have heard of, 51
    as nominee for Democratic presidential candidate,
        51
Rollerskating
    your participation in, 43
Roosevelt, Franklin
    approval rating, 161
        retrospective versus actual ratings, 161
Rose, Pete
    as greatest baseball player, 46
Rowing
    your participation in, 43
Running
    your participation in, 43
        by men, 43
        by women, 44
Ruth, Babe
    as greatest baseball player, 46
        national trend, 46

S

Sailing
    your participation in, 43
        frequency of participation, 44
San Diego
    safe to live in or visit, 119
San Francisco
    safe to live in or visit, 119
Satisfaction
    why are you dissatisfied with way things are going
        in the United States, 141

United States (*continued*)
　　national trend, 24, 85, 126, 137, 141, 148
See also Census, U.S.; Soviet Union; Vietnam War

V

Veterans' benefits
　　reduce spending on domestic programs such as, 129
Video cassette recorder (VCR)
　　does your household have, 133
Vietnam War
　　any Americans prisoners of war still in captivity, 48
　　as a result, Americans have less trust in their leaders, 49
　　as a result, Congress became more assertive in limiting our involvement in foreign war, 50
　　as a result, United States is more cautious about involvement abroad, 49
　　as a result, U.S. government became more responsive to the opinions of the people, 49
　　commitment to fight communism in, helped bring about current decline in communism, 49-50
　　did American soldiers die in vain in, 50
　　did the United States win or lose, 47
　　did you demonstrate against, 48
　　did you serve in the military in, 48
　　do you wish that you had made stronger effort to protest against, 48
　　expense of war led to growing American budget deficit, 49
　　have Vietnam veterans been treated well by the people, 50
　　have Vietnam veterans been treated well by the U.S. government, 50
　　in which war, greatest number of American troops lost their lives, 47
　　a just war, 47
　　Korean War a just war, 47
　　likely that U.S. involvement in Saudi Arabia could turn into another, 95, 99, 106
　　　　national trend, 99, 106
　　our participation strengthened America's position throughout world, 49
　　　　national trend, 49
　　pace of communism in Southeast Asia was slowed, 49
　　United States fighting on side of North or South Vietnamese, 47
　　United States made mistake sending troops to fight in, 48
　　　　national trend, 48
　　United States should have cut its losses earlier, 48
　　United States and the South Vietnamese could have won, 48
　　U.S. policy to maintain our military strength throughout world, 47
　　　　national trend, 47

visited Vietnam War Memorial in Washington, 50
war an outmoded way of settling differences, 46-47
　　national trend, 47
we should have gone all out to win, 48
which president was most responsible for getting our country involved in, 47
which president was most responsible for getting out of, 48
World War I a just war, 47
World War II a just war, 47
your opinion of person's or group's (listed) role in, 49
Volleyball
　　your participation in, 43
　　　　participation changes by decade, 44

W

Walesa, Lech
　　as most admired man, 176
War
　　fear of, as most important problem, 38, 84, 149
　　　　national trend, 84
　　See also Nuclear war
Washington, DC
　　safe to live in or visit, 119
Waterskiing
　　your participation in, 43
Wealthy people
　　Republican or Democratic party best serves, 144
　　See also Financial situation *for rich people*
Weight and weight reduction
　　attending a hospital-based program, as effective way to lose weight, 164
　　attending a weight-loss program, as effective way to lose weight, 164
　　at what age did you first try to lose weight, 164
　　avoiding alcohol, as effective way to lose weight, 164
　　eating less, as effective way to lose weight, 164
　　eating low-calorie foods, as effective way to lose weight, 164
　　ever caused you health problems, 163
　　ever caused you to be depressed, 162
　　ever caused you to lose out on job opportunities, 162
　　ever caused you trouble with relationships, 162
　　exercising, as effective way to lose weight, 164
　　how many times have you seriously tried to lose weight, 163-64
　　how often do you worry about your weight, 163
　　if you had to take a physical fitness test, what shape would it show you to be in, 165
　　is this weight loss program working for you, 163
　　psychotherapy or hypnosis, as effective way to lose weight, 165